SILENT ADMIRER

Claire Stibbe

United States of America

BOOKPRENEUR

Copyright © Claire Stibbe 2019
Silent Admirer
Published by Bookpreneur

This is a work of fiction. Names, characters, places, organizations, businesses, places and events, other than those clearly in the public domain, are the product of the author's imagination or are used fictitiously. Any resemblance to actual persons, living or dead, events, or locales is entirely coincidental.

All rights reserved. No part of this book may be reproduced or transmitted in any form or by any means, electronic or mechanical, including photocopying, recording, or by any information storage and retrieval system, without prior written permission of the publishers.

Claire Stibbe has asserted her right to be identified as the author of this work.

ISBN-10: 0-9982027-7-0
ISBN-13: 978-0-9982027-7-8
eBook: 978-0-9982027-6-1

Printed in the United States of America

Cover Artwork by Esther Kotecha
ekdesigns.co.uk

Editing by Jeff Gardiner and The Book Lab

www.clairestibbe.com

ACKNOWLEDGMENTS

My thanks to New Mexico for providing the inspiration for the Detective Temeke Series. To my mother for giving me a safe and loving home, and to my father who gave me his love of language and books.

Special thanks to the Albuquerque Citizen's Police Academy, the Albuquerque Sheriff's Department, to all the police officers, deputies and detectives I have worked with, especially for their dedication and sacrifice. For the invaluable services of Twisted Ink Publishing, The 13th Sign and An Tig Beag Press. A huge thank you to editor, Jeff Gardiner, and the wonderful proofreaders at BookLab for molding the clay into something worth reading.

As always I owe the greatest of thanks possible to my husband Jeff for his love and support, and to Jamie for his encouragement and humor.

Claire Stibbe
Albuquerque, New Mexico
February 2019

ONE

She heard shouting. The words were muffled through the bathroom wall and her stomach was on fire with terror.

Whenever her mom raised her voice it made her cry. Made her want to apologize even when she knew she hadn't done anything bad.

Something lurched in the back of her throat and she gripped her stomach, leaned over the toilet and threw up.

Stop... please, please, stop.

The sound of scraping made her flinch: drawers opening and closing, and then things thumping on the floor. After a few minutes it went quiet.

She grabbed her blanket and crept down the corridor to mom and dad's room. Wanted to ask for a hug, except recently mom had begun shrugging her off. Said it was 'creepy'.

She inched further toward the door, running her hands along the wall. The cramping in her stomach had gotten worse and she was scared she'd throw up again.

A scream. Then another sound, louder than a fire cracker.

Fingers flat against the frame of the bedroom door, she peered in.

"Cover your face!"

She gasped, and must have stood there for a few seconds because he rushed over and pressed her hands up against her face. Between her fingers she could see a stain of crimson on the sheets and she could hear dripping. Not like rain drops against a pavement. Thicker. Slower. Sliding down one side of the bed and slapping against the carpet.

A hand grasped her collar and yanked her downstairs. Told her to keep her eyes closed as he dragged her along the corridor.

Thud, thud, thud. The toes of her shoes barely patting each step.

"I feel sick," she said.

Then a glass rammed against her mouth and a palm full of pills.

"Swallow! All of them."

She tried to swallow and he kept tipping the glass higher and higher until she almost gagged. The pills tasted like bitter lemons and salt.

"You won't tell?" he asked.

No, she wouldn't tell. She didn't want to. Looking and tattling only got her into trouble.

Didn't want to wait in the kitchen either and smell soapy water. Hearing the plunk of the bucket handle and the swish of the mop.

Back and forth. Back and forth. Roll it up. Make a burrito.

Then the car swerving along the back roads, higher and higher until her ears popped. Houses rushing past like the images in her mind. Couldn't remember when her mom stopped making pancakes and eggs, and PB&Js became boring because that's all there was.

Sometimes the neighbor lady let her pet her dog. A

whippet, she said it was. Always shivering, tail looped like a jug handle. Sometimes the lady gave her snacks. A bag of assorted nuts or chips.

One night she padded out of the house when no one was looking and peered in through a back window. The computer inside was a neon glow and she could make out ladies in underwear. She knew they weren't supposed to look like that. Like when a dog only had three legs. She felt sorry and disgusted all at once.

It made her heart beat fast because she knew she shouldn't have been looking. She wanted to tell her best friend at school, almost did in recess two days ago. But somehow the thing just stuck in her throat and wouldn't come out.

She was sick and she was tired. All because of that damn computer.

TWO

It was five o'clock on a Thursday afternoon when Detective David Temeke entered El Pinto, a hacienda style restaurant in Albuquerque's North Valley.

On a cloudy day like this he would have been hiking the rocky slopes of La Luz Trail—eight or so miles—from the foothills of the Sandia Mountains to the top of the world. It was well worth the spike in adrenaline and elevation, although it was the brunt of the sun on a hot day he didn't miss on the way down.

He grabbed a newspaper off the front desk and followed the waitress outside. A canopy of vines covered the patio dining area, quiet, except for her clacking heels on the tile. It was his favorite restaurant, where he brought his ex-wife, Serena, on their first date.

Twenty people hunched over menus, eating enchiladas and drinking beers. There was a lone man near the kiva fireplace sucking on a Bloody Mary, nose nudging a cocktail parasol. He gave Temeke the eye.

The waitress showed Temeke a table near the gardens, placed salsa and a basket of tortilla chips on the table and asked him what he wanted to drink.

"Iced water. And one for the lady," he said, pointing at the empty chair. "Oh, and a coffee while I'm waiting, love."

She looked at him sideways and smiled. A look that required clarification about his culture. English and Ethiopian, he assured her, and even though he'd been living in the US for over ten years he still couldn't shake off his sodding accent. The drone of how much she loved London, except for the biting wind and rain, elicited a few nods and he was relieved when she left. At least she didn't try putting on a British accent. That was something he hated.

His mind filtered and evaluated every sound, instantly alert to the warm August wind that whipped around the patio. Policing the west side had been big-city stress over the past week and he hadn't been able to get to the usual nuisance calls of the day.

The metro area had seen a crime spike in drug trafficking, which had netted nearly fifty pounds of heroin and meth. He tried to rid himself of how hard law enforcement worked to crack down and keep offenders behind bars but the fact remained, crime was rising with the heat. Drug traffic, gang wars and domestic violence continued to plague society and pending cases choked the courts. Even when those cases were finally brought to trial, no prison cell could remove hatred from hearts and madness from minds.

His phone jangled with an incoming call: Unit Commander Hackett.

"I've sent you a memo about a new trainee," he barked. "Officer Midgely. She'll be starting next week."

Temeke recalled an image of a rugged blonde, hands on hips. "You're kidding. Scarlet Midgely? The one who got her knuckles rapped for flipping Captain Fowler the bird. *That* officer Midgely?"

"Seems since her return to the unit, she's made obscene gestures a bit of hobby. She's also got a mouth like a chainsaw. But that makes two of you doesn't it?"

"Sir—"

"You'll find it on your personal email since I'm aware Malin has the password to your work computer. I wouldn't want her seeing this."

"Absolutely, sir."

Have a nice day."

The dial tone set Temeke's nerves on edge. Hackett was a far cry from warm and fuzzy. Had the effect of wanting to make everyone feel invisible, where they ran for cover every time he arrived in the office. Since he was on the cusp of retirement it was a toss-up as to when.

The waitress scuttled back with a cup of coffee. He downed two mugs, while flicking through the newspaper.

A small article caught his eye, something that had fascinated him every time he set off for a hike from the Elena Gallegos Open Space. It was the anniversary of a senior journalist who had typed up the article over sixty years ago and still the memory lingered.

A TWA plane with sixteen aboard had taken off from Albuquerque on February 19, 1955, bound for Santa Fe. Temeke's eyes sprinted over the headlines:

Plane Found; None Survives.

Flight 250 was heading north out of Albuquerque, apparently following the Rio Grande Valley before making a dogleg east-northeast to Santa Fe. Soon after takeoff the pilot radioed the tower, but there was no further communication for twenty-four hours. Until a glint of metal was spotted in the Sandia Mountains by a cargo pilot the following morning. The mystery of how it happened had put a hammerlock on the citizens, and along with The Civil Aeronautics Board probable-cause report, problems with the plane's fluxgate compass on the wingtip had been cited as a possible reason.

With debris strewn among the rock and a plaque to commemorate the incident, it was hard not to look at the rock face and imagine both crew and passenger's last moments. He had the GPS coordinates permanently set in his phone. Did the hike on cloudy days such as this and as often as he could.

But today he was meeting Serena. Today he was hoping for good news.

They had closed a case involving a brave teenage girl who had been held at gunpoint in a large office building. The lowlife predator was latterly shot and the article in the *Journal* commended Temeke and a member of the SWAT unit, Officer Hardy, taking into account the difficulties both officers had faced. They said he was due a promotion. They said it would be this year.

Temeke had to hand it to Journal Staff Writer, Jennifer Danes, whose less than complementary articles had once described him as *a crazy Brit from darkest London*. Restraint was hardly her strong point.

When he did school visits, he often emerged from his unit to a gauntlet of cell phone flashes. The kids loved his talks and one of the teachers told him a toy manufacturer had already named a police doll after him. It was a sodding joke.

He looked up at the archway that led to the patio and then at his phone. Five ten. Scooping salsa on the edge of a chip, he crunched his way through the basket. He liked eating dinner early to escape the rush. Plenty of people to watch, conversations to listen to.

He patted the pager in his belt. Even though he was off duty, his fingers twitched impatiently on the leather case, mind clattering away like a diesel engine.

The waitress asked him if he was ready to order.

"Let's give her ten more minutes," he said, taking out his phone and checking his calendar.

Right place, right time. Where the heck was she?

It was a golden opportunity to patch things up with Serena yet each opportunity seemed to slip away with every word. He could never get to grips with marriage, whereas chasing suspects was as natural as riding a bike.

He flipped his camera to self-portrait and gazed at a head atrociously shaved and burned black by the desert sun. Was there anything about him Serena might despise? In his opinion, everything looked orderly.

He shook out his napkin and placed it on his knee, glad to be away from it all. Commander Hackett had dug out a cold case from a dusty closet and left it on Temeke's desk. Andrea Irwin and Maria Velasquez, 2004. Killed in the foothills. They never did find the person responsible.

It was funding. It was *always* bloody funding.

His cell phone lit up with another incoming call; Brother-in-law, Lieutenant Luis Alvarez.

"Sorry to bother you, David. There was a call made to dispatch about ten minutes ago. A man on Talmadge Avenue. If it wasn't for blood in the bedroom and a missing ten-year-old, I would have asked someone else."

As the one detective who had worked in the CAC Unit—Crimes Against Children—Temeke knew Luis wasn't going to let this case go to another man.

He slapped the napkin on the table and scraped back his chair. "On my way."

THREE

Temeke gave his call sign and location, swung out in front of a blue minivan and was met with the blare of a horn before running code all the way to Talmadge Avenue. He pulled up behind two police units and an ambulance crew, unhooked the radio and gave dispatch a status check.

It was a two storey, white stucco house in Cottonwood Heights. The mailbox displayed a plaque which read, *4219 Trandahl*. Quiet neighborhood with a median income, he guessed, at around thirty-five thousand a year. A baize of green lawns and yuccas, and the scent of a single cigarette that soiled the afternoon air. He had given up smoking recently and the smell always got to him.

There was no call history on the house and he ran the license plates of a Harley Davidson parked outside. Came back clean. Belonged to the homeowner, Dai M. Trandahl.

He grabbed a handful of latex gloves and shoe covers and shoved them in his pocket. Took his notepad and walked to the curb to where Officer Manning was standing under a tree with ninety pounds of quivering

German Shepherd. K-9 Brock had been given two personal items belonging to Trandahl's wife and daughter, smells known as 'agitators'.

"Anything?" Temeke asked.

"Scuff marks on the block wall in the back yard. Nothing around front. Brock didn't give any alerts away from the house but he gave a few in the garage and the back porch. It indicates the mother and the little girl had been in both areas recently."

"So they can't have walked down the street."

"No. But they could have been driven away. It's hard finding a direction if the dogs can't pick up a trail."

Temeke shook Manning's hand and then greeted a sprawl of officers standing in front of the mobile command center, which was parked on the opposite side of the street.

Lieutenant Alvarez relayed how many cruisers were patrolling the area between the time of Trandahl's call-in and now. He suggested a perimeter of not more than five miles given the amount of blood found in the bedroom.

The speed traveled by someone, either with extensive wounds or carrying a person with extensive wounds, would be minimal. Someone *had* to have seen them.

Temeke put on shoe covers and gloves, sauntered toward the front door and signed himself in with a female officer. He nodded at Officer Jarvis who was chewing, as usual, on a toothpick.

"Any reason why you're not wearing gloves, son? Because I don't want to get excited about a few latents and find out they're yours."

Jarvis started digging around in his pocket. "Sorry, sir. I took them off after I'd finished up here."

Temeke then nodded at a man slouched on the porch. Dai Trandahl was shaking his head, the butt of a cigarette peeking out from under his heel. He appeared to be blabbering to ambulance personnel about a stranger he had seen sniffing around the neighborhood. Blond, thick set. Probably wouldn't remember him if he saw him again.

The front door was wide open and Temeke could see as far as the living room. Nice and orderly, nothing remarkable.

He crouched in front of Trandahl, noticing a child's backpack in the entryway. "How are you doing, sir?"

"Not so good. There's blood all over the bed."

There were no cuts on Trandahl's hands, no blood smears, nothing to indicate that he needed medical assistance, but Temeke asked anyway.

"No, I'm fine. It's my wife. My little girl, Hannah. She's only ten." Trandahl's brow creased into three deep lines and his fingers toyed with a cell phone. "I don't know where they are."

"Can you tell me your wife's name?"

"Rachael."

"Have you called her?"

"I keep getting voicemail. Same with Hannah."

"Can you give me their numbers?"

Trandahl rattled of two ten digit numbers, faltering a little at Hannah's. "I think the last number's a four not a six."

"About what time did you call?"

"I don't know. About fiveish. I called her cell phone. Asked how Hannah did at school. She never called back."

"What was your wife wearing?"

"Blue pajamas... bows on the collar. Hannah was already up. Jeans, blue t-shirt. Had words on it." He closed his eyes as if that would give him a better view. "*Her Royal Ten-ness.*"

"Get it for her birthday?"

"Yeah, I got it online." Trandahl yawned.

"Early shift?"

"Board meeting. Takes it out of you."

"So where does Hannah go to school?" Temeke asked.

"Lincoln Middle School."

"What time did you get home?"

"Around five." Trandahl frowned and sucked in his bottom lip. "Hannah usually comes running and shouting, 'Dad!' But she didn't today. I checked the garage and Rachael's car was there so I thought they were home."

"See anything odd when you first got in?"

"Just the patio door open. We never leave doors open. Apart from the electricity bill, it's not secure."

"Do you have any guns in the house?"

"No. I'm not a fan. Sorry. Just don't like them."

"You stay here." Temeke said. "I'd like to check the house."

"They're not inside."

"I know, sir. I just need to look around."

Temeke beckoned Jarvis into a small living room beside the front door and lowered his voice. "What was Trandahl's state of mind when you arrived?"

"Agitated. I think he'd just finished making a call when I pulled up. I cleared the house. There was no one else here." Jarvis ran a hand through popcorn colored hair, cheeks plump like a hamster hoarding food.

"Any signs of blood apart from on the bed?" Temeke asked.

"Bedhead and wall, and there's possible spatter on the stairs. You don't think the mother killed the kid?"

"I don't think anything, Jarv. Not until I've seen it. And when I've seen it, I still won't be thinking anything."

"The windows are intact. No forced entry." Jarvis handed Temeke an evidence bag containing a yellow Post-it note. "Found this wedged into the mirror frame. Think it's a suicide?"

"Suicides rarely leave Post-it notes, Jarv." Temeke turned it over in his hand. The handwriting was cursive. Could have been written by anyone.

*'Death lies on her like an untimely frost
Upon the sweetest flower of all the field.'*

"*Romeo and Juliet*," Temeke said.

Jarvis nodded and then fixed his eyes briefly on a pale sun through the window, blinking in and out of smoky clouds. "Maggie Watts is on her way to take Mr. Trandahl back for an interview. She also called all the hospitals to see if a woman and a little girl had been admitted today. Nothing so far."

"Find any hidden firearms?"

"I didn't look under the bed if that's what you're saying."

"Any cars in the garage?"

"A red Toyota Highlander. Hers. Well, there's a pink fluffy flip-flop hanging from the review mirror. Can't be his."

"Computer?" Temeke asked.

"There's a laptop in the spare room."

"When Maggie arrives, ask her to get details of any POI's in the area."

"I already did, sir. No persons of interest. Well, not persons that would interest us. In case you hadn't noticed, there's a serious lack of nosy neighbors rushing forward to offer assistance, except for that kid over there."

"Do me a favor, Jarv. Talk to that kid and do a knock-and-talk ASAP."

"What if I knock and nobody wants to talk?"

"You're not here to sell tickets for a police picnic. And you don't care about the drug hive they've got around back. Just ask them if they saw anything. And while you're at it, call Lincoln Middle School. See if Hannah or her mother were there today. Anyone issued a BOLO yet?"

"Yes, sir."

With a *be on the lookout* issued for Hannah and Rachael, all units were alert and active.

Jarvis angled his cheek to his radio for any updates and Temeke followed him out into the street. He smiled at the questioning looks of a kid, hair soaped into a four foot Mohican and riding a tricked-out bike. Astro metallic blue with alloy rims and blue streamers hanging from the handlebars. Temeke made a circle with his fingers and mouthed *wicked*.

He looked down at Trandahl. "Know that kid?"

"Yeah, he lives opposite. Jack. Jack Colby. Hannah hangs out with him sometimes. We vaguely know the parents."

"You friendly with any other neighbors?"

"Not really." Trandahl let out a huge sigh. "I wish I'd taken the day off. Hannah wasn't feeling well."

Temeke placed the Post-it note in the evidence bag on Trandahl's lap. "Recognize the handwriting?"

"Never seen it before."

Temeke patted Trandahl on the shoulder and walked back into the house. Placed the evidence bag in the box and dialed Rachael's number. No point in thinking she'd pick up. But in case she'd topped the kid and done a runner he left her a message. Asked her to call him and told her he understood if she wanted to be alone.

Up the stairs were three investigators suited up in protective clothing and taking swabs on the railings. One was a female whose voice turned almost falsetto when she looked down at him.

"Hi, Detective. Good to see you."

"You too, Alice." Attractive. Annoying voice.

"Agnes is still taking photos and we're running UV over the sheets. We'll be ready for you in about ten minutes."

"That's OK, love. Take your time."

Temeke glanced back at the front porch where a

member of the ambulance crew was stooping over Trandahl. The light from the street flooded the hardwood floor and from the threshold to the study door there was a rectangular demarcation, darker than its boundary and indicated the absence of a rug.

Temeke squatted and ran a gloved hand over the planks. No dust. Had to have been cleaned recently.

He sketched everything he saw—the back yard, the sitting room—knowing photos of the street, and the approach to the house, were being taken by the Agnes Kjellson, the photographer regularly used by Dr. Vasillion.

He measured the gap between the open patio door and the frame: four feet, three inches. Plenty of space for an adult to step through. No footprints leading in from the back wall to the threshold, which there would be since the lawn was heavily irrigated, almost waterlogged.

He noticed Trandahl's head was tucked down, hands capping his knees. Temeke could hear a series of long and short breaths, and the hitching in his chest. He hoped the man hadn't seen anything that might have branded his mind; an indelible image of death and slaughter he couldn't possibly process.

That didn't mean Temeke couldn't put a little pressure on him at an interview.

FOUR

Trash scuttled across the pavement, lifted into the air and soared over a sand-colored wall rising between Trandahl's property and the neighbor's yard.

Technicians were already digging through the dumpsters, hauling bags of trash into a waiting van.

Temeke stood a few feet from the doorstep, cell phone rumbling in his hand. It was Jarvis. Neither Hannah nor her mother had been seen at school and the principal hadn't heard from either Rachael or Dai. She'd already left a message on Rachael's phone.

Sodding marvelous, Temeke thought, noticing several cigarette butts snuggled between the cracks in the concrete. He could almost taste them.

"She not let you smoke inside?" he said, taking a step toward the house.

Trandahl lifted his head. "Oh, no. She doesn't like me smoking at all."

"They'll make you sick and if they don't make you sick, they'll kill you."

"That right?"

"My dad... he smoked several packs a day. 'Course, he was also a pot-smoking slacker, an alcoholic and a few other things I could name. He was absent more than he was present. Never could hold down a sodding job and money trickled out of his wallet every time he walked past the bookie. I often wondered why his headstone read *I was hoping for a pyramid*."

Temeke noticed Trandahl was fully alert to the distraction he'd provided. And he noticed something else. The comment got a chuckle out of him.

"Were you close to your mom?" Trandahl asked.

"Very. Well, someone had to look out for her."

Trandahl looked down at his phone, pressed the home button and stared at a blank screen.

"Your wife or Hannah have any allergies?" Temeke asked.

"No."

"Any arguments last night or this morning?"

"No, nothing."

"We'll need to take a few pieces of clothing for Rachael and Hannah."

"I don't understand."

"Dogs need a target scent, sir. Amazing how they do it. Apparently, they can smell a substance diluted to five parts per trillion. That, my son, is the same as detecting a teaspoon of sugar in a million gallons of water."

"You gotta be kidding."

"No joke."

The purr of a Ford Explorer disturbed the frown on Trandahl's face. Detective Malin Santiago pulled up next to the curb, slid off the driver's seat and onto the pavement with a loud smack.

It had been almost a year since she had joined the Duke City Police Department giving Northwest Area Command a sense of order. Local girl, through and through, and solid under pressure. Mid-thirties with pale skin freckled around the nose. It was her eyes Temeke liked the best. Not a hint of the cynicism prevalent in the hardened police veterans, rather the curiosity of a deer foraging for food. Working in a male dominated-environment, her career mattered to him. Always dodging a volley of male opinions, male intrusion and male stares. He didn't know how she did it.

And here he was studying a crisp white shirt and black pants that underlined her femininity. Lace-up combat boots, same as his. Dark hair tied back from a finely chiseled face; too serious to offer a smile and probably too shattered to care. She cradled a bottle of water, eyes scuttling up and down the front façade and stopping at the doorstep.

"You Dai Trandahl?" she asked,

"Yes, ma'am."

"Here," she said, handing him the bottle. "Have you called your wife?"

"Several times. She's not answering."

"Do you remember what you said in your messages?"

"I asked her how she was doing, that kind of thing. In my last message I asked if Hannah had got an 'A' today. She never called back."

"Mind if I go inside?"

"Yeah... yeah, that's fine."

Temeke studied the grin that bracketed Malin's mouth and ushered her in. "I can always count on you to make a witness feel at ease."

"Witnesses usually a little more responsive when you offer refreshments, sir. I made some brownies this morning."

"Brownies? I *love* brownies."

She gave him a wink. "So, what have we got?"

He showed her the yellow Post-it note in a box of evidence pouches in the hall. "Husband on door step marveling why his wife's not answering the phone. Bed's covered in blood and the wife's car is still in the garage. Jarvis called the school. She wasn't there today. Nor was the kid."

"Does Mr. Trandahl have any idea where they went?"

"Hasn't a clue."

Temeke didn't have to tell her to keep quiet. She knew the drill. Complete silence during the first twenty minutes provided them both with the necessary time to do a mental examination before asking questions.

Outside, more officers were searching the perimeter using concentric circles, widening to the main road and any nearby parks. Others were searching child-sized boxes, dog kennels and abandoned houses.

According to dispatch, an Amber Alert had been issued in concern for Hannah's safety. Too much blood at the scene. Too much uncertainty

The living room opened up into a kitchen and at one end they could see the back door was open. Whether it had been left open by Trandahl or by an intruder was not obvious. Temeke expected footprints on the tile. There had been rain, which would mean plenty of mud to trample in.

He walked toward the sound of loud chatter coming from the garage. The floor was painted in a gray epoxy and there were two tool boxes standing against the far wall. It was hard to see much else between the technicians and the open doors of the SUV.

"Can one of you guys give me the license number?" he shouted, not wanting to barge in.

One of the technicians looked up and helpfully rattled off the sequence. Temeke jotted it down on his pad.

"Oh, and one more thing. Is there a sprinkler system controller in here?"

The same technician pointed to a gray box mounted half way up the wall near the left side of the garage door.

"Give me the scheduled times," Temeke asked.

The technician opened the box and squinted at the screen. "Five in the morning and nine at night. Both for thirty minutes."

Temeke waved and nodded his thanks and turned to leave. "Doesn't look like Trandahl spends much time in here, Marl. Either that or he's a neat freak. Most people have some kind of storage. Kids toys, gardening equipment. There's nothing here."

They headed back to the kitchen. Temeke checked the drawers and cupboards, which were neatly stacked and the refrigerator was well stocked with a collection of cooked meals in Tupperware boxes.

He noticed the blinking light on the landline phone. Turning on his tape recorder, he reached for the play button. The messages were from Trandahl, asking where Rachael was and when she was coming home; each one showing more concern throughout the day. None were from any strangers containing a ransom request or any mention of a kidnapping.

Temeke stood at the bottom of the stairs and shouted up at Alice. "Any sign of Mrs. Trandahl's cell phone?"

"Yes," Alice shouted back. "Come on up."

Temeke followed Malin upstairs to the master bedroom and that's when the smell hit him. A thick, coppery odor that always made him gag. He had seen enough gore in the twisted metal of auto accidents, cars lying belly up like smoking turtles and a driver trapped behind glass. Shooting tragedies and meth-related homicides; some so heinous they kept him up at night. He focused on his breathing. A bloody pillow wasn't the worst he'd ever seen.

The cell phone was already bagged and Alice pointed to where it had been. Temeke called the number Trandahl had given him just to be sure it was her phone. The screen lit up but there was no sound.

"What's the use of a sodding phone if the sound's

turned off?" he muttered behind a hand. The battery was at ninety percent.

Malin wince at the scene. "Maybe she was taking a nap."

"There's a few unread messages on the lock screen, including mine."

He handed the bag back to Alice. "Can someone keep an eye on it for calls?"

Alice nodded. "We always do, sir."

They made way for two investigators who were taking samples beside the king-size bed, where the sheets had been peeled back to reveal a large spatter of blood on the pillow. It was no longer dripping from the bedframe and the large volume blood stains on the floor had congealed. Temeke knew a significant area of carpet and bedding would be taken for processing.

The fingerprints on the tufted head board Jarvis had mentioned were mainly smears and on the wall behind it was one print with visible friction ridges. Spatter arced above it; tiny red beads which from a distance reminded him of an abstract painting he had once seen in London's National Gallery.

Even though the bed was ruffled—duvet on the right side pulled back where blood had soaked into the bottom sheet—on the left side, the top edge of the duvet was still tucked underneath the pillows, meaning Trandahl had either made his side of the bed before he left for work or he hadn't slept there last night.

Clothing was scattered across the room, drawers upended and a laundry basket lying on its side under the window. Angled in the corner was a fabric chair paired with an ottoman, where a pair of pantyhose lolled over one arm. The contents of a jewelry box and a purse had been dumped on the floor about a foot from the door.

Temeke crouched, took out a pen from his top pocket and tapped open the purse. The usual feminine articles were inside, including a set of car keys and a wallet. Wedged against one leg of the bed was a shoe, minimal blood spatter on the sole but enough for Alice to bag for urgent analysis.

Temeke looked through the box of sealed evidence pouches and asked Alice if there were any DVD's or videos of *Romeo and Juliet*. She shook her head. He then asked where the yellow Post-it note had been. Alice pointed to the bottom left-hand side of the vanity mirror.

Temeke turned his head toward Malin's ear. "Odd Trandahl never mentioned it."

"I've always thought you were a good judge of credibility," she whispered back. "First impressions?"

"We may find ourselves thinking Mr. Trandahl's guilty. So far, there's circumstantial evidence and very little actual evidence. He could say he didn't kill his wife or do anything to harm his little girl. That an intruder did it. If that's the case, he better start praying for witnesses."

"So you're saying Trandahl isn't a cold-blooded killer. But rather a victim."

Temeke glanced at the pillow and direction of blood flow. "I'm saying he'd better hope they're still alive."

The ceiling fan clicked above his head, sending a breath of cool air down his spine. Being on the second floor the room should have been warmer than the rest of the house. But not today.

"Looks like crap in here," Malin said.

"That's the intention, love. If it is a burglary, time's not on their side." He paused a beat. "Trandahl mentioned a stranger in the neighborhood. Wasn't sure if he could identify him in a line-up."

"It's surprising what witnesses can remember."

Temeke looked down at the floor to a picture frame where the glass had shattered across the image of a young woman. Deep green eyes contrasted with dark hair and pale skin. She had the look of someone assertive;

someone who knew exactly what she wanted.

"Rachael?" he asked.

"That would be my guess."

Temeke jutted his chin at Alice who was in the bathroom. "Find any slugs?"

"Nothing, sir."

"Anything in the medicine cabinet?"

"Paxil for Rachael Trandahl, six tablets left. Toothpaste, nail scissors, a bottle of antacids—half full—and a new box of analgesics still in its seal. Tampons, about six left, and a bag of cotton balls. Oh, and a retainer."

Hopefully, there would be a few dental X-rays to go with that retainer, Temeke thought. "There's three pillows on the bed. Two on one side and one on the other. Any sign of the fourth?"

"No, sir."

"Thanks."

Temeke and Malin proceeded down the corridor to the spare room which accommodated a queen-size bed, computer table and chair, and a window that faced the street. It was small, investigators almost shoulder to shoulder. The laptop was open; LCD display off and LED lights blinking.

Temeke let his finger glance over the touchpad and the screen opened at a logon window. No point wasting time searching for a password; a minor inconvenience like that had never stopped the media compliance officer, Mac Webber. He'd have a report for them in the blink of an eye.

Malin opened the closet, rifled through suits and dresses, glancing down at the shoes. Then she stood on tiptoe and patted the upper shelf. Pulled out a firearm storage box and studied the spongy interior.

"Empty," she said. "There's a receipt inside for a nine mil. Bought two weeks ago."

Temeke felt a crackle of tension. Many of these guns were commonly used for concealed carry and could hold on average fifteen to seventeen rounds in the magazine. In any case, Trandahl was wrong. Someone in the house definitely liked firearms.

"We need the search warrant to include all storage sheds and vehicles on the premises," he said. "That includes the crotch rocket outside and the Highlander in the garage. We also need to know if Rachael had a license to carry a firearm."

They moved down the hall to Hannah's bedroom. The bed had a bottom sheet and a quilt with a blue horse. A plush bear lounged on the pillow and on the desk was a book on basic geometry. No sign of a phone. On the walls were two posters of Captain Jack Sparrow and a picture of a young boy sitting cross-legged in a wood surrounded by fairies and playing a pipe.

An investigator came out of the en suite bathroom with a small jar in a sealed bag. "Vomit in the toilet," he said, making his way out to the corridor without looking back.

Temeke caught the look on Malin's face. "Her father did tell me she was sick."

He opened the closet door, eyes grazing over a sprig-print tea dress and feeling the same pang of sorrow and emptiness he always did at every crime scene.

Missing wife. Missing child. A shit-load of blood.

He knew Malin would do what she did best. Poke around and ask all the right questions, putting her finger on whatever it was he was sensing. He only had to wait a few minutes before she inched her way toward him, looking somewhere past his head toward the street.

"Trandahl's shivering," she whispered, voice trailing off.

"So would you be if you were left behind at a crime scene." Temeke rolled his shoulders and grimaced.

He saw the liaison officer, Maggie Watts, arrive and

muscle her way through a wall of brass to shake Trandahl's hand. She'd been tasked to take him to the command center for interview. Temeke almost pitied the interviewing officer who would have to dig deep into the background of a distraught father, scratching away at the surface without a hope in hell of ever reaching the core.

"Poor old bugger," he said. "Got to be the worst day of his life."

FIVE

Malin wanted to talk to Trandahl a little more. Preferably without having to tune out two more officers who stood in front of the witness in a tight, suffocating clump.

She stood in the hall behind Temeke, unable to tear her eyes from flawlessly sculpted cheekbones and impossibly perfect lips. He was handsome.

Beautiful would be a better word.

Smoothly shaved head and intelligent eyes, and up close he had this scent—some kind of exotic cologne—that stayed under your nose for hours. He was the only person she knew who could rock standard government-issue khakis and polo shirts, *and* hold open doors for female officers at a crime scene.

She left him to Captain Fowler who, in comparison, was a stench of narcissism. He reminded her of a poisonous spider, upper lip quirked as he raked his fingers through the stubble on his head. Why the look of disgust, she couldn't fathom, until his eyes latched onto hers. He'd never liked her.

Malin inhaled sharply and closed her thoughts away.

Walking through the foyer, she saw an investigator videotaping clear droplets on the floor, ones she would never have noticed. He reported most of what the others had seen and added that there was no castoff from the bloodstains.

She kept hearing voices remarking on the lack of spatter caused by a blunt-force blow. While other voices suggested it had to have been from a gun or a knife.

Matt Black, resident crime scene specialist walked in from the garage. A fresh-faced intellectual with the hint of a stutter and a tendency to talk compulsively. He had asked her out a few times and as far as she knew no one else had a line on him. But there was something about him that ruffled her feathers.

"What do you think happened in the bedroom?" she asked.

"No medium or high-velocity patterns on the sheets and very little cast-off spatter on the wall. Just the headboard. Might rule out blunt force trauma." He pinched his chin. "Most of the blood seems to have pooled on the pillow. There's very little void there or on the sheets."

She knew blood distribution patterns told the relative positions of victims and objects. How far the blood flew and at what speed. What she didn't know was the estimate of impact and time between impact, and whether or not someone tried to clean the place up afterward.

"The victim probably didn't fight back against her attacker or try to get away," he said. "There's no drag marks, no smears or wipes. Looks like the carpet in the rest of the house has been freshly vacuumed."

Matt's eyes shot over Malin's shoulder to Alice who was waiting for him to nod her in.

"I just wanted to let you know we found trace amounts of blood on the interior of the car," Alice said. "Steering wheel and gas pedal. Driver's side door handle and frame."

"Any larger amounts?" Matt asked.

"None."

"If bodies had been taken out to the car there should be trails leading from the master bedroom to the garage. Assuming the stains in the car are connected to those in the bedroom."

Malin noticed Alice gave a lazy smile and then sucked in her bottom lip.

"We used luminol in the garage and hallway," she said. "Didn't see anything, except for a small stain near the front door frame. Left side. Also the rear seats in the car are lying flat. Should I start in the kitchen?"

"Yes, thanks." Matt gave her a pat on the shoulder as he walked out to the living room.

Malin followed, recognizing a blatant flirter when she saw one. How old was Alice? Twenty-five? Matt wasn't one to spend lonely evenings in his apartment on Old Airport Road and he had already intimated how much he wanted to take things further with Malin. If she dithered any longer, she'd only regret it.

She had been wrong. Someone did have a line on Matt.

He turned to face her and lowered his voice. "If there were no large amounts of blood in the car either the bodies weren't placed in there or they were tightly wrapped in some kind of protective material."

"But Alice just said the rear seats are flat," Malin said. "That indicates something was put there. When you consider the blood in the master bedroom, we've got to be talking about a body. What about the clear liquid?"

"Possibly an attempt to dilute the blood or get rid of it."

"Clearly we're not looking at someone who broke in because all the doors and windows are intact. We're looking at someone she knew. This person shot or stabbed her, and possibly Hannah, and then transported them both by car. You'd think someone would have seen that."

"Not necessarily," Matt said. "The back of the property faces 7 Bar Loop Road. It runs from Ellison to Coors. The block wall between the back yard and the road has a gap of about five feet between the west and the north side. Very likely punched out by a speeder. But the bricks have been stacked neatly, as if the wall was about to be rebuilt."

"Too close to a school zone and it's 30 mph along Ellison."

"Doesn't mean drivers adhere to it. You know the complaints in this area for speeders making a short cut to Coors."

Malin nodded. Too many to count.

Matt edged a little closer still and stared down at her with a deep frown. "Can I ask you something?"

"Sure."

"I overheard Trandahl telling Temeke that the patio door was open. It's a straight shot from the front door, so he would have seen it when he came in. But he sounded more concerned about his air conditioning bill than a missing wife and kid."

"That was his first reaction, Matt. Let's not forget he hadn't seen the bedroom at that point."

"He didn't say much about the bedroom to Officer Jarvis. Although he did tell him he'd called a few hospitals and the doctor's office. I think—and don't repeat this—maybe he's right about an intruder." Matt huffed out a breath. "Must have scared the shit out of him."

"Well, he looks scared."

Malin tried to imagine it. Nobody in Albuquerque would leave their back door unlocked, especially one exposed to the street. It was unlikely Rachael and Hannah were lifted into a car in broad daylight unless the bodies had been wrapped in something. The houses either side were two storey and neighbors were usually nosy. She hoped Jarvis had some good news.

"Listen," Matt let out another loud breath, "I know I shouldn't be discussing this but—"

"Then don't."

"Can you come over later tonight?"

She shook her head. "A bit unrealistic, don't you think?"

"Tomorrow night then?" He lowered his voice even more. "I reckon we'll have this all wrapped up in twenty-four hours."

"I'm glad you feel so jazzed, Matt, because Trandahl's not talking and there aren't any witnesses. Not exactly a walk in the park, is it?"

"Yet."

Without offering a smile, Malin shrugged. She wanted him to think she had a guarded nature—the type men found to be a challenge. The fact was, no one was taking time off with a high profile case like this. *No one.*

"About six?" he asked.

Malin could see Alice out of the corner of her eye, lifting prints on the master bedroom door handle. It gave her a twinge of satisfaction and she made sure she responded loud enough to be overheard.

"Six then."

SIX

Dr. Vasillion, forensic pathologist and Chief Medical Investigator pulled up outside the house. It was six forty-five.

Temeke had always known the doctor to respond to high profile cases personally and he rarely sent forensic investigators in his place. He shrugged off a dark gray jacket and suited up over a pair of brogues.

"Nice night for it," Temeke said.

"You always say that." Dr. Vasillion shook his hand, then snapped on a pair of gloves. "Agnes here?"

"I believe she's already finished upstairs, doc."

"You given up smoking?"

Temeke could still feel the stump of a cigarette lolling between his lips. Worse whenever someone mentioned it.

"Gave up over three months ago, doc. Got a patch instead. Can't say it's a good substitute but it's a start."

"Apart from the nauseating smell, which, by the way, gets absorbed into everything, even a slice of bread on the kitchen table. I can't say cigarettes ever looked cool hanging from the corner of your mouth."

"My wife never liked it. She kept telling me to be careful where I put my ash. Always fanning smoke out of an open window. Well, it's too cold in the winter and too bloody hot in the summer."

"I heard Serena left you. I'm sorry." Dr. Vasillion ran a hand through a neat crop of gray hair. "Can't be easy with a job like yours."

"Yeah. And now I've stopped smoking. Sod's law, isn't it?"

Dr. Vasillion feigned a smile and walked upstairs to the bedroom. "So you just want me to take a look?"

"If you don't mind."

Dr. Vassillion stared at the scene from the doorway first, while his limber photographer took a few more shots. Then he examined the pillow and the sheets. "There's two pillows on one side and only one on the left. Any sign of the fourth?"

Temeke shook his head. He'd asked himself and everyone else the same thing.

"There is sufficient blood to have caused the death of an adult or a ten year-old-child," Dr. Vasillion said. "Or a serious injury. But the wounds would need to be taken care of. Any blankets missing?"

"We don't know yet. But there's evidence of a hall carpet, if that helps."

"OK, I'll take it from here and I'll get you a preliminary report by tomorrow."

It was Dr. Vasillion's way of saying sod off and let me think. "Thanks, doc."

"You're welcome."

While the doc was crouching and studying the bedroom carpet, Temeke sauntered downstairs.

A breeze whispered through along the corridor and made him shiver. He nodded at a few technicians as they marked objects with small yellow tents and noticed Matt Black whispering to Alice in the study with a handful of clear evidence bags. He took a slip of paper she offered him and slunk back toward the garage.

Temeke wanted to learn everything he could about Rachael Trandahl. Friends, work colleagues, interests. Where she would go if things got bad. His attention was seized by two photographs hanging on the hall wall. One showed a woman around thirty years old wearing a pale blue dress and brown hair cascading onto bare shoulders. The other was a little girl; a close-up of blond curls and a dimple in both cheeks. Pretty. Had her mother's eyes. Must have been five years old then.

He watched Agnes working the scene in a clockwise pattern, usually from all four corners. She carried a boom to take pictures from ceiling height in case anything was missed on the ground.

She turned and gave him a 'Hey, detective', her voice lost behind the whir of the shutter.

Temeke felt the build-up of a sneeze and covered his nose, which did little to disguise a high-pitched squeal.

"You OK?" she asked.

"Allergies," he said, angling his head to take in more of the Swedish accent. "You?"

"Gotta hand it to them, haven't you? I mean, there's Trandahl sobbing his poor little heart out and the captain, what's his name…"

"Fowler."

"…inferred that Trandahl should have been running up and down the street looking for his wife instead of sitting on his doorstep waiting for her to come home. She's not coming home, for crying out loud. Did you see the blood on the pillow? And another thing, why's Fowler permanently stuck to that Cornwell woman? Anyone would think they were joined at the hip. And before you say anything, I'm not interested. Just concerned, that's all."

"Well, that's good of you, Agnes. I'll be sure to tell

Cornwell to watch her goods next time I see her. A word of advice. Pretty woman like you should keep your lens as far away from that cocky bastard as possible. I've seen you shoot a few in his general direction and if he gets wind of your forensic curiosity you'll be needing a restraining order before the weeks out."

"You don't miss a trick, do you?"

"No, love. It's my job."

"I better be doing mine then," she said, adjusting the camera setting.

Temeke knew Agnes was attracted to Fowler's honey-in-your-ears voice, where a six foot frame and cold eyes added to the feral veneer every woman felt the need to tame. What gave her away was the second time she had taken shots of the front door. He had been counting.

"Sir." Malin eased around the corner, sliding her phone back in her pocket. "Sarge called. Maggie's coming to pick up Trandahl, but he wants me back there to interview him."

So it was Malin, poor old sod, who'd been assigned the tricky task of interviewing their witness.

"That's fine with me. But make sure you ask him if he heard anything when he arrived home."

"Like what?"

"Screaming, shouting, shots fired."

"Jarvis already asked."

"Well, *ask* again." Temeke looked at his watch, heard the light patter of rain. "Ask him if he's had anything to eat."

"Why? Do I need to make him a sandwich?"

"You know what I mean. If that were me, I'd be worried sick. Unable to think of eating. Only there's a jar of peanut butter in the kitchen and breadcrumbs on the counter."

"Well you're not him, are you? And some people eat when they're worried."

"What's got into you?"

"Nothing. In any case, it could have been the kid. Kids like peanut butter." Her eyes flicked up the corridor and locked onto Matt. "I'll be on my way then,"

Temeke didn't like that look. "You OK?"

"Yep."

"Want to talk about it?"

"Maybe."

"Tomorrow then," Temeke said. "Around six?"

"You overheard, didn't you?"

"Well, it's a small house, Marl. For your information, Matt took the phone number little Alice offered him. Just a hunch, but I'm betting he'll follow through."

Malin huffed out a loud breath. "You're so full of it."

SEVEN

She awoke to pulses of rain against the windshield. The car had stopped. Where were they?

Dad? Mom?

She tried to spread her fingers across the back seat, but they twitched rather than stretched.

Her cell phone was out of reach. The sound, she remembered, had been turned off. Mom couldn't stand eternal pinging *every time someone texted.*

And kids do text. All the damn time when they should be doing their homework. Not sending cat videos.

Grades, little girl. Grades. Then you can be a big girl with big dreams.

Her toes curled. A warm feeling of socks. The waistband of her jeans cut into her belly and the rivets left tiny dents on her hips.

You're getting fat, little girl. Don't you hate fat little girls? You should, you know.

No, she didn't hate fat little girls. They can't help being fat and anyway fat's *a bad word. Can't say* fat *at school. It makes people cry.*

She was slouched in the rear seat, breeze brushing against her cheek. She tried to shout for help but out came a gurgle no louder than a hitch of breath.

Something her mom had said. Something about being quiet.

Be quiet, little girl. Or you'll be sorry.

It hurt to turn her head, to move her eyes. Below, her knees were covered in a plaid blanket. Looked the same as the one in her room. She was too drowsy to move.

"Mom?"

She didn't recognize the view beyond the car window. It was possible they had gone to get food and left her there because she was sleepy. Had been sleeping. Deeply.

Rain, she thought. Big, heavy drops falling against the roof of the car. Tap, tap, tap!

There were three bottles of water tucked under the front seat. She only needed to pluck one out, break the seal and drink. But she couldn't move.

A sick feeling came over her as she focused on the phone. A beam of light. Someone was calling. Her arms wouldn't reach and she tried to stretch her fingers again but something in her brain wasn't connecting.

Tall street lamps to the left of her and to the right a gray sky. Straight ahead was the familiar ridge of the Sandia Mountains. She could have been anywhere.

There was a break in the rain, silent for the count of sixty, and no more had fallen since. Had she been sleeping? Had it really been raining?

She couldn't lift her body to take a better look. But she remembered something.

Words. Muddled. Like another language. A deeper voice. When they were spoken she had felt hot breath against her cheek. If she could imagine any character that had teeth and a cloud of vapor coming out of its mouth, this was it.

And if it hadn't been for the low grade she got in

geometry, her mom wouldn't have been so mad.

The worst of it was being grounded from iTunes for a week. Fat lot of use that was when she'd been hoping to download the new album from Séance. If she was lucky, she might get two songs.

Mom? Dad?

Her eyes were heavy. Closing to darkness. Then silence.

EIGHT

Malin called Hannah Trandahl's phone. No answer always made her jumpy.

She took a breath and straightened her jacket. The time, according to the clock on the wall was seven fifteen. She had been advised by Sergeant Moran to keep Trandahl in the interview room and away from the media, which was congregating outside like a bat swarm. Commander Hackett was giving a press conference.

Hands flattened on the evidence file, she gave Dai Trandahl a long hard look. Her line of questioning wasn't to go through each detail in order, but to ask the same questions in several different ways.

"I'm Detective Malin Santiago. I've been assigned to the case. Is your name Dai Trandahl?"

"Yes."

"And you've waived your right to counsel?"

"Yes."

"Coffee?" she asked, sliding a fresh cup toward him.

"Thanks."

"This was made by one of our officers." She offered him a slice of key lime pie.

She knew how odd it must have looked, but Dai Trandahl was too well connected to be starved into talking. What were the odds? He was Mayor Oliver's nephew.

She saw him give the tape recorder a casual glance. Recessed into the wall and bolted down like the rest of the furniture because items had been hurled across the room by less than chirpy guests.

Malin recorded the date, time and names of those present. She pushed a plastic bag containing pictures of the crime scene toward him and spoke into the tape recorder.

"Detective Santiago is now showing Dai Trandahl a photograph of his bedroom and the blood on the pillow and carpet. So, how did your day begin?"

There was a shuddering motion of Dai's shoulders before he slumped forward with his face in his hands. He looked up, vacantly at first, and then with dawning nod as if suddenly aware she'd just asked him a question.

"Your day?" she repeated.

Dai dragged his eyes away from the photograph. "Hannah was up. Rachael was still asleep. I noticed her phone was ringing."

"You heard it ringing?"

"No, no. She always turns the volume down before she goes to bed. The screen lit up. Anyway, it was her mother. It's always her damn mother."

"Does she call every day?" Malin noted the expression *mother* as opposed to *mom*.

"More or less. She and I don't get along. Never liked my political views or the fact that I worked for a European car dealership. Rachael is an only child. I expect Hannah will be too."

"Why do you say that?" Malin asked, scrolling through the questions on her notepad.

He hesitated before answering and she realized how awkward he felt. "We're not intimate anymore. I wonder if it's the medication she's taking. Leaves her dizzy and sleeping most of the day. She overreacts. Gets mean."

Malin studied a long face that tapered into a thin drip of a chin. His mouth seemed to twitch into a grimace one moment and a tight smile the next. It made her wonder if he was nervous.

"Anyway, she doesn't have to be at work as early as I do," he said. "I left around seven-oh-five. Got to work at seven thirty. I'm a service advisor at the Porsche dealership on Pan American. Been there four years now. I usually call her around lunchtime. Only today there was no answer."

"Did you leave a message?"

"Yeah. I asked her how she was doing. I didn't hear back, so I left another message at around three on my way to delivering a car to a customer in the heights. When she didn't call back I was concerned. But then things got busy at work so I didn't have another chance to call again until I was driving home."

"What time was that?"

"Around four thirty." He glanced around the gray-walled interview room and wiped an eye. "Got home around five something and parked my bike on the curb. I was going out later with a few biker buddies. When I got inside, I saw the back door open so I assumed they were in the back yard. When I considered she hadn't called me back all day and we never leave the back door open, I was a bit concerned. I called her name. Then I went down the hallway to the garage. Her car was still there."

"How did that make you feel?"

"At first I just thought they had gone for a walk. So I went upstairs and checked Hannah's room first. She wasn't there."

"But when you go upstairs, isn't the master bedroom the first room you see?"

"The door was half-closed and I thought Rachael was taking a nap. When I went in I saw blood... on the bed and on the floor."

Malin was still stuck on why he hadn't gone into the master bedroom first. "Did you touch anything?"

"I don't remember. I called nine-one-one and the lady I spoke to told me to stay calm because I was ranting on about the blood. She told me to go outside and wait for the police."

"Does Rachael take naps during the day?"

"Sometimes. She's a light sleeper. Gets woken up by a door creak. Me? I sleep through anything."

"What did you make of the note on the mirror?"

"What note?"

"You're saying you didn't notice a handwritten note on the mirror?"

"No."

Malin leaned over toward the tape recorder. "I'm now handing Mr. Trandahl a copy of the note. Mr. Trandahl please read the note out loud for the benefit of the tape."

Trandahl picked up the clear evidence bag and took his time reading it. Squinted a few times. "It's Rachael's writing. But I don't remember ever seeing it."

It was possible he was too distracted and never noticed it. Which meant it could have been there for at least twenty-four hours. It could have been placed there after he'd left for work.

"Any idea what it means?"

He shook his head. "No."

"Rachael a religious woman?"

"We used to go to a church but, to be honest, I found it hard. Rachael's Catholic. I was raised Baptist."

"She like movies? Books?"

"Yeah. She has a kindle. Watches movies on the computer. We have Netflix."

"So tell me about Rachael," she asked, sliding the evidence bag in the folder. "On a scale of one to ten where would you put her as a wife?"

"Ten. She's great. Really great. Works at Lincoln Middle School. They like her there. The kids made her a poster for her birthday and some of the moms sent cupcakes."

"Does she belong to any clubs? Women's groups?"

"Yes. Women in Philanthropy and a couple of school groups once a month. The others are about three times a month."

Malin admired women who empowered others and supported local businesses. "So I take it she knows a lot of people."

"Yeah, she does."

"How was she last night?"

"Happy. Chatty. She told me she had been given a pay raise. So we ordered a pizza and watched *The Bachelor*."

"TV or Netflix?"

"Netflix."

"Was this at home?"

"Yeah. Just the three of us. Then Hannah and I went upstairs. Rachael wasn't tired. Said she'd be up later."

Malin watched him yawn and asked him if he needed another coffee. He shook his head, eyes dropping to this hands which were curled on his lap.

"How would you rate your neighbors?" she asked.

"Quiet. Mostly keep themselves to themselves. Hannah likes to hang out with Jack Colby opposite and Bailey Parker in the next house. Food tastes better there apparently."

"So… would you say you live in a safe neighborhood?"

"For the most part. There was a break-in a year ago. Three houses down on the right. But I think the son was a drug addict. He was stealing from his own parents."

"You told Detective Temeke you'd seen a stranger in the neighborhood. A man, right?"

"Yeah. Stocky with spiky blond hair. Wasn't the neighbor's son. He was too old. Probably around thirty-five."

"Was he doing anything suspicious?"

"No, he was just wandering about. Looked lost really."

"Any identifying features?" Malin watched his eyes as they strayed to the ceiling. If he said a do-rag and a tattoo, she'd slap him.

"No."

"Did he have a car?"

"No. No car. He was on foot."

Malin made a mental note to check on the description of the man, meager as it was.

"Does Hannah have a cell phone?"

Trandahl nodded. "It's new."

"You know all phones have tracking features. Provided it's switched on and the battery hasn't died, we can trace it to her last location, that is before it was powered down."

Malin watched his face. The heel of one hand was pressed against one eyebrow and his eyes were glossy. Then wide open.

"So you guys can see where she is right now?"

"They're looking into it." Malin took a breath. "Own a gun?"

"No. I told the other detective I don't like them."

"Want to tell me why there's a firearm storage box in your bedroom?"

"A what? I don't know anything about a storage box."

"The fact that there was one without your knowledge concerns me. As I'm sure it concerns you."

"I didn't put it there."

"I never implied you did." Malin nodded slowly. "Have you always lived in New Mexico?"

"Yeah. Rachael's from Hobbs and I'm from Roswell."

"Would you say your marriage is a happy one?"

"We have the same struggles as everyone else. Money. Not enough time. But our marriage is strong. She's a beautiful person and I'm a lucky guy."

"So there's never been any bad arguments?"

"Not really." His stomach growled. "Nothing big anyway."

"You say you were going out with one of your biker buddies last night. Did you call him and tell him you weren't going?"

"No... I forgot."

Malin looked at her watch and jutted her chin at him. "You hungry?"

"I could do with a sandwich."

Malin tapped out a quick text to her colleague, Maggie Watts asking for food. Also asking for any sign of a license to carry a firearm for Rachael Trandahl. She also texted Temeke to see if he was on his way back to the substation.

"Do you like peanut butter?" she asked.

"Hannah does. I make her a PB&J every morning although she says she's getting too old for them."

"Did you make one this morning?"

"Yeah. For her lunch box."

"Since neither Rachael nor Hannah were at school today, any idea where they might have gone?"

She was clinging by her fingernails to the best case scenario. Rachael and Hannah would be found before the night was out, staying perhaps with a friend or driving to another state in a rental car. Unlikely with so much blood at the scene.

He looked at his phone, forehead creased into three deep lines. "She does counseling. But it's an online thing. WebDoc or something. Apparently, he's Nobel Prize-winning psychiatrist from Harvard."

"You don't know his name?"

"I forget. But she says the counseling has really helped her. Now I'm really worried. What if… what if someone's killed them? Oh God…"

Malin held up a hand. "We don't have a body and that's a good thing. So, let's hang onto that, okay?"

NINE

Malin watched Trandahl peel the plastic wrapper from his sandwich and squint at a wedge of beef.

"So tell me, Dai," she said, eyes floating up to the clock. It was just past eight. "Can I call you Dai?"

"Sure. Everybody does."

"Rachael have any other cell phones? One for work maybe?"

"No. Only the one."

"How old is Hannah now?"

"Ten. She's smart." He beamed.

"Does Rachael work in Hannah's class?"

"Yeah. There's a period where she grades papers and they work on assignments in the morning." He took a large bite of his sandwich and chewed for a few moments. "She leaves school around eleven forty-five. Goes shopping and goes back to pick up Hannah. I usually call her sometime in the afternoon to see how she's doing. But today I didn't get to talk to her."

"But yesterday everything was OK?"

"Yeah."

"She didn't tell you she was going away? No bags packed?"

"No."

"What time does Hannah go to bed?"

"Around ten on school nights. Later at weekends."

"And Rachael?"

"A few hours after me. Eleven."

Judging by the look on his face, Malin realized he didn't really know. Could have been eleven. Could have been in the early hours. "Hannah got a favorite stuffed toy? Blanket?"

"Bit old for toys. She has a blanket. Brown plaid. Had it since she was three."

Malin caught the sob way back in his throat. "You doing OK?"

"I feel like I've been put through the ringer."

"Do you think something bad happened?"

Dai nodded. "I keep thinking someone hurt them. Took them, you know. You saw the blood."

"As far as you remember, where was the blood?"

Dai frowned at Malin and then looked down at his lap. "On her side of the bed. It was dripping on the carpet. She must have been bleeding pretty bad."

"Was there blood anywhere else in the house?"

"No. But that's good, isn't it?"

Malin looked down at an incoming text. According to Maggie, the news vans were leaving. And no, there was no license to carry a firearm for Rachael Trandahl. "Did you see anything strange in the house? Anything unusual?"

"Like what?"

"Anything broken into. Anything disturbed."

"Well, the jewelry for one. In our bedroom. Rachael's handbag was on the floor." He held up a hand. "I don't remember seeing Hannah's blanket on her bed. Maybe it was in the laundry basket but I didn't think to look. It was the blood... really freaked me out."

Malin saw an image of Rachael sleeping before being attacked by an intruder. But that scenario got murkier by the minute, especially if she was, as Trandahl claimed, a light sleeper.

"Do you have any enemies, Dai?" she asked.

"No. Not that I know of."

"Any other family in Albuquerque?"

"Only Uncle Bill."

Only Uncle Bill, the mayor of Albuquerque. The comment was almost flippant and if she hadn't been sitting opposite Dai she would have laughed.

"Do you remember touching anything? Sometimes when we're in shock, we touch things and we don't remember what things."

"You're right. I don't remember. I looked around the house. Must have touched a whole pile of shit. I assume you mean door handles and that kind of thing."

"For instance, which phone did you use to call nine-one-one?" she asked.

"My cell phone."

"You didn't feel like using the landline in the bedroom?"

"No. I always use my cell phone. We only keep the landline for emergencies. I know how it sounds. But when you have a cell phone you reach for that first."

"Right. So you're a close family."

"Very." He looked down at his phone and checked his messages.

Malin noticed a flush to his cheeks at an incoming text. He switched the phone on silent and placed it face down on the table.

"Won't you need to hear that if Rachael calls?" she asked.

"It's just someone from work."

Malin studied his posture. There was a seriousness about him. An earnestness. She couldn't put her finger on it but the determined edge to his composure kept her from believing him. "Are there any problems. Physically, I mean, between you and your wife?"

"It's the depression I can't handle. Hard to know what makes her mad." He stared at the back of his phone. "I never know if she's gonna make it through the day. She told me depression is like being inside a collapsing building. You can't get out from under it. So I thought a vacation would help. I thought—well, assumed really—that it would bring her back."

"Did it?"

"She said it was madness. We don't have the money. I didn't have the nerve to disagree."

Malin looked down at her notepad at a question she had about his laptop. "I understand you use a computer."

"We all do."

"With your permission, we'd like to look through the hard drive."

He shrugged and leaned forward a little. "I have no problem with that."

And if you did, we'd look anyway. "Do you have an alarm in the house?"

"No. The house is wired up with an alarm system but we never bothered to renew the subscription. For the most part, it's a safe neighborhood."

TEN

Temeke parked outside Northwest Area Command. Like all the substations in Albuquerque it housed a state-of-the-art gym, a lockup and a detective's unit.

The gray brick building was dedicated to two fallen cops. One officer had been his friend. The other he barely knew. There was something disturbing about recalling a sad memory and feeling nothing. Perhaps he was too afraid to put a jinx on his own career.

There were three flags to the left of the front façade, rolling like billows of silk and masking the glare of a dying sun. He couldn't remember the last time he rasped a match on the outside wall and puffed away a few precious moments. The cravings were fewer now. Life was cheaper.

Sergeant Moran was in the lobby eating a plate of key lime pie. He wiped a dribble of cream from his chin and buzzed Temeke in.

"Trandahl's a lucky sod. Already had two slices."

"Blimey, Sarge, what else does he want. A charred steak from The Rancher's Club? This is a police station not a sodding café."

Sarge must have interpreted the frown on Temeke's face as requiring explanation. He leaned over the desk and lowered his voice. "It's because the mayor just happens to be a relative and Malin knows on which side her bread is buttered. By the way, you just missed your favorite journalist. She said its time you two hooked up."

"You can tell Jennifer Danes I'm very flattered, but I'm also very married." Hiding behind an ex-wife had its merits. "Malin still interviewing?"

"Far as I know."

Temeke sauntered toward the incident room with the smell of crime scene still lingering on his shirt. Looking around, he noted Captain Fowler was absent. But so was Detective Cornwell.

Suzi Cornwell was the Jessica Rabbit of the unit. A flame that had already guttered in Fowler's pilot light. According to Maggie Watts, Suzi had been tweeting her dirty laundry in public which, in Maggie's words, rendered her *insanely vulnerable*. Apparently, Fowler had had a little moment with a waitress in the coat closet at the Hispanic Cultural Center. Now Suzi was past tense.

Hackett's assistant was hooking up a laptop to the flat-screen mounted on the far wall. On the table was a box of fresh donuts brought in earlier by the *Stand True 4 Blue* team; volunteer citizens who supported local law enforcement.

Temeke took a seat between Maggie Watts and Officer Jarvis, both looking down at their laps and consulting Facebook. Lieutenant Luis Alvarez hurled a banana skin in the trash and four other officers gave hurry-up yawns.

"So, what have we got?" Temeke asked.

"Looks like a neighbor thought she saw Rachael's car last night." Hackett pushed a photograph of Rachael's Toyota Highlander toward him. "Jarv has the details."

Jarvis put down his phone and sat a little taller. "It was

a Mrs. Rhonda Milow, sir, from number 4217. She was walking her dog. Said she thought she saw Rachael driving down the street around ten, ten thirty last night. Thing is, there are three Highlanders in the area, same color, same year, and since she didn't see it come out of the Trandahl's garage she couldn't be sure."

Hackett pushed his half-moon glasses further up his nose and scanned the flat-screen. "Manager at the Chevron gas station on Coors dropped off video footage at the front desk half an hour ago. I'd like to hear your opinion, Temeke."

"Well, I'm here now, so let's crack on."

"He knows Mrs. Trandahl quite well." Hackett laced his hands over his gut and peered over his glasses. "Said she mentioned receiving an anonymous death threat. When he asked her to call the police she seemed reluctant. Said it was probably some high school prankster."

"What's his name, this manager?" Temeke asked, narrowing his eyes at the security video. The man behind the store counter appeared to have blond hair, athletic, possibly early thirties.

"Josh Childers. He was concerned about his friendship with Rachael. Didn't want her husband to think he was moving in on his missus. But he thought the tape was relevant to our enquiries."

Hackett's assistant maximized the window on the big screen, which showed a short clip of Rachael Trandahl filling up her car and then walking into the store. The time stamp showed four-fifteen on Wednesday afternoon.

"Due to the reflection on the windshield, we can't see Hannah inside," Hackett said. "But from the in-store camera we see Rachael buying two bottled waters."

Temeke watched a clip of Rachael, sheathed in what he understood from the manager's description as a red dress. Since the security footage did not have audio, he had to interpret her sucked in lip and hands pressed against her stomach as nervousness. She nodded frequently at the manager while making her purchases.

"The store manager recorded the conversation," Hackett said. "And before you ask why, he said she was jumpy. He was concerned about the death threat, enough it seems to follow her to the back of the store. That's when he heard her talking on the phone. Didn't want to interrupt, but she seemed distressed and he felt it was his responsibility to tape her."

"With what?" Temeke asked.

"The app on his cell phone. He said he might have missed about ten seconds but he caught most of it."

The final portion of the video showed Rachael at the mid-section of the store facing the window. The store manager stood a few feet behind, cell phone in his hand.

Hackett's assistant froze the video so they could listen to the audio tape.

"… just calm down, will you?" Rachael said. "What am I supposed to do? Hide under a stone?"

Several seconds passed, then she said, "Well, if you must know I'm tapped out. In serious trouble. Do you have any idea what it's like to tiptoe around a suspicious husband? One minute you're up and the next you're down. Don't get me wrong but you and I seem to be going in two different directions… That's not what I signed up for. Am I what? Oh, knock it off, will you? Of course I'm not drunk. Just because I was half in the bag the other night doesn't mean I do it all the time? Do you have any idea how humiliating this is?"

She went quiet again.

"It's no good tap dancing around the truth. I'm not taking second place and you're not going to hurt her either. I'll call the cops. I mean it. Just stop with the threats, OK?"

Temeke counted three seconds of silence before Rachael hung up. Meaning the person she was calling had hung up first *and* that Rachael knew exactly who had sent her the death threat.

Hackett ran the video forward, picking up Rachael inside her car before cruising out of shot. "I'm guessing she went home, had dinner. Then somehow disappeared this morning."

"Is Trandahl being consistent?" Temeke asked.

"So far, yes."

The room fell silent as the impact of the scene began to strike a chord.

"Any CCTV on the south side of the building?" Temeke asked. "Going out in the street and beyond would help."

"None." Hackett's stare was dark and cold, like the coffee in Temeke's hand.

"In a city populated by nosy eyewitnesses and cameras posted in every parking lot, you're telling me Rachael Trandahl ceased to exist?"

"We do have video from a nearby ATM machine. About a block away that captures her withdrawing some cash."

"We'll need medical records, sir, which could take a while without a warrant."

"Not if they're needed to identify a suspect and two missing persons."

"One other question. Since this case is being covered by the press I'd like to ensure discretion where Mayor Oliver is concerned. We don't want it being compared with the near kidnap of his own son."

"Agreed." Hackett removed a sharpened pencil from inside the spiral binding of a Weight Watchers notebook and began scribbling. "Captain Fowler is taking care of all media enquiries."

"Do you think that's wise, sir? Considering his chatty nature."

Hackett stopped writing and met his gaze. "Unless, of

course, you'd rather—"

"Not at all, sir. The ladies at the *Journal* have come to enjoy Fowler's type of discretion."

Hackett gave the shadow of a smile. "I need you to take a look at every website Trandahl's ever visited, every transaction he's made and every person he's ever spoken to. I want this guy nailed."

ELEVEN

Malin sat alone in the interview room waiting for Trandahl to return from the bathroom. It was almost nine o'clock.

Her fingers tapped the surface of the table, mind focusing on her call to the Porsche dealership. According to the service advisor's recorded message the place closed at seven. She hung up with a note to herself to call early tomorrow morning.

Her phone then lit up with an incoming text. *Wingman*, an anonymous caller who had helped her with so many cases, she had begun to think of him as a friend.

Wingman: You can learn so much from a marriage. A seemingly perfect family. A vulgar secret. A frantic search. There's only ever one way out.

Malin tapped out a response: You gonna tell me who you really are anytime soon?

Wingman: We were talking about two missing women. More important, don't you think?

Malin: How did you hear about it?

Wingman: In the same way I hear about everything.

You never want to let a case get as far as age progression photos of missing people. Or a human leg dangling out of a backhoe bucket at a landfill. I'll leave you with one tiny question. Who's Ella?

Dread inched up Malin's throat, before the door opened and in walked Trandahl. She returned her phone to the table; facedown.

"How are you feeling?" she asked.

"OK. I guess." He looked down at his hands and grimaced. "Any news?"

"I'm afraid not. But while we're waiting, I would like to ask you a few more questions." She took a breath. "Did you change your clothes when you got home?"

"No."

"Do you have a locker at work where you can put your clothes?"

"No, I don't need one. I never change clothes at work."

"Any mental health problems?"

"No."

"Ever been in trouble for anything when you were a kid?" She knew he hadn't but even priority background checks took time. "By that I mean have you ever been in juvy?"

"Shit, no."

"What about Rachael?"

"Only the depression, although I wouldn't call it full-blown depression. Not if she doesn't have to take her medication all the time. Just gets down from time to time. And no, she's never been in trouble."

"Apart from the vacation Rachael said you couldn't afford, have there been any serious financial problems?"

"The mortgage is high. We bought the house when Rachael worked at Mountain Financial. Our joint salary was bigger then. She used to be an assistant branch manager. Now she's an assistant to a school principal."

"How much do you make a year?"

"About fifty thousand. Not much when you've got a

$200,000 house. She earns around $29,000."

Malin understood the financial burden on a two storey house would have been stressful, but they were earning a shit-load more than she was. "Are you Hannah's natural father?"

"Yes."

"Are you close to Hannah?"

"Yeah. I rarely get mad at her. Except the time when she slammed the car door with the force of an F5 tornado. Said it was the wind. She can be funny sometimes. Hilarious actually. I'm not funny. Ever."

"Does she play soccer?"

"She's trying on a range of activities at the moment. It was soccer last week. It'll be karate next. She's discovered sarcasm and eye rolls. Got a shoe box hidden in the back yard for the foxes. The ones, that is, that can't fend for themselves. She wears her mom's make-up. I know because I found some in her backpack. I think she's wonderful even when she's having a meltdown."

"Would you say you're close to your parents?"

"So-so."

"Does Rachael have brothers and sisters?"

"One sister. Lives in Dallas."

"Are they close?"

"Not really. I can't remember the last time Rachael spoke to her. Probably last Christmas. Louise is married to a stockbroker. Big money."

"Does Rachael have any close friends?"

"I wouldn't say anyone really close. There's a woman at work she talks to. They go out for lunch sometimes but that's about it. Bev somebody-or-other."

One person she could cling to, Malin thought. "Have you ever had any affairs?"

"Affairs? Oh, no. Just the mild flirtation. The boys at work like to go out on Friday nights and sometimes things get a little wild. Nothing too out of hand though."

"Does she have girls' nights?"

"Yeah. They do dinner. I don't think they do clubs."

"Would you say you were moody? Easygoing?"

"I'm easygoing. Pretty calm for the most part. Rachael's tantrums don't bother me as much as they bother Hannah. If only I could find the *off* switch."

"Rachael has tantrums?"

"She pitches a fit when she's overwhelmed. It can be explosive sometimes. That's why she gets on the phone to her damn mother. They go on for hours. I don't know what they talk about. What do women talk about?"

"Clothes, boyfriends, husbands."

"Do you have a close friend?" he asked.

"Yeah." Malin thought of Maggie first and then Temeke. They had both been loyal. Both been close.

"I don't have anyone I could call *close*," he said. "There was this gal at work. Naomi Michaels. She was the admin assistant at Porsche. Left about six weeks ago. But we'd talk a little. I liked her. We weren't—you know—intimate. Just friends."

"Do you prefer women to men?" she asked. "I mean to talk to?"

"Yeah, I do. I work out three times a week at the gym nearby and there's this woman there. A manager. I can tell her anything."

"Can you give me her first name?"

"Emma. Emma Burnett."

"Might want to give me her number. And while you're at it give me Naomi's."

He swiped through the contacts on his phone and read them both out to her.

"Are you seeing Emma?" she asked.

"No, of course not. Before I got married I found it hard to put roots down. I could never find a woman to suit my temperament, someone with a little excitement. Now, I'm settled, Rachael's the best thing that's ever happened to me."

Malin looked down at her left hand and wondered what it would feel like to be married. Holidays flooded with family and evenings curled up on the couch. Warm images began to settle in her chest and she swallowed a swell of emotion. It would never happen.

"Does the name Ella mean anything to you?" she asked.

"No, can't say it does."

TWELVE

Faint, rhythmic sounds woke her.
 "Dad?"
 Her tongue was swollen and her nostrils were full of mucus. Dad was snoring again. He always snored when she slept beside him. Big hairy dog snores, wet against her ears.
 Sometimes at night the little rabbits shrieked. Skinned alive in their back yard by the coyotes. That's when dad let her climb into bed beside him, even though mom said she was too old.
 But there were no little rabbits. She wasn't in bed and he wasn't beside her.
 The smell of leather had jogged her awake. A yellowish tinge came from the dome light and a mosquito buzzed along the ceiling.
 It was dark outside, except for a street light. It seemed to be wearing a halo, misty against a black sky. On the right was a gray building set high up on the side of the mountain. A white roof. A large stone sign too far away to read.

"Mom?"

This was all happening too fast. The dark, the sudden awakening from a deep sleep. There was a green air freshener fixed to one of the air vents that smelled of pine needles and something else. Nail varnish remover?

Not her mom's car. Then whose?

She unhooked herself from the seat belt, plucked at the blanket and brushed it off her legs.

Pulling herself forward, she reached around the seat, one hand slapping against leather. But looking up into the rearview mirror confirmed what she already knew. There was no one there.

She plucked a bottle of water and snapped off the cap, chugging half of it before she felt normal again. Wiping her hand across her mouth, she grabbed her phone, thumb pressed against the home button, and saw what the flashing light had tried to warn her.

Battery dangerously low.

She slipped through the gap between the front seats and popped open the glove box. No charger. There wasn't one in the console either.

She turned on the volume of her phone and texted three words to her mom. Where are you?

Three seconds passed. She decided to spam her.

Mom.

Mom.

Mom.

Which was quicker? Scrolling through contacts or dialing? She dialed the number and heard her mom's voice, lips mouthing the words she had committed to memory. 'This is Rachael Trandahl. I'm sorry I can't come to the phone, please leave a message after the beep.'

"Mom, it's me. Where are you? I'm in the car."

And then it hit her.

"You've gone and done it again, haven't you? You've gone and damn-well left me!"

Pulling the blanket around her shoulders, she opened the passenger door. A cool breeze and the smell of tree sap.

"Mom. Pick up!"

She felt nauseous at the silence.

"Mom, you better pick up. There's no one here…"

The light on her phone began to dim and she rammed the home button with her thumb.

No, no, please… don't… not now.

No little gray apple. No slider to reset the phone.

The black screen of death.

THIRTEEN

Malin studied Dai Trandahl as he stifled another yawn. Lifting weights three times a week had left him in good shape and she couldn't deny how it made her feel nervous.

"Can't we finish this tomorrow?" he asked. "I'd like to go home now."

"Since we've got custody of the house, I suggest you stay with a friend for a while. Got anywhere in mind?"

He nodded.

"Just a few more questions then."

"I've already told you I don't know where they are. I came back and found the house empty. Don't you guys get it? Or have you already decided who your so-called suspect is? Because I can tell you, it's not me. I have witnesses to prove it."

There was a rise to his voice that was out of proportion to the complaint, and Malin tapped out a quick text to Maggie, asking her to call family friends for character references.

"Let's talk about marital problems. Because all marriages have them. Anything you want to tell me?"

"I thought we'd already talked about that."

"No, Dai, I don't think we have."

He swallowed down another yawn. "It's usually about money. Sixty grand a year was one hell of a hike on what we've got now. Scratching a living together is bound to cause fighting, especially when you can't have the things you're used to."

"I was referring to the last few weeks. Let's keep it there for now."

"Sure. I... I wanted to add that although we love each other we don't always sleep in the same room. I snore. She gets mad. So it's the couch or the spare room for me."

"Was it like that last night?"

"Yeah."

The spare room, as Malin recalled, was surprisingly clean. "Do you always make the bed?"

"Always. She gets mad if I don't."

"How would you describe Rachael? Physically."

"She's a beauty. Five-seven, green eyes, brown hair. She doesn't wear that much make-up. She doesn't need to. I could never understand what she saw in me."

"You get horny thinking about her?"

"What kind of question's that? Do I need an attorney?"

"Not unless you have something to confess?"

"I don't."

"How much does she weigh?"

"At the beginning she was around a hundred and thirty pounds. More recently a hundred and fifty. So, a bit overweight."

Fine lines spidered the corners of his eyes and his smile seemed false. If Malin wasn't imagining it, he was giving her a good looking over. Then his lips suddenly clamped together and he nodded. "I'm sorry if that was offensive."

Malin shrugged it off. What was weight to her when she was gaining every day?

Dai, on the other hand, was—what?—five eight and about a hundred and eighty pounds? He worked out, so he could have carried Rachael... through the house to the garage. Laid her in the back of her car...

"Any reason why the back seats were down in Rachael's car?" she asked.

"Yeah, we took some old furniture to the dump last week. Garden tools and a folding table. Just never got around to putting the seats back."

Yet he could have used the car earlier in the morning to transport a body before going to work on his bike.

"Tell me about Hannah? Is she tall, petite, blonde, what?"

"She's tall for her age. Went through a growing spurt recently. Had to buy all new clothes. She's skinny. Hair's got darker over the years. It's kind of a dirty blonde now. She's a social media whiz. Calls me a *rad dad*. Is it bad to say I love her more than anything else?"

Malin didn't answer.

"Being an only child, she's independent," he said. "We had her tested for ADHD when she was in preschool, around three years old. But the doctor said she was fine. She's happy going up to strangers and exchanging names. So an extrovert, I guess."

"How do you discipline her?"

"Bargaining mostly. She'll do anything for a milkshake. We do time-outs but I've never spanked her."

"Would you say you were the stronger disciplinarian?"

"I'd say it was more Rachael. She can be a little harsh sometimes." He massaged his head. "Listen, shouldn't I be out looking for them? Because sitting here is ripping my guts out."

"There's no point going out and driving around. We have a team looking at every possibility. And I mean, *every* possibility. That's why I'm here to talk to you. Just in case you come up with something I can pass on to them."

Her phone buzzed with an incoming text from Maggie and Malin angled her phone away from Trandahl to read it.

Jarvis concluded his interviews. 4 neighbors and 6 work buddies claim Trandahl a good honest guy. Same with Mrs. T. Hannah well liked at school. No incident reports. Gunshot was heard by Dr. Fredericks at 4217, although he thought it was a car backfiring. Time: Sometime between 7 and 8.

"Is there anyone at my house?" Dai asked.

"Yes. There's someone there in case your wife comes home. Why don't you give me a place… somewhere we can look? I know you're tired, but the more information you can give me, the better it is. Sound good?"

"I don't know where to look. I don't know where they'd be."

Malin wondered if she needed to go through any of her previous questions to see if there were inconsistencies, but settled on, "Would you do anything to harm Hannah?"

"No." His brows knotted into deep V. "I couldn't hurt her."

"Did you take them somewhere?"

"You mean drive them and leave them? No. I would never do that."

"Can you explain the damage to the back wall of your property? You having a gate put in?"

"No, we think it was an accident. Someone must have driven into it. In any case, we'd need permission to put a gate in. It's a main road back there."

Malin took the answer to mean he'd thought about it, done the research and decided it wasn't worth the bother. "What do you believe happened in your house this morning?"

"I think somebody took them, don't you?"

Again Malin didn't answer.

"I think someone hurt them," he said. "Perverts do that, you know. Watch little girls. She's cute. Really cute. You don't think…"

"We don't *think* anything yet." Malin took in the smooth skin that appeared to have taken on a stony pallor. "Would you be willing to provide us with a written timeline of your activities over the past two days?"

"Yeah, sure."

"Before I let you go, during your interview were you at any time threatened, promised anything?"

"No, I wasn't."

"And is this statement made of your own free will?"

"It was."

"Were you treated respectfully, allowed regular breaks, refreshments?"

"Yes, I was given everything I needed."

"Anything else you'd like to add to this tape recording?"

"I'd like to say I'm sorry this happened to my wife. I wish I could pretend it had never happened. But you can't with stuff like this."

Malin went to join Temeke in the viewing room next door.

FOURTEEN

Malin watched Temeke as he stared through the window, eyes following Trandahl as he walked back and forth with a phone pressed to his ear.

It was Rachael's mother Trandahl was talking to and it was clear by his responses she hadn't seen or heard from her daughter.

"Trandahl doesn't look the type to hurt his wife," Malin said. "But I doubt he'd turn the other cheek to an affair."

"Turning the other cheek is about as useful as a pillow fight in a nuclear war, love, and this particular marriage was a combat zone not a vacation spot." Temeke chewed on a Nicorette. "Is he a cocaine... heroin user?"

"Neither. No track marks." Malin gave Temeke a long, hard look. "Why are you all dressed up?"

"Felt I owed it to Trandahl, him being related to the mayor and all."

"Baloney. You were out on a date."

"So?"

"Who with?"

"Since when is it your business who I go out with." His rope-muscled body suddenly went rigid.

"She stood you up again, didn't she? I bet she hasn't even called to apologize." Malin was itching to say it. "If you want my opinion—"

"I don't."

"You should call her and tell her *three* times is enough. Although even that might be invasive. Honestly, sir, it's disrespectful. Of course you never listen. Always running that mouth off and pretending you're better. What is that?"

"What's what?"

"That? You know, the superiority thing you always do."

He just grinned, shoulders trembling with laughter. His loyalty wasn't one of those blink-or-you'll-miss-it things. It was out there like a big waving flag. He held things close to the fence and wouldn't discuss Serena. But Malin wished he'd take her advice and get closure for once.

"It's not funny, sir. You should call it a day."

"It's not my marriage on the line here, Marl. It's his. Look at him. Head in his hands one moment and then mouthing something to his invisible friend. Maybe he's praying. He better be praying. He doesn't have an alibi for the hours leading up to his wife's disappearance."

"I think he was trying to set up an alibi by calling home so many times," she said. "Even though he knew Rachael was already dead. His actions don't jibe with what he claims. When he came in he said he called out 'I'm home!' but didn't check on Rachael immediately."

"Didn't need to. Told me he checked the garage for her car *after* entering the house through the front door. His bike was parked in the street, meaning he didn't use the remote to access the house via the garage. If she habitually took a nap in the afternoon, for whatever reason, then why bother checking? He might have woken her up."

Malin knew Temeke had done that many times with his ex. Graves' disease had kept Serena up during the night and she routinely took a nap when she got home from work, which would have been around six in the evening.

"Trandahl said Rachael has a friend at work called Bev," Malin muttered. "I'd like to talk to her ASAP in case Rachael ever confided in her."

Temeke nodded. "Trandahl strike you as someone with an explosive temper? The type who doesn't remember shit afterwards?"

"You mean triggers?"

"Yeah. Marriage isn't an easy street. Too much stonewalling, dismissing comments, put downs. When aversive chains last too long things can get violent."

Malin couldn't help watching Temeke out of the corner of her eye. Along the back of his neck was a whirl of a scar, the relic of a knife wound inflicted by his father when Temeke was seven years old. She'd never really studied it before. But it revealed the life of a little boy in Brixton, London, struggling to escape the torment of a lunatic alcoholic who regularly beat his mom. No wonder Temeke went to such lengths to protect the kids.

"The *Journal* want to publish an article in tomorrow's paper," Temeke said. "No names, no suspects, just a brief explanation. Of course, there's no knowing what else they might come up with."

"They'll print names and they'll print suspects. When has Jennifer Danes ever kept a promise?"

"It's not in her job description to keep promises."

"It's our job to stay off the phone and stop feeding the rumor mill."

"What are you saying?"

"Fowler."

Temeke pulled his gaze from her and returned his attention to the window. "Are you sure he was talking to Jen?"

"Of course I'm sure. She gets a little something. He gets a little something. Everyone's happy. Except the family. When does anyone think of the family?"

Temeke narrowed his eyes, fingers massaging the dome of his head. "Any character references on Trandahl?"

"Maggie says there's been a steady flow of calls from friends and neighbors, sir. All very flattering."

Temeke rocked slightly on his feet. "I called the number Trandahl gave me for his bank manager, Calvin Dowie. Went straight through to voicemail. So I spoke to his assistant, Kate Harroway. She could only give me a few minutes but it was an informative few minutes. According to her, the Trandahls have had an account at Mountain Financial for several years. Loyal customers. No complaints. She also confirmed Rachael worked there as an assistant branch manager. She was cheerful and good to work with. But latterly she was let go. It upset Kate because she didn't know why. Then Rachael came to see Dowie two weeks ago and wanted to open a second bank account in her name only. Deposited a large sum of money. Kate remembered the day quite well because she saw a lot of hand gesturing through the open blinds. If she could bet on it, Rachael was having financial problems."

Temeke glanced away, eyes tracking the glass through which he could study Trandahl. "I appreciate Kate Harroway is legally obligated to protect her customer's privacy, but I got the impression she might have liked to talk some more."

Malin knew what he meant. Had he have spoken to Kate face-to-face it would have been a look, a gesture. It was all there when you studied it in slow-mo. "You want me to interview her?"

Temeke nodded. "Get an interview with Dowie as well. I'll text you the details."

"If Rachael wanted to keep a second bank account a secret from her husband, sir, why open one at the same bank where they had a joint account?"

"Her old place of work. *Family* so to speak."

Malin looked through the observation window at Trandahl. "Looks like he's finished his call, sir. Better get back."

"You keeping him up all night?"

"If he'll talk then, yes. I wouldn't mind following him after he leaves here."

"He doesn't need twenty-four hour surveillance, Marl."

"If you were him where would you go?"

"Home, in case my old lady happened to walk in through the front door. There'd be a shit-load of questions. Unfortunately *home* is off-limits for him. But he won't go to ground, Marl, not now his face and name's all over the papers. Besides, his neighbors will be watching if he decides to hop over a fence or two."

"Baloney. Did you see any neighbors stumbling over themselves to give us a statement? Trandahl knows something, sir. So how do we get ahead of him?"

"Speak to his boss, friends and Internet love interests. There's someone out there who's just about to become our favorite worst nightmare."

Malin gave him a quick nod and searched her phone for an email from Detective Mac Webber. The preliminary report was already in her inbox.

"Looks like Trandahl's using a dating site, sir. Screen name; *SilentAdmirer*."

FIFTEEN

Temeke jogged upstairs to the bull pen he shared with Malin, a room they affectionately referred to as the Oval Office. If it wasn't for a large window that faced north, it would have been dark and uninhabitable.

He was proud of it: a moderate sized space with two desks pushed together, walls and carpets a commercial-grade gray. It was small and functional, although back in the eighties a room like this would have been the toilets.

It was the first time he'd ever sat at a desk older than himself, where he crammed all kinds of things in his drawers, because he couldn't be bothered to do any filing.

He pulled out a pink piggy bank and shook it. A few quarters for coffee in the vending machine when he'd drunk everything in the pot. His mind couldn't stop spooling over Malin's voice.

If you were Trandahl where would you go?

He had responded with one word. Home. It seemed unfair of Temeke to do a little surveillance of his own, especially after telling Malin Trandahl didn't need to be watched. But now seemed an excellent time to do it.

Firing up his computer to check for mail—those with long attachments his smart phone didn't seem to handle—he found one from Lieutenant Alvarez.

Like to have a word about Sergeant Thompson's request (attached). Would also appreciate an update on Trandahl ASAP.

Temeke tried opening Sergeant Thompson's attachment but the little red box, which assured him there was a PDF attached, was lying.

He sat back and sighed, eyes intuitively swinging to the corkboard hanging on the wall. Twenty-eight smiling faces pinned in chronological order, a timeless collection of cold case victims.

His *Lost Children*.

He'd salute them sometimes when no one was looking, tell them he'd find them one day. But killers never talk and victims remained hidden in the mud, or the concrete or whatever sandy hole the ugly-ass bastards had dug.

Years of wading ankle deep in the filth of what killers left behind, Temeke refused to be put off by lack of evidence and strained resources. With new technology in DNA and automated fingerprint matching, he was hell-bent on taking on the most challenging cases.

It was hotter this year than last, although he said that every year. Leaves clinging for weeks longer due to a lack of wind last fall, brown peeking through a canopy of green. If Hannah was out there, she'd have a fighting chance.

Serena still hadn't called and he'd been pouncing on every text for the past few hours. Calling her, as Malin had pointed out, was probably invasive. Serena would only say, "It's good to hear from you, David, but you *shouldn't* call so much. Promise me you won't?"

A whiny hinge and then the face of Lieutenant Alvarez. "Glad I caught you. Did you get my email?"

"I haven't opened it yet, Luis," Temeke said, knowing he'd need Malin's soft touch for that. "I was on my way out to the Trandahl house. For a drive, as it happens."

"You mean a little surveillance."

"Can't hurt."

"No, no. Right."

It had never been awkward working for Serena's brother. In fact, Temeke had skillfully managed to maneuver most subjects in his favor, as in where she was living and which stores she frequented. He had followed her countless times since their separation and, as far as he knew, she hadn't suspected a thing.

"So what's the latest?" Lieutenant Luis Alvarez combed a hand through freshly clipped hair and pulled out Malin's chair. "Think he knows something?"

"Hard to say. But the internet report wasn't in his favor."

"Torture porn?"

"Dating sites mostly." Temeke swiveled in his squeaky chair, first one way and then the other. "Dog team's out searching and Hackett wants me to look through Trandahl's bank accounts. Sodding waste of time when it's past ten and everywhere's closed."

Luis glanced at a tower of three-ring binders: cold cases dating back to the late seventies and stacked on top of the two desks. "If Trandahl's wife wanted to leave him, where would she go?"

"Maybe her sister." Temeke leaned his head back against his locked fingers. "We have to hit on all possibilities; the most glaring one being that Rachael could already be dead. According to the blood at the scene, the victim would have needed immediate medical assistance and none of the hospitals reported any new patients with sizable wounds. Sure, Trandahl was scared of the amount of blood. It's a nightmare no father and husband would want to go through. But they're missing. You can't help thinking the worst."

"When he arrived home, did he change his clothes?"

"No. Malin already asked."

"What about child discipline?" Luis asked. "When you think about it, you wonder what his temperament is like. Or hers, for that matter. Time-outs and denying sleepovers doesn't always do it."

"Malin went over all that. Sounds like he's a regular guy with regular habits. Of course, things could change the more she pushes him."

"That's my point." Luis yawned. "Maybe Hannah did something bad and he lost it. How many cases have we seen where parents went too far? Didn't see a bloody rolling pin lying around in the kitchen while you were there?"

"No, Luis. I didn't see a bloody rolling pin."

"Any prescription medication in the bathroom?"

"Paxil for her. Nothing for him, but that's not to say Trandahl didn't indulge in any recreational drugs. Not exactly the type of medication you stumble across, is it? He could have been all coked up that morning or needed something to slow himself down. Then they had a fight and boom!"

"She ever talk about suicide?"

"I'm not the one asking the questions, am I?" Temeke suddenly felt like drinking the brace of scotch he'd kept hidden on top the filing cabinet.

"Did *he* talk about suicide?" Luis asked.

"No and I'm not in the least bit curious as to whether sorry-ass Trandahl wanted to top himself. It's the mother and kid I'm worried about."

"We're *all* worried about them."

Temeke was extremely concerned about the fate of Rachael Trandahl who, judging by her picture, looked almost virginal. But who could really tell? He decided to chase away any chivalry that had been stirring in his chest, or desire to protect her.

"Listen," Luis said, lowering his voice. "Malin's logged enough overtime this week. Maybe it's best if you take over the interview."

"I wouldn't hear of it. She's doing a damn fine job. Always on the pulse and gives me a live read of everything. In return I want to give her more opportunity for senior exposure. Think you can pull that?"

"What did you have in mind?"

"Detective second-grade and a pay increase to match."

"That would mean she'd almost be on the same pay scale as you..." Luis' eyes floated around the room. "Which is almost as much as me. If it means that much to you I reckon I could swing it."

"It does."

"Anything else on your mind?" Luis said.

"Like what?"

"You seem distracted that's all."

Temeke had the distinct impression Luis expected him to be distracted. He didn't feel distracted nor did he look distracted.

"Ran into Serena at the diner on 4th Street," Luis said. "She's lost her job."

Ah, there it was. Temeke unlocked his hands and placed them on his desk.

"She admitted having a *thing* for the doctor she works for," Luis continued. "But he enjoys a wide variety of female company, a beer or two in the evenings and then home to the hell-hole he calls his wife."

"He's married?"

"Yeah. Kept that minor hurdle quiet apparently. Serena found out this morning. Said it made her feel dirty."

Dirty... had they been intimate? Temeke took a breath.

"It was a minor flirtation." Luis had read the panic on Temeke's face. Then went on in a rush. "They talked. She resigned. Well, you can't exactly work for someone like that, can you? All hands and no promises."

"You mean, a second-rate bastard who makes up the bulk of the sodding human race?"

"Yeah. You lose your self-respect and it affects your work. We've all been through it."

And guilt always interferes with the head. "How's she feeling... with the Graves' and all?"

"Lost a little weight, but she's sleeping better."

"Tell her, if there's anything I can do..."

"Yeah, yeah, I think she'd appreciate it. Well," Luis slapped his thighs, "back to work, eh?"

Temeke listened to the click of the door and leaned back in his chair.

Alone again. Silence.

He looked up at the light fixture—one pale light bulb and one empty socket, rays spoking out to the corners of the room. He gave a half-ass grin and shook his head. No point in salving his wounds with she'll-come-back-stories. Besides, he was too sodding embarrassed to tell Luis he'd been stood up.

Leaving the piggy bank on his desk, he grabbed his keys and headed out.

SIXTEEN

Temeke gassed up his Explorer and approached the rear of Trandahl's house from 7 Bar Loop Road. If anyone was tampering with evidence, now would be a good time.

He parked along the curb and studied the left side of the rear wall. He noticed it sagged inwards, having taken most of the force but the right side appeared stable, even down to the footing. There were no tire treads to read the angle of impact and any car colliding with a solid wall would have suffered accordion damage. There was nothing to suggest the bricks had been deliberately removed prior to the incident, although cracks from weathering may have weakened it.

He pulled a barrier of yellow tape wide enough to climb through. The back yard appeared deserted; so quiet, he could hear the wind breathing through the trees. His nose was filled with the fragrance of sage and juniper, and damp flagstones from the sprinklers.

The patio door was locked and through the windows he could see a portion of the living room through angled blinds. Nothing had been touched and there was no sign of any monkeying around.

Walking around to the front of the house, he found more yellow tape across the front door and garage doors. Both intact. There was a metal gate separating the front yard from the back, and maneuvering the beam from his flashlight along the side of the house, he could see a maple tree in the far corner. A swing was attached to a lower branch but a child would have been hard to see behind an eight foot yucca; thick spiky leaves spreading up to the sky and dead fronds drooping downward like a grass skirt.

So far, there were no leads to suggest Rachael and Hannah had been abducted by a sadistic stranger and he hoped neither of their bodies had been left in business park dumpster or a remote area to hide the crime. It happened all the time.

The neighboring house to the left had one small frosted window facing the Trandahl house, suggesting a bathroom with no clear view of the outside. This belonged to the on-call doctor, who had just arrived home at the time and was taking a shower when he heard what he thought was a car backfiring. The house on the right, however, had a window on the ground floor, blinds drawn to a panoramic view of the Sandia Mountains.

Officer Jarvis had interviewed the neighbors and no one had seen anything suspicious. According to the log, people got up around six and left for work at seven-thirty. Temeke doubted they would have heard a bang, placing the incident closer to eight or sometime thereafter.

Leaving the property, he headed east toward Riverside Drive, making his way to the mayor's mansion. A pale yellow stucco house barely blending with the neighboring houses and made all the more conspicuous with a plaque bearing the state seal over the front door.

The gate was closed. He wasn't expected.

But there was nothing to say he couldn't park outside the gate and read a newspaper. He spent an hour jumping every time the phone rang, reaching for it and getting a dead signal. He had a nauseous feeling it was his ex calling from an unavailable number. But it was Jennifer Danes whose message informed him of her responsibility to provide updates to loyal readers the *Duke City Journal* and would he please call back.

Serena had left zip.

He gave the street and the house a quick sweep and then opened the newspaper. Another woman killed. Her body was found behind Smiths supermarket on the corner of Golf Course and McMahon, gunshot to the back of the head. The police hadn't revealed any further details, Temeke thought, because it was likely they had no leads.

His eyes skimmed over the second page. A prisoner found dead in custody—police arrest man for eleventh DWI offense—argument leads to a shooting at a bar—killer raccoon finally captured after being found in a dumpster behind a restaurant—and a well-known weather man wore a silly hat at a car show.

Then something caught his eye. A shadow passing behind an upper window, possibly a bodyguard, watching the driveway from the second floor. Then the carriage lantern lit up over the front porch and the door opened a crack. Wide enough for a man with a black German Shepherd, which bounded toward the front gate, raised an ear and growled.

Temeke powered down his window and nodded a greeting at wire-rim glasses on a thirty-something face with a close cut beard. His hair was swept back into a ponytail and jaw appeared to be working over a wad of gum.

"Good evening," the man said, peering over the gate. The dog stopped growling. "You be security, by any chance?"

"No." Temeke pointed down at the word POLICE on the side of his cruiser. "Everything OK, sir?"

"Yes, thanks. Dog was going a little stir-crazy when you pulled up. I'd offer you a cup of something in the kitchen but the mayor's already gone to bed."

"No problem. I was just driving through."

Patrolling the neighborhood was nothing short of ordinary and cruisers were often seen gliding up and down the lanes. Only his cruiser was somewhat conspicuous with its dings and scrapes along the front fender and nudge bar.

"Name's Storm Champagne," the man said, as if reading Temeke's frown. "Been in the US four months. Before that I was in Arizona with a few crop-pickers. A kind of don't-ask-don't-tell policy because none of them had any papers. The mayor found me in the local bus terminal with a zip-up bag and a bottle of booze... Just kidding."

Ha, ha. Very funny.

"I'm assistant bodyguard to Art Ingram, Press Secretary. Ever met him? Six foot four. Armani suit."

Temeke remembered Art well. "Played for the Oakland Raiders."

"That's the one."

Temeke's mind was working overtime to keep Champagne talking. "Is it a good place to work?"

"Good benefits." Champagne leaned over the gate to spit his gum on the road. "Can't complain."

"Mayor doing OK?"

"Oh yeah. He's got his nephew staying at the moment. Wife's gone missing. But you cops probably know all about it. No use me standing here gossiping."

"Missing?"

"Looks bad. There was blood in the house and it didn't sound like nosebleed." Champagne lowered his voice and leaned further out toward Temeke's open window. "I heard them talking over dinner. They think it was an intruder. Someone who'd been lurking around the house. Maybe a delivery guy."

"Did they get a description?"

"No. They said it could have been. Not that it was. I can't help wondering when all those FBI guys turned up with their big guns and flak vests that whoever it was might have slipped around the back and scarpered. Yeah, well he's a good guy. Must be awful not knowing where his wife and kid are. Know what I reckon? I reckon they've run off. Wives do that."

"How do you explain the blood?"

"Could have been fake. She could have been planning on leaving him. Pigs are said to be similar in DNA to humans. Then I had to ask myself who'd drag a live pig to a residence and slaughter it? Or a dead one for that matter?"

Temeke began to realize a trip to Riverside was probably about as redundant as Champagne's imagination. There was no way he get a handle on whether Trandahl was still inside and safely tucked up in bed.

"Then I got to thinking what if *he'd* slit her throat with a kitchen knife." Champagne's eyes floated up to the stars. "But he seems too nice to do a thing like that. Came over all queasy when they had squirrel tonight. You could see it in his eyes."

"And you believe him?"

"Yeah. I guess. I almost asked for his autograph but you can't ask, can you? I mean, it would be awful if the sucker was guilty. Be like having O.J. Simpson's initials on your favorite football."

"I suppose it would."

"Well, must be sod-awful to lose your wife. Bad enough to lose a kid. He kept saying the same thing over and over again. That he'd left for work and when he came home they were gone."

"I hope he gets a good night's sleep."

"Oh, trust me, he's out for the count. Drank three whiskies, four glasses of wine and two beers. Saw him throwing up in the downstairs toilet. You'd think he'd had a few more by the way he was grappling with his bedroom door. I did check on him. Passed out fully dressed on the bed. Anyway, I better get back."

Temeke waved and muttered, "Nice talking to you."

He felt the phone shimmy on his belt and cupped a hand over his ear at the passing traffic.

"Just got off the phone with a Gloria Marquez," Sergeant Moran said, clearing his throat. "Said she'd been watching the news and wondered why the name *Rachael Trandahl* rang a bell. She found a piece of paper with Trandahl's name and number in her granddaughter's room about three days ago. Wants to talk to you ASAP."

"Granddaughter's name?"

"Ella Gibson."

SEVENTEEN

Temeke rang Gloria Marquez's bell and took a few steps back so he was standing under the porch light.

It was a small ranch house in Skyview Acres. Peeling paint along the window frames and gutters stuffed with last year's leaves—the type of house he had imagined her to have.

Ella Gibson's RAP sheet included petty theft, breaking and entering, and possession of marijuana second degree. All these were five years previously, although she had been arrested recently at an Albuquerque car wash for concealing a marijuana cigar, just a day after pleading guilty to careless driving.

Rachael Trandahl, on the other hand, was a speeder. It wasn't exactly her only brush with the law. She'd had a citation in June for making an illegal U-turn at an intersection and when stopped, her driver's license and vehicle registration were found to be out of date. She appeared before a judge and got off with a fine.

Temeke walked around the corner of the house, peered down a dark alleyway that led to the back yard. No sound of a popping fly screen and someone climbing out of a back window.

He ignored an incoming phone call and walked back to the front door. Rang the bell again and checked the time. Eleven ten. The wait seemed interminably long; cicadas buzzing in a tree and the whine of a siren along the main road. He couldn't help wondering if she was eyeing him through the peep-hole.

The grinding of a bolt and the door opened a crack. An elderly woman, eyes blinking through blue-rimmed glasses and head bobbing like a car ornament.

"Gloria Marquez?" Temeke opened his jacket a little and her eyes scooted to the badge in his belt. "I'm sorry, I hope I didn't wake you. Detective Temeke, Police Department."

"How did you find me?" she said.

"Finding people is what I do, ma'am."

"I didn't expect anyone so soon." Quiet voice, permanent frown. Didn't ask him in. "She hasn't been home for over a week. Hasn't returned my calls. Always been so good at looking after her nan. I'm worried, that's all."

"Ella Gibson?"

"Yeah, that's her."

"Do you have a number for her?"

Gloria gave it to him, eyes blurry with tears. "I hope you find her."

"I hope so too, love. Does she have a boyfriend?"

"Yeah. Some rich guy in the heights." She spread one arm as if silencing a din in the street, skin puckered like a bat wing. "Big house. Ella said it was green. Somewhere near a buffalo field."

"Any idea where she works?"

"She works from home mostly. Uses a laptop."

"Any friends?"

"Nah. Not much of a girls' girl and, in any case, most of them have moved away. Wasn't easy growing up and God knows we never had any money. Her mom ran off when she was five. Damn good thing, if you ask me, 'cause she's always drinking and cranky."

"You mentioned something about Rachael Trandahl when you called. A piece of paper with her name on it?"

Gloria slipped back inside for a few moments and then reappeared with a crumpled piece of paper. "Just her name and phone number. I heard Ella talking to her boyfriend about her. Something about her being his ex and how it wasn't right how he handled it."

"Was Ella upset? Mad?"

"Mad I'd say. Then she left in a hurry."

Temeke handed her his card. "If you hear from her you'll let me know?"

The one thing Temeke hated about his job was trust. There wasn't enough of it. The old lady had no idea where her granddaughter was or what type of life she led, and it was likely a few drug deals went on under her nose without her knowing.

He verified Ella's cell phone number with dispatch and made his way to the only buffalo field he knew in the heights, smelling dung through his open window.

There was a green stucco house situated on the border of Sandia Reservation and where the casino, wreathed in a floodlit pinks and blues, was visible on the other side of the field. It was set back from the road with a grove of Austrian pines on the west corner. Whatever Ella Gibson's boyfriend did for a living, his salary must have been sodding *huge.*

Temeke called in his position to dispatch and asked for information on the house. Hunters Residential, a real estate firm in California had listed the home as a modest contemporary in Albuquerque's northeast heights with a mortgage payment in the region of $16,148 a month.

Nothing modest about that, he thought.

Surrounded by a wall, where the only access was through a gated archway, the house appeared like a sheet of glass against a black sky. It offered a voyeur's view into the bedroom had the lights been on.

Except for an amber glow downstairs, it appeared deserted, as if by some invisible prompt the occupant had seen him and hauled ass out of the back door. Maybe Ella's nan called ahead to warn her.

Tucking a pair of gloves in his pocket, the first thing that struck him was an inch of space between the front gate and the stone frame.

He pushed it open.

The second thing that set him on edge was the sudden glare of motion sensors as he approached the house and the fact that the front and garage doors were open. As he crunched across the gravel, he heard the orchestrated rattle of leaves overhead and even though he was oblivious to the melody, his mind would be instantly alerted to any note out of the place.

A white Range Rover stood half inside the garage with a trail of soil that ran from the tailgate to a large pot by the front door. Probably explained why both doors were open. There were no lights on inside and no evidence of broken bulbs or any that might have been removed. He rang the doorbell and waited.

Then rapped hard. The door yawned wide.

"Hello! Anyone here?"

There was no response.

After looking over his shoulder at the front gate and at the house next door, he walked in. The door jamb wasn't shredded nor were there any scratches on the locks.

His voice sounded hollow in the hallway and resting one hand on his holster, he shifted forward, angling his body sideways as he followed the curve of the wall.

"Ella? Ella Gibson?"

No footsteps rushed toward him. He didn't recall seeing any windows open from the outside but there were three open in the back, now that he was counting.

The interior of the house was focused around a central hallway with a wide staircase, which appeared to provide the main egress to the rooms on the second floor.

A large portrait hung on the east wall: a young woman, staring through a screen of dark hair. Her arms were crossed over a bare chest and hands resting on her shoulders. There was a hint of expression in the arched brows, as if a whisper was about to be uttered through full lips.

"Ms. Gibson?"

Still no response.

He looked out across the expanse of tile where a pair of sandals appeared to have been kicked off. A flicker of light was evident through the glass door of the kitchen and there was no lived-in odor; rather the scent of freshly-mown grass and some kind of fragrance.

And then a movement to his right. He unsnapped his holster and removed the Glock. Focusing through the arch of two decorative columns, a cat sniffed the air before scampering into the shadows.

The sensible thing would be to call for backup, rather than respond alone. But there had been no calls to dispatch to report a felony suspect, no immediate threat. He wondered if that was the reason for his—not suspicion, exactly. That was overstating it. Reservation.

He drew his flashlight into his off-hand and eased along the north wall, where a thermostat read eighty-five degrees. Guided by a glaze of blue which seemed to come from the colored glass panes in the top panel of the kitchen door, he strained for any sound—a footstep on the stair. A creaky door.

Keeping his flashlight and pistol trained, he walked toward the kitchen; a U-shaped arrangement with row upon row of white cabinets, a double-door refrigerator and a high-tech oven. A fan droned in front of the patio doors and the under cabinet lights glared brassily on the polished surface of the countertops.

Temeke eased around the doorframe and just as his gaze dropped to the floor, he spotted her.

EIGHTEEN

Ella Gibson never made it out of the back door. Her body lay on its side; one arm following the line of her belly, the other thrown out in front.

A red stain had blossomed on the back of her skull and the floor, at first glance, was drenched in a bloody dew. At second glance he found it to have congealed. She was barefoot and wore a white shirt and mini-skirt. Temeke holstered his pistol, snapped on his gloves and shone the flashlight in one of her eyes.

No response. He couldn't locate a pulse on either side of her neck or wrists, and called for backup.

The windows had been cracked open and the back door was wide enough to let in the sweltering August heat.

Dividing the room into a grid, he worked outward from the body. Saw a bloody footprint near the back door and a handbag on the countertop, wallet and keys spilling out from the zipper and three open bills: one for gas and one for the rental.

There was a pack of bank cards, an out-of-date medical card and an ID in the name of Ella Gibson—the same face in the portrait.

He continued down the hallway and heard the hiss of wind through the eaves. Then another sound, lower than the first. He pivoted sharply and held the Glock out in front, saw a leaf scuttling across the tile floor driven in by an errant breeze. It spooked him enough to turn a complete circle, ear angled for sound.

The living room had white painted book shelves on one wall and a row of windows on the other. Two couches, two easy chairs and on the coffee table was a photograph album he made a note to read.

Upstairs, an open doorway provided a glimpse of an office filled with suitcases and storage boxes. Opposite, a master bedroom faced east with sliding doors onto a narrow balcony.

The quilt on the bed was folded down on one side and the pillows starched flat. The only hint of character was a picture of two adults on the bedside table.

Ella and her boyfriend, wearing baggy sweaters and lopsided smiles.

In front of it was a small laptop and a book: *Bodie's Collection of Short Stories: Gripping thrillers with shocking twists.* The type of subtitle he didn't trust. And a charging cell phone with four missed calls displayed on the lock screen. A doctor's office and three from someone called *NightC*.

Temeke nudged open the bathroom door with his boot. He saw a pedestal sink with a tube of toothpaste in the soap holder and an electric toothbrush plugged in and flashing.

Closets were large and clothes wedged into every available space—women's dresses and men's suits—some still wrapped in transparent garment bags.

No blood spatter either on the ceilings or walls and nothing to suggest a thorough clean up. He didn't see a skylight or attic above but the moonlight streamed through a large bank of windows, leaving the corners of the room cast in shadow.

Plenty of places for a perpetrator to hide.

He opened the balcony doors. The lawn stretched south to a patch of wasteland, which in the breeze had become a heaving surface of grass. The Sandia Mountains lay to the east, sharply ridged and iron-gray in the moonlight. This was the same view Ella Gibson would have experienced every night.

But not tonight.

Through the rattle of leaves, he could hear the loud wail of sirens and voices calling out from downstairs.

While officers and crime scene technicians took over the scene, Temeke ended up in an easy chair in the sitting room poring through a few photo albums. Photos of Ella aged five, fifteen, twenty-five; enough to give him a good understanding of a brief life she shared with a boyfriend.

"Want these, sir?"

Temeke looked up at a halo of golden curls with a buttery sheen. Officer Jarvis stood over him with a pair of shoe covers.

Temeke slipped them on. "Doc here yet?"

"Just arrived, sir. I wanted to update you on Trandahl's neighbors. Mrs. Judy Parker lives in the house opposite. She said Rachael Trandahl usually leaves the residence between eight and eight-fifteen. But there was no sign of her this morning or anyone who might have given her a ride. She's pretty sure about that."

"Did Mrs. Parker see them coming home?"

"No. She took her daughter Bailey to school, came home and then went up to her quilting room at the back of the house. Didn't see shit."

Temeke had that nagging sense of dissatisfaction. Something about Rachael's car being in the garage with trace amounts of blood in the interior. He had to force himself to ignore a convulsive lunge down the driveway to his unit and conduct the search himself.

Whoever had taken Rachael and Hannah had a few hours' start. No reason to give him any more.

Temeke walked into the kitchen and watched Agnes snap a few close-angled shots and Dr. Vasillion completed his examination. Looking first up at the ceiling and walls and then down again at the victim. Fingers sliding over the body and parting a strand of matted hair, revealing a small crater in the back of her head.

Temeke's eyes strayed to a rape kit on the kitchen counter that contained swabs, combs, a checklist and envelopes to preserve any DNA evidence.

"She was shot twice and at close range," Dr. Vasillion observed, pointing at the powder burns around the entry wound. "Since the body has cooled to the surrounding temperature, I would say somewhere in the last twenty-four hours."

"Looks like he got at least one round off—"

"Two. And we don't know that it's a *he*. Any cartridge cases?"

"Nope and I didn't find a weapon."

"Those your footprints?" Dr. Vasillion asked, looking at a partial near the back door.

"No, doc."

"Do we know the victim's name?"

"Ella Gibson."

"Rather beautiful. That her picture in the hall?"

"As far as I know. If not, it's a dead ringer."

Dr. Vasillion stood and mustered a brittle smile. "She own this property?"

"I believe it's a rental. Nice place. No sign of any ransacking."

"I'll need to know if she had a primary care physician." He glanced around briefly, eyes settling on the hand bag.

"Her insurance card's two years out of date but it looks like Dr. Henderson, at least that's who called on her phone upstairs."

"I'll give him a call." Dr. Vasillion paused and studied Temeke for a moment. "Not a spree killing. Could be drug related rather than someone rejected by society. I mean, look at her? I doubt she's a random target."

No one was *ever* a random target, thought Temeke, conscious that the face in the portrait bore none of the ravages of drugs, in spite of the pallid coloring. It was strikingly beautiful, unmarked by anything other than curiosity.

"Might be a former employer or employee," Temeke said. "Her links to gangs are relevant and the computer upstairs will tell us more."

Dr. Vasillion's brow furrowed as if he was thinking hard. "Next of kin."

"Gloria Marquez. I'll text you the details."

"Well, you'll have my report by tomorrow afternoon."

"Thanks, doc. I'll leave you to it."

So far, the shooter was unknown. No name and no history with which to build a reliable profile. Given the most recent visual provided by a neighbor and the fact that no one else had come forward yet with any information, the police were hunting for witnesses.

The only witness they had was Trandahl himself and, from what Temeke had seen, he wasn't exactly giving a rapid-fire version of events. He was stalling. Going slow. Rubbing his eyes and yawning. Hell, he'd even stopped looking at his phone. Who was he avoiding?

And now Trandahl was lying half cut on his bed. Who gets drunk, Temeke thought, when their wife and kid go missing? Who goes to sleep?

Challenges like this excited Temeke, got him going. But today, he didn't feel like he was going anywhere.

His phone did a little jig and he clamped it to his ear. "Yep."

"Detective Temeke, this is Alice. We tried to call you several times. You asked me to let you know if anyone called Rachael's phone. Well, someone did. It was Hannah."

NINETEEN

If it wasn't so dark, she would have enjoyed being out on her own. The clock on the dash said twelve-sixteen.

The view was familiar.

She remembered it from a school trip when Josie Rich-Bitch Henderson had been learning 'cheer vocabulary' and practicing tumbling in the parking lot.

Later Mom caught her texting the B-word, said she'd get a spanking and no TV for a week.

Looking back at the car, she wondered if closing the doors would be the right thing to do. The car light would keep the animals away, wouldn't it?

"Mom!" Where the heck was she?

Sooner or later she'd have to come back. Surely she'd realized she'd forgotten something. Who leaves their kid all alone in a car at night?

Maybe she was smoking in the bushes and soon she'd come out of her hazy hiding place and shout, 'What the heck are you looking so down and out about?'

Happened once before at the mall. There was a carousel outside Dillard's and she wanted a ride. No sign of her mom when the carousel stopped. Lucky she had a phone. But boy that was a bad day.

It wasn't kind to think bad things. That's what the neighbor lady always said. Whatever bad thoughts she had about her mom, she mustn't think them. Whatever anger she'd held inside about what her mom had done, she mustn't feel it.

Maybe that's why she felt so sad about the yesterdays. You couldn't go back and change them.

But there were the nights when her mom wouldn't leave her at home. Told her a little drive would do her good. But the drive took them to a house in the heights, where they'd sit outside watching people in the window.

It was so boring. She hated it.

She looked back at the car and wondered how easy it would be to drive it. All you had to do was turn it on, put it in drive and steer. Her legs were long enough if she leaned forward a bit. Only she wasn't quite sure where home was without using her phone.

With all that dripping under the hood, she had a strange feeling the car wasn't going anywhere.

She could see the Albuquerque lights from where she stood and she could see how the road curved down the hill.

Probably jog most of the way to the bottom. She was fast.

A distant shriek. Somewhere to the left of her. It put chills on her skin.

She wrapped the blanket tightly around her shoulders, gripped the bottle of water against her chest. Maybe staying by the car wasn't such a good idea.

Maybe leaving her phone behind was. She'd heard of kids being traced if they left something personal behind.

The phone was her personal something.

She started walking away from the car, toward the edge of the parking lot, racing to get to each patch of light cast from a street lamp.

The shriek again, a little louder this time. Somewhere in the trees where it was too dark to see. It sounded like a skinning, only it was louder than that.

She felt like she should do something, but she didn't know what.

Were there starving coyotes up here? Teeth like jagged points. Did the little rabbits in their back yard ever get away? She couldn't remember if they did. She could only remember how many didn't.

On, on, on. Blanket dragging along the pavement and churning up dust like Linus in Charlie Brown. If the noise happened again she would do something. Follow it. Save the rabbits.

What day was it tomorrow?

Clean sheets day. She'd take a shower when she got home and wash her hair with the new shampoo her dad had bought her. Green bottle with fruit on the front. She was dying to use it.

Another shriek.

Made her flinch this time. No use pretending it wasn't closer than the last time and no use thinking it wasn't an animal.

She paused, her heart pounding as she tried to take a steadying breath. Time to make a decision.

She stepped off the pavement and into the woods.

TWENTY

The first call came forty minutes past midnight. An abandoned vehicle had been spotted at the Peak Tram parking lot at the same location Hannah's cell phone carrier relayed back to the emergency response teams.

The caller had also found a wallet belonging to Rachael Trandahl and blood spatter she thought the police should see.

After having spent forty-five minutes in the command center scanning the Trandahl's social media sites, Temeke logged out of his computer, slapped on a black baseball cap and headed to the foothills.

He was second on scene, pockets already filled with evidence bags. The nearest unit to respond was officer Scarlet Midgely from Foothills Area Command. A woman who had the solid build of a carthorse and always had a personal stake in each case. She stood waiting for him, wrists perched on her duty belt and fingers glazed in black leather.

She wasn't a hand-shaker. More of a palm slapper.

"Checked the wallet, sir. No cash but there are two bank cards with Rachael Trandahl's ID."

"Anyone been notified at the Sandia Ranger Station?"

"Yep. Ken Whitman. Said he's on his way."

Midgely introduced him to a teenage girl who was perched on the nudge bars of Midgely's cruiser. The female displayed rapid, shallow breathing and lackluster eyes. Temeke shook her hand and found her skin to be cold and clammy. She wore a hoodie and combat boots with neon laces. He thanked her for making the call.

Next to her was a male wearing a pair of butt-dragging jeans and plaid underwear visible over the waistband. He was already cuffed and smirking like it happened every day.

Officer Midgely beckoned Temeke away from the cruiser and lowered her voice. She was less intimidating without her Oakleys.

"Apparently, they were supposed to meet someone up here, sir. But when they arrived, they noticed a car angled across two parking spaces, interior light on, triggered by two open doors—driver's door and rear passenger door. There was blood and smears on the window. It bothered her enough to call dispatch."

"IDs?"

"Hers is clean. She's pretty shell-shocked. I doubt believing her is going to come back and bite me in the ass. I mean look at her. Puny little arms and legs. Couldn't lift a two-by-four."

"You know what they say about looks."

"Yeah. Look at me, case in hand."

Temeke straightened a little. Midgely wasn't pretty, barely attractive actually. Blonde hair scraped back in a tight bun, and on the rare occasion she wore it loose, she had what Malin described as a teal ombré. Eyes unusually striking, although he couldn't see what color they were without shining his flashlight directly in her face. Single and, from what he knew, enjoyed her singleness.

"What I actually meant," he said, "was that she could have had a gun in her pocket."

"I've already done the honors, sir. Fat chance unless there's one up her ass. Him? Now that's different. Big wad of fifties stuffed down his pants."

"Drug deal?"

"That'd be my guess. Only there's no sign of the people they were supposed to meet."

"A siren and a black and white probably put them off. Don't you have any blankets in the back of your unit?"

She cocked her head sideways. "What for?"

"They're both in shock. He's whiter than a store mannequin."

"Possibly on account of what I told him I'd found on my computer. Petty larceny, possession, vandalism, criminal mischief and to add to that, meddling with evidence. I'd say he was facing, oh, seventy-two months. I think what he needs is an attorney not a blanket."

Temeke walked over to a dilapidated white Crown Victoria which, in its current rusted out state, shouldn't have been on the road. It was a junker. Period.

"First and last registered owner was in 2001," Midgely said. "A Samuel L. Petit. He's dead, by the way. Already checked." She pointed her flashlight on the ground. "You'll notice the puddle under the hood. Radiator leak. Maybe that's why the car's here and not on the road. And you'll also notice a minor scrape along the lower corner of the passenger side fender. Probably took a corner too sharp."

Temeke noticed how the water had trickled down a slight camber in the asphalt before merging with the curb and as for the scrapes, Midge was right. There was no paint transfer from another vehicle so it would have come from a highway barrier or something similar. "Any other personal items?"

"None."

"Car charger?"

"Doesn't look like it. The keys are still in the ignition and the trunk's empty. You can see dark stains on the rear bumper and fender. Couple of shoe impressions over by the dumpster; size four adult, leaving the road and heading downhill. And a plastic bottle of water I picked up while I was over there. I shouted a few times. Nothing moved."

Temeke felt his cheeks burn. Even he wouldn't have moved if he'd seen Scarlet Midgely gripping her Glock and shouting at the top of her lungs. Not if he wanted his backside peppered with lead.

"I looked around the immediate area, sir, including the perimeter of the information center and the east parking lot. No sign of a break-in and nothing to suggest anyone was hurt and in need of assistance."

"You been here long?" he asked.

"Let's see. Just finished a call at The County Line twenty minutes ago. An intoxicated guest thought he needed to receive a beam from the mother ship in order to recharge his brain. Usual crock of shit. So reckon on a good fifteen minutes."

Temeke nodded. The restaurant was less than five minutes' drive from the Peak Tram. "Since you've done a general sweep of the area I'll take a look at the car."

"When you say *general*, you mean like this?" she said, flicking her flashlight from left to right. "Cause nothing's as good as aerial and, in any case, it's darker than crap out here."

"Right."

"Crime scene techs are on their way," she said, angling one ear toward her radio. "Might need some little orange flags on the ground before I touch anything else."

Temeke crouched about ten feet from the driver's door, flashlight dancing over the asphalt. There were no identifiable signs of disturbance, no glossy spatter visible in the beam. But with all the recent activity, the area around the car had been severely compromised.

His attention was drawn to a fine mist of blood on the rear tail light, unlikely from an exit wound but he couldn't be sure. "Those kids hear any gunshots?"

"Nope."

"I guess you already asked."

"I guess I did." Midgely hit the home button on her phone, face illuminated by the neon beam. "I thought I had better mention that Hannah Trandahl and her mom are already headline news. It says here: *A thirty-year-old woman and her ten-year-old child have been missing since this morning. Rachael and Hannah Trandahl of 4219 Talmadge Avenue in Cottonwood Heights were last seen yesterday. Due to circumstances inside the house, the police department believe they could be in danger. Mr. Dai Trandahl is not considered a suspect, however he is being questioned.*"

"Anything on a Ms. Ella Gibson?"

"Just a one-liner saying her body had been found in the heights and that the cases were thought to be unrelated."

Temeke knew if he asked Captain Fowler for information on how the story had leaked to the *Journal*, it would be met with the usual silence. He thought he knew Fowler well enough, while the police officer in him understood he didn't know anyone at all.

He trained his flashlight at the driver's side of the car. Nothing remarkable. The rear passenger seats were a different matter. Trapped behind one of the buckles was a dead cell phone.

"Got a charger?" he asked Midge, taking an evidence bag from his pocket.

"What kind of phone is it?"

"An iPhone?"

"Yep."

It was the trunk that bothered him; gel-like puddles had troughed in the door sill, along with smears, as Midgely had pointed out, on the rear fender. A beige-colored floor mat had been placed in the trunk, mottled with passive blood stains, some of which had run into the rubber channels leaving tiny pools in the reservoir trap.

Keys dangled from the ignition, no doubt yielding a print or two. "So why here?" he said out loud. "Why all the way to the Peak Tram?"

"Maybe she was reliving an old memory. Maybe she took a wrong turn." Midgely lowered her head and peered through the passenger door. Gripping her flashlight, she shone the beam under the rear seat footwell, running it back and forth over the rubber mats. "Antiseptic wipe soiled with reddish-brown stains. Could be blood. Four sealed bottles of water in a pack—minus two—and no sign of the empties. No indication of how many passengers."

"Gives you a twinge of hope, doesn't it?"

Midgely pressed her lips together and gave a slow shake of the head. "Anytime there's blood in a car and nobody in it, yeah."

"The way I see it is the car broke down so they called for help. But who did they call and did they get help? Or did they stumble on someone else? Either way, you'd think they would have trekked along the road to Tramway. Someone must have seen them."

"If they went west, there're residences along Sandia Heights and further down on Juniper Hill Road, sir." Midgely referred to a topographical map she pulled up on her phone. "If they went east, it's a maze of trails. One of them could have met with an accident, got dehydrated and disoriented. Children have been known to go missing in open country. Happens all the time."

"True. You're on a gravel road and then it becomes rocky and when I mean rocky, I mean big rocks, scattered about the steep hillside. There's not a hope in hell they would have gone that way."

"What if Rachael Trandahl was hooking up with someone? Someone she recently met but didn't really know?"

"Too much blood in the Trandahl house, Midge. She wasn't hooking up with anyone."

"But what if she was?" Midgely's brow seemed to furrow and then smooth at the sudden realization of what that meant. "Hannah and her mom could have been taken…"

Temeke could hear a multitude of possibilities in that open-ended statement. "Probably best not to assume."

He was briefly interrupted by the pulse of a siren. A cruiser swerved into the parking lot followed by an ambulance and the crime scene van.

"Before I forget," she said, breathing in and raising her chin. "I'm joining you for training next week."

"I had heard."

"I just wanted you to know that I've got a few football injuries. But apart from that, I'm in good shape."

Temeke tried not to look her up and down, but despite any physical limitations she looked anything but frail.

"I've already met Captain Fowler," she said with a smirk. "He asked me if I was always this rude. I told him yes, while my brain's on duty. Think we'll get along?"

Temeke chuckled. "Want my best advice? Don't rattle his cage."

Temeke studied the perimeter while she sauntered toward the crime scene techs. To the east was a steep incline to the peak, which no one in their right mind would tackle and to the north, more brush and rugged terrain. Bears and mountain lions were known to range as far as the foothills, driven to the streets if they were hungry.

He ran the flashlight from the door sill, following it along the ground to where the road met the parking lot.

A pile of sand had bunched up against the curb and he could make out part of a footprint.

Midgely was right. Impossible to tell shit in the dark.

TWENTY-ONE

It was nearly one thirty in the early hours when Malin stood on the front steps of the command center with Trandahl, watching the mayor's car drawing up alongside the curb.

The breeze had dropped to a whisper and the sky was riffled and dark. Trandahl hesitated before ascending the steps to the waiting car. Malin followed him.

"Mayor Oliver," she said, peering in through the driver's window.

Mayor Oliver gave her a tight nod. His body was rigid but the interplay between his mouth and eyes revealed what she could only describe as conflict and anger.

"You saw the news, I assume," he said. "I hope they don't start trash-talking the family now he's under surveillance."

"Mr. Trandahl's not strictly under surveillance—"

"Oh, that so? I thought I saw a cruiser outside my house. Scratch on the front left panel and a dangling wing mirror. Sound familiar?"

It did. She cringed.

"Domestic violence is a terrible thing," the mayor droned one. "I don't want Dai ostracized. If the *Journal* so much as writes an article accusing him of killing Rachael, I'll find the sorry piece of human waste and pray he burns in hell."

Malin felt the same way herself but didn't add that the *he* the mayor referred to was likely a *she*.

"I know a lot of people," he said.

Malin didn't doubt it.

"But there are two on my radar," he said. "Cyn Wrigley, Chief Editor at the *Duke City Journal* and Raymond Brewster of the *Daily Tribune*. Fact is, Brewster doesn't like me. Thinks I beat the crap out of my own wife a few months back, if you remember. He probably thinks domestic abuse runs in the family. But putting Dai through the mill on account of me is just plain stupid. In any case it's a violation of civil rights."

Malin remained skeptical that the media wouldn't reach into Trandahl's private life and pull out something damning. Hooking up with women online was a case in hand.

Added to that, the *Journal* had already sent out tweets headlined, CONCERNS MOUNT IN COTTONWOOD HEIGHTS DISAPPEARANCE and another tweet saying TIME FOR A NEWS CONFERENCE. TRANDAHL'S GOT SOMETHING TO HIDE.

Trandahl had showed little emotion during his interview and when asked if he had called the school to find out if Hannah was there, he calmly said no. Not the response you'd expect from a distraught father.

The mayor gripped the steering wheel and gave her a rapid nod. "I can be an asshole—a troublesome one—if anyone can get to me at all."

Malin gave a stiff smile. "Now would be a good time to advise that Mr. Trandahl's house may be in custody for some time."

"How long?" Mayor Oliver asked.

"The investigators are still collecting items, then they'll go for processing. Could be a couple of weeks."

"I see." The Mayor turned and gave Trandahl a cursory glance. "He'll just have to put up with me then."

Malin stepped back from the curb and lifted a hand as the car pulled away.

Mayor Oliver come very close to losing his twelve-year-old son Adam to a kidnapper earlier that year. Although it almost cost him his career, it most certainly cost him his marriage. Malin wondered if the mayor had reservations about allowing Trandahl to stay. Whether it might re-open old wounds.

Footsteps tapped down the steps behind her and Sergeant Moran's voice broke the silence. "No activity on Rachael Trandahl's bank account or any credit card for that matter. None of the family members have heard from her, although it's early yet."

"Any ransom or hostage exchange?" Malin asked.

"Nothing."

"Any similar incidents to link it with?"

"None." A deep breath. "Looks like you're running on empty, Santiago. Go home and get some rest."

"Yes, Sarge. On my way."

She quickly tapped out a text to Temeke to update him, then unlocked her car. She was finding it tough to remain focused and on task. Four hours sleep was usually all she could manage during a case, but four hours was better than nothing. Her body needed it and her mind demanded it.

As she drove home, she wondered if Rachael Trandahl had reported any kind of abuse to legal services. As she pulled into the parking lot of her apartment, she called the number of a caseworker she knew.

Sally Saavedra had an eidetic memory. If anyone would remember Rachael Trandahl, she would.

Malin's call was picked up after the first ring. "I'm sorry for calling so late—"

"Don't be," Sally said, voice surprisingly perky. "I'm guessing you're calling about Rachael Trandahl. Kept me up too. Awful business. I was just looking at her pictures on Facebook. It's definitely her. She came to the office a month ago with a friend."

"You sure?"

"Positive. My first impression was that she was tense. Friend's name was Beverly Herrera. I asked Rachael if it was domestic violence and her words were, 'I think so.' Thing is, we can't assign a caseworker unless victims fill out an intake sheet for the attorneys to review. I handed her a divorce form and told her she could get a restraining order at ten the next morning. But it didn't look like she ever did."

"Why? Why didn't she follow through?"

"Probably too scared, especially if she believed all the threats she may have heard. Often the abuse a victim suffers is the hardest to communicate. Sometimes they don't know how violent an episode has to be before an attorney will take the case. And sometimes they figure they're not worthy of help at all. I always want to run out after them. Especially the ones that can't make up their minds. It won't be long before investigators find out what kind of life Rachael led. Whether it was abuse or if she fell prey to a stalker. We'll know something soon."

"Thanks, Sally. I appreciate it."

"Anytime."

Malin hated the thought of hanging out in her safe place while Rachael and Hannah were still missing. But with the assistance of Agent Stu Anderson of the Albuquerque FBI and members of the Bernalillo County Sheriff's Office (BCSO), she was confident they would get a sighting soon.

She bounded up the steps to her second floor apartment at Puerta de Corrales; a small one bedroom she affectionately called the 'kennel'. She was met with the usual darkness as she opened the door. Thick fumes of burnt French fries wafted up the stairwell from her neighbor downstairs, thick enough to stick.

She unclipped her phone and set it on the coffee table, then opened the sliding door to the patio. Water from the fountain at the front gate tumbled over a palisade of rocks, emitting a steady patter that seemed to calm her nerves.

She had to admit that with no calls for a ransom demand typical in a kidnapping case, the whereabouts of Rachael and Hannah looked gloomier by the minute. It was only the first day and provided they hadn't been separated, their chance for survival had gone up a notch.

Her phone gave a counter-turn on the table and one look told her who it was.

Wingman: A suspicious end is only just the beginning.

Malin: Oh cut the crap.

Wingman: They also say that the twisted truth hides out in the darkest corners. I'd say the woman you're looking for isn't a bit shy about shaking things up. In fact, true to character she may have gone a little too far this time.

Malin tapped out a response: Which woman?

Wingman: Remember the vulgar secret I was telling you about? That woman. While you're thinking through scenarios of why and who, consider the reactions of close family friends. They don't always yield telltale signs.

Malin: Do you think Trandahl did it?

Wingman: I wouldn't be that hasty. Think about risk factors. Ask yourself if he fits the profile of an abuser. The most important thing is finding Hannah and her mother.

Malin: What about cell phone tracking?

Wingman: I suspect it won't help. Perhaps they're switched off or lost. Vast open spaces. There's no accounting for recklessness.

Malin didn't bother asking him what he meant. She knew he had signed off. His way of getting the last word.

Setting her pistol on the nightstand, she unfastened a heavy belt burdened by cuffs and ammunition. It would have carried a Taser and flashlight in the old days when she worked the graveyard shift as a field officer. Radio on her right shoulder and a bulletproof vest beneath her shirt. The first sergeant she ever had called her The Polyester Princess, but then he called her a number of other things she didn't care to remember.

Now it took seconds to peel off a polo shirt and khakis, stare in the bathroom mirror at a heart-shaped face beneath a cap of black hair. Not bad for thirty-something, only she could never shake the air of sadness in a face that no one kissed goodbye when each day could be her last.

Breathing in the steam, she felt tiny needles of water against her back. It always helped to sift through the mental data and filter out the junk. There was one question that kept pounding at her brain.

Was there anything about Rachael Dai didn't like?

TWENTY-TWO

The cell phone they found in the abandoned car was confirmed to have belonged to Hannah Trandahl. Temeke texted the information to Malin.

His mind kept rewinding the comment Officer Manning made upon arrival at the Trandahl house. K-9 Brock couldn't follow Rachael and Hannah's scent further than the back patio because they had been driven away. At first glance, it ruled out Trandahl because he rode a bike. But it certainly didn't rule out the possibility of him using the Highlander earlier that morning.

The car had been in the garage, rear seats folded down and blood stains found in various locations on the driver's side. Trandahl could have seemingly left for work and then re-entered the premises through the rear of the property via the broken wall. But that didn't work either because there were no tire tracks on the back lawn.

Trandahl also worked for Porsche, where run-around cars were sometimes provided. Certainly not a 2001 Crown Vic, but Porsche had its own version of an SUV.

However, this wouldn't explain the bloodstains found in the Highlander.

Trandahl's fingerprints, including those of his wife and child, were found inside the house and the car—as one would expect—but the investigators had yet to find any belonging to a possible killer/kidnapper.

Nausea kept roiling in Temeke's gut. No matter how hard he tried to replay each scenario, he kept coming back with the same thought.

Trandahl may have done it. Temeke just didn't know how.

Then his radio started crackling with activity. An anonymous call came into dispatch at one thirty in the early hours. It was a male voice, possibly calling from a gas station on Tramway Road. The caller claimed Hannah was last seen around midnight, somewhere between the trailhead and Juniper Hill Road.

Pity it hadn't been called in earlier, Temeke thought. Juniper Hill Road was roughly 0.4 miles, which equated to a ten minute walk from where they were.

With all the hoax calls and sightings flooding in Temeke had no desire to rouse Trandahl. This particular call was worth looking into since the sighting corresponded to the correct origin point and with the use of two way radios, GPS units and computer generated maps, they were covered.

K-9 Commander Phil Ashton had arrived on scene along with volunteers from Sandia Search Dogs. While some officers stayed behind to review footage in the mobile command unit, Temeke decided to head out with the search party.

He opened the trunk of his cruiser and grabbed his radio. He then shrugged on an AR-15 fitted with a 2-point sling and decorated with a small British flag on the pad. The high-definition sighting had four times the magnification, and he knew if they were dealing with a hostage situation it was one hell of a target acquisition. A backpack of water and medical supplies and a handful of protein bars which he slotted into every zipper he could find in his pants. They might be gone a while.

The park ranger was on his phone, barking out orders to some unfortunate individual whose night off had just been interrupted, and seven state police officers stood in a tight huddle, shrugging on backpacks and talking in whispers.

Temeke's throat was thick with emotion when he saw Ted Hardy, the young officer who had made both the fatal and life-saving shot in their last case. Shaking Ted's hand, he patted him on the shoulder, felt so much gratitude he almost burst out of his own skin.

"Thought you were with SWAT, son."

"I put in for the K-9 unit after the Jessie Bowman case." Hardy patted his dog on the head and looked down at his four-legged companion. "This is where I belong."

"What's his name?"

"Mauser. He's a real trip. I'll see you out there then."

Temeke nodded, making out four more handlers with K-9s wearing military style vests and pockets filled with gear. They were focusing on the clothing from the Trandahl house and specific scents near the car.

Midgely had not only managed to separate herself from the huddle of crime scene techs but to palm off her felon and his companion to another field officer. She had already shrugged on a backpack and had retrieved a shotgun from the trunk of her unit.

"You coming?" Temeke shouted over the distant drone of a chopper.

"Wouldn't miss this for the world." She carried her rifle with the muzzle sloping downward, stock against her shoulder. "You ought to know I don't share my protein bars on the first date. If that bugs you, there's plenty of officers you can try your luck with."

"Believe or not, Midge, not every detective is looking to dive in your backpack the first chance they get. And anyway," he patted his pants, "I've got my own."

"Righto. After you, sir," she said, head thrust forward and flashlight burning a hole through the trees.

The emergency medical teams went through high and low angle technical rescue situations. Equipped with backpacks and collapsible titanium litters, they split into teams of five, each with their own medical specialty. It was the terrain that would give them all the ultimate stress test with drops of anywhere between fifty to a hundred feet over the limestone cliffs. If Hannah or her mother needed lifting, zip lines would be used so the strike teams could reach her.

The commander wrapped up his debriefing, search teams fanning out in different directions. There was wasn't much hope of seeing broken twigs or torn clothing, any natural disturbance a tracker would find during the day. There had been rain recently which meant the ground could yield a footprint along the trail.

With the aid of stealth cams and DCPD Air 1 hovering overhead, they set off at a slow pace remaining within calling distance of one another. Temeke knew that the trail they took was probably hours cold and the chances of finding the victims were slim. He watched as some teams took five steps forward, looked up, looked down and then repeated the process, while others worked in spirals and diagonals. He counted four different agencies and everyone had their own method.

Pepper, Rex and Diesel—dogs that had won bravery awards during the last two years—were trained specifically in tracking missing victims. They trotted briskly beneath the piñon trees despite the weight of their Kevlar vests.

But after two hours of calling Rachael and Hannah's names and with no hits from the BOLO, Temeke wondered if the girls were long gone. Driven out of state by someone they barely knew or running for their lives from the enemy indoors.

Since there was blood in the abandoned car, the latter option was less likely.

The K-9s picked up a northerly trail, nostrils flaring in the dirt. Why north? Temeke wondered. It was a thought worth considering. Did Rachael's kidnapper have a destination in mind or was the direction just a whim? While Temeke identified coyote and bear scat and knowing there were cougars traveling along the ditches, he realized something must have driven them that way.

The trudge of boots and the occasional rustle of a wrapper behind him, reminded him Midgely was tucking into her first protein snack. When she wasn't wolfing down food she was training her flashlight at overgrown brush, crouching low and looking for disturbances just as he was.

There were scattered boulder fields in the foothills and juniper and prickly pear added to the topography. Spines that might have dug into his ankles and gone through his socks if it hadn't been for a study pair of boots. An officer's best friend.

TWENTY-THREE

The sounds were coming from a patch of high grass and boulders and where trees were at their thickest.

A man shouting and fisting the air at a coyote.

There was a rolled up rug at his feet and she couldn't work out why he was talking to it.

"You saw something. You did something."

What had the rug seen? What had it done?

Was it so bad he wanted to splatter it dead with the rock he just picked up? He stood there for a few seconds then hurled the rock behind him. Sobbing.

"At least I didn't go snooping into other people's business. You knew what it was right from the start. I never promised anything!"

Then he said something about how it was all in the heat of the moment. That he didn't have any love left to give and how that was the problem.

The heat of the moment.

What did that mean exactly? It was something sudden, wasn't it? When you didn't think it through properly.

She was still groggy from the drink. Yes, it was drink he'd given her. Poured it down her throat and told her to swallow.

Then he shouted that he wasn't a liar and that other people lied all the time.

People needed to un-lie. They knew how to do it, they just didn't want to be the first. Like it's a game of who can do it last because it looked better that way.

There were no real hiding places out here, not like in the closet or the broom cupboard where it was dark and you could hold the door closed. Nobody could get in unless they were strong.

She started to shake, feet dragging like weights through the grass, ankles torn by spikes and jagged things. When the man stopped shouting, he shook and panted and turned in circles.

Then he stopped, stared and saw. "What are you looking at?"

She took a few steps back but the man ran forward, took her arm and brought her to the rug. She could see a head, a hand.

"Look. Look at what she's done!"

She wasn't doing anything, wasn't moving. Something dark and glistening on the side of her face.

His hand felt sticky in hers. He tugged. She pulled.

Then a hand swung around her face and clamped against her teeth. She bit down hard, teeth tearing through flesh.

He howled but he wouldn't let go.

She felt herself being dragged uphill and instead of turning right to the parking lot, they turned left.

It was then she saw the gun.

TWENTY-FOUR

It was dark and even though a big moon blazed high in the sky, everyone used a flashlight.

Occasionally, Temeke could hear the word 'fuss' for heel, or 'such' for find. A dog whined about thirty yards ahead, tight at his handler's heels and snout raised to test the wind. He alerted on the spot.

The sound stopped two other officers who were trailing the animal, and Temeke paused to slide the imaging scope from his rifle and scour the landscape.

"There's something under that tree," he said to Midgely who was intrusively close to his left shoulder.

He felt his knees go soft, moving toward the object on autopilot. Some things he didn't expect, even when he'd seen everything and thought he was made of stone. He wanted to feel strong and in control and yet nothing ever prepared him for the utter hopelessness that came from being too late.

"Over here!" he yelled.

The dogs barked again, telling him what he needed to know. Wrapped in a rug and tied with rope, she lay on her side. The lower half of one leg was exposed and near the ankle, Temeke could make out four bloodstains that resembled a tear drop with a tail; drips that may have fallen from the open wound of a perpetrator.

The silence then was like walking into a tomb. Nobody said anything.

"It's her, isn't it?" Midgely said, playing the beam of her flashlight over the victim's head.

There was no movement or sound, and Temeke could see a matting of crimson hair. The woman had been shot. No pulse.

As officers and paramedics pushed through, Temeke called dispatch and asked them not to give any information over the radio. The worst part of any case was keeping it from the media, and it would be a few hours before the medical examiner had made a positive identification before visiting the family in person.

With no sign of Hannah, Temeke took a long hard look at the area, shining his flashlight into the trees and the surrounding clumps of sage. He heard a scuttle in the undergrowth and knew there were coyotes and bears in the mountains. No point thinking about it.

Judging by the amount of blood he'd seen on Rachael's pillow, it would appear she had been attacked there and left here. They were too late to help her.

"Any sign of a weapon?" he asked Midgely, whose flashlight skittered about over the terrain.

"Nothing," she muttered, cuffing away a tear.

He could hear the sob in her voice and it surprised him. The hard-hitting veneer had been eroded by stress and if he didn't help her through it she might cave in to a damn good cry. It was tough relinquishing a victim to the medical teams. Worse to stand there helpless.

"We did everything we could, love. It's not over yet. We still have to find Hannah."

"She could have fallen… What if he's locked her in a basement? What if we never find her?"

"Remember, these dogs are highly trained," he said in an effort to cheer her up. "Hackett once said they're just as intelligent as man, only a little more thorough."

"It's not my first," she whispered, wiping her eyes with the heel of both hands. "I always cry when I see them, what's been done to them. I guess you could call it angry tears. You know what, sir? I'm tired of running across parking lots, chasing burglars and pot pushers, when I could be helping the people who need it the most." She turned her back on the victim, frozen in the glare of oncoming officers. "I'd hate to take my last dying breath knowing my kid was still at the mercy of the person who'd just killed me."

Temeke knew she watched in pinched fear as the forensic teams went through the motions of an investigation. Faces sagging with defeat.

They watched the victim being lifted onto a scoop stretcher and rushed to a second ambulance parked in a lower parking lot on Tramway Road. This ambulance had not yet been seen by gangs of press and volunteers who were still stationed further up the hill. It was a ruse employed to keep the press from publishing pictures before the family had been notified.

A K-9 snuffled in a nearby thicket and then barked. The officer held up a silver watch engraved with the words *My only love*. Looked as shiny as if it had just been left there and the broken leather strap indicated signs of a struggle. It was the blood spatter on the glass that suggested it was linked to the scene—a scene heavily compromised by foot and paw.

Wading knee-deep in cacti, Temeke tried to see how the scrubland presented itself through young eyes. Not as a detective, looking for evidence. But as a ten-year-old girl, trying to escape.

Hannah would have gone downhill, surely, to where the lights were. To the main road. Then he had to ask himself, had she run off because of what she had seen? Or had her body been dragged uphill to the mountains? Speaking of which…

The dogs were already tuned in to a new scent, heading uphill. As Temeke trudged behind a persistent team of searchers, he thought of that case.

It was dogs that found Kizzy Williams' notebook in a barn in Cimarron State Park. A brave nine-year-old victim of one of the most heinous crimes Temeke had ever investigated. Her older sister had been fourteen when she was abducted outside her school by the very same man. Due to running four hundred meters cross country and clocking the fastest time ever for track and field in New Mexico, she outwitted the 9th Hour killer. Then there was Mayor Oliver's son, Adam, a twelve-year-old who had put his scouting skills to good use when he too was abducted.

Temeke had every confidence that a ten-year old could do the same. Whoever she was with might be mentally sick and assume he was equally invisible, but that didn't mean he was stupid. He must have heard the police calling for her and her mother. Must have dug himself in deep.

Temeke lifted his scope, felt a stiff wind against his cheek while studying heaving miles of grass. Boulders shimmered under the moon, too high to climb and too smooth to get a foothold. He would have seen something from that vantage point but climb those rocks in the dark and you were toast.

Leading with his weapon, he followed the dogs as they chuffed and rumbled through the underbrush. The air suddenly seemed like damp cotton, muggy and saturated the higher they went. Rivulets of sweat ran down his face with the feel of crawling insects across his flesh. His jaw ached and the saliva inside his mouth tasted of brass. He stopped and took a few swigs of water. Then started uphill again, driven by the compulsion to do something, anything to hurry the search.

"How far do you think he went?" Midgely asked.

"Depends how fit he is. We get a second wind, he'll get one too. According to the dogs, he's headed uphill."

"So we just follow him. All of us in a straight line?"

"What type of stupid ass question is that?"

"Well, do we?"

"Don't let me influence you, Midge, if you've got a better suggestion."

"I have actually. Why not split up and go off in teams. Different directions is good because then the bastard will be surrounded."

"Don't you think Commander Ashton's already thought of that?"

"Well, he might of thought of it but we're not doing it."

"Keep your voice down, love. A field officer giving out loud opinions is never appreciated."

She made a depreciating gesture. "Rather elitist, don't you think?"

"Now's not the time, OK?" His parade-ground bark seemed to turn a few heads. He lowered his voice. "Keep searching with that scope. Then you can have an opinion."

She threw him a brief look of lazy insolence as if out of mere curiosity to see what would happen. "Yes, sir. I'm just conscious of the wasted minutes, and the fact that he could be some sadistic bully with a RAP sheet as long as your arm."

"Let's hope that even a sadist has rational intervals."

"I think he's made it quite clear that he hasn't. That's my opinion, sir. Take it or leave it."

Temeke decided to leave it for now. They were both running on adrenaline and anger. The thought of Hannah was pouring through everyone's minds and he tried to barricade himself against what might happen if they didn't reach her in time. And then…

"Every time I look at you," Midgely said, "I see dozens of public service and community awards. That's why they don't like you, isn't it? Maybe I'll get a few awards from now on and they won't like me either."

"It's not about breaking the city's most notorious case and getting recognition, Midge. Or totting up felony arrests and countless brushes with death. You could be desk-bound for days."

"Anything's better than those downtown hotshots looking to steal a big case. All that posturing and jealousy over who gets the big jobs and who runs the investigation… Who is running this investigation?"

Temeke chuckled. With so many agencies on the mountain it was anyone's guess. "Do you really want to play departmental politics with top brass and take civil services tests towards promotion? Work the streets. Make arrests. That's what counts. Quit bitching about the bitching and just get on with it."

What was that saying? Temeke thought. Do what you can and quit thinking about what you can't.

TWENTY-FIVE

Malin flicked her eyes open at a glimmer of light. It was nearly four in the morning and the horizon was a thin line of burnt orange.

Her one-bedroom apartment at Puerta de Corrales was on the second floor with brown stucco walls and white frame windows and a large cottonwood outside. She had begun to like its flaws. How the light flooded through the patio doors and how she could see the road from as far back as the kitchen. That's how small the unit was. Minimalist and so very brown. Just like her.

Wafting up from downstairs was the constant reek of fried potatoes and fish cakes from Old Man Topper. He'd be sitting on his doorstep with a muffin tin clutched in one hand and a bottle of beer in the other, hoping the food would appeal to her, assuming she was hungry.

Then there was Laura Glass. Small, blonde and well into her ninth boyfriend since last Christmas. A seamstress by day and an exotic dancer at night. There had to be medals for girls like her. But the thump, thump, thump of her bedpost against the wall accelerating to fever pitch before dying down and then starting all over again, had kept Malin awake.

She had been staring at the ceiling for what seemed like minutes. Matt always called to say goodnight but last night was different. She kept hoping for an email, text... something, but the screen was stubbornly blank.

She swung her legs off the bed conscious of an ache in her neck. Not from sleeping with her head thrown to one side, but remembering that she had also woken at the sound of her ringtone.

A text from Temeke confirming they had found Rachael's body in the foothills.

She felt part anger, part guilt, that she should have been out there searching with him. The text mentioned an abandoned car at the Peak Tram and a request for her to look into the previous owner, a Mr. Samuel L. Petit. Then another text telling her to forget it, he'd do it himself.

She gave a loud groan and tapped out an apology. Said Sarge told her to go home because she wasn't any use to him with her gas gauge on empty. Of course, Temeke's scenario kept working through her head. How he and all the other officers had been out all night without a wink of sleep or a change of clothes.

Enough time wasted, she thought, standing under a hot shower. Pellets of water stabbed her forehead and her flesh prickled with unease.

For some strange reason an old memory pulsed into life. Hazy. Laughing. Jumping through the sprinkler on Aunt Freda's lawn. Freda wasn't really an aunt. Just a friend of mom's. A good friend.

Only she had a bad husband with a generous left hook.

Malin had been eight when Freda first came over. A lady who, if Malin recalled, always bought French fries on Friday nights. Malin's eyes welled at the vision and the sound of her voice. "Ready, then? Let's go get a bag of fries."

It wasn't just one bag. It was always five. A fast-food banquet. Soft fluffy buns and the smell of cheese.

Fast-forward five years and there was a grunt to Freda's voice and she'd clutch her stomach every so often: "Best thing about French fries is the ketchup. Take one and give it a good dipping. Not like that. Like this."

Malin never saw her after that. Never went back into that musty old house because Freda died all alone from cancer. A gruesome television appeal for citizens to look after their elderly and the memory of the ambulance as it took away her body.

Another chance to help someone gone.

There was silence when the water stopped. Then the steady *drip, drip, drip* as Malin wiped her eyes and toweled herself dry. Spitting out a glob of toothpaste into the sink, she watched the froth slide down into the plughole wishing it was just as easy to dispose of shame and guilt in much the same way.

She blew out the breath she'd been clutching inside as her phone rallied to an incoming call.

Commander Hackett.

"Hannah's still missing," he growled. "If Trandahl was with the mayor last night, and I mean all night, then we're screwed. Know how much security the mayor's residence has? Nobody could have got out or in without being the star of all that CCTV footage. We got the blood samples back from the bedroom. All Rachael's. No matches for Hannah. The blood in the car also belonged to Rachael."

"Any other blood types, sir?"

"None. I'd like you to meet Trandahl this morning. Update him. Go easy and don't ask him on a scale of one to ten how he rates himself as a husband and a father. Any relation of the mayor's…"

Malin hardly had the words, 'right, sir,' out of her mouth before Hackett hung up.

Interviewing suspects was the one thing Malin least enjoyed, especially if you were shut in a gray room with a psycho rambling on about how it was always someone else's fault. Since there had been no sign of bloody clothing or a murder weapon, Trandahl was their prime suspect.

So far, he hadn't indicated any signs of an explosive temper and nothing that implied a mental disorder of any kind. If anything would have pushed him over the edge it would have been his missing child.

She pulled on a pair of pants and a polo shirt. Removed her pistol from the holster, racked the slide back to show an empty chamber and then dropped it back in her holster.

She listened to the slumbering rumble of her unit as it warmed up in the parking lot. Tapping through the most recent incident reports on the computer, she found a homicide at Smiths, an accident on Paseo and an alarm going off at Target on Coors.

She had no idea why her stomach continued to twist with anxiety. Her meetings with Beverly Herrera, Naomi Michaels and Emma Burnett still had to be arranged. Then there was Kate Harroway at Mountain Financial, whose proximity to Rachael at one time was invaluable.

Maybe it was because she missed doing interviews with Temeke, watching his sharp mind navigating around the lies and shooting down the avenues of most resistance in order to see the perps squirm.

She hadn't realized how alone she'd felt during these last few days. As if she had suddenly become aware that he was her friend, her *most cherished* friend, and if she didn't do something soon he might be snatched away from her.

It was suddenly unbearable.

Malin took a sharp right-hand turn, mind focusing on the recent updates on Hannah. SWAT's tactical unit had made a possible sighting on the northeast edge of the city in the Sandia foothills.

A bum living rough? Or a frightened little girl?

Either way, it was nowhere as simple as it sounded. Hannah might well be disoriented and unable to find her way back because she wouldn't know which way *back* was. The accumulated errors of navigating the terrain at night was so great she wouldn't know up from down within thirty yards of where she was.

Parking in the rear lot of Northwest Area Command, Malin made her way to the front lobby, where Sergeant Moran's head was obscured behind an open *Albuquerque Journal*. The headlines read, *TRANDAHL CASE BAFFLING* and the article went on to add how the police department were still determining if it was a burglary, robbery, kidnapping or some combination.

"Hey, you," Sarge said, folding the paper.

"Morning, Sarge. Do we have any more information on the car found in the heights?"

"Officer Midgely described it as a white Crown Vic. Well, those weren't her words exactly. More like a crapped-out piece of junk. It was licensed to a Sam Petit. Deceased."

"Yeah, I got that." Her fingers massaged the back of her neck. The description of the car, the color, the age… anxiety began to hum inside her like electricity. "Have there been any calls about Hannah?"

"If you count the three crank calls I had this morning claiming they'd seen her at the laundromat on Alameda, Starbucks on 528 and sitting in Tuscany Park on Bandelier. I wish people would get a life."

"Maggie here?"

"Nope. She left over an hour ago with Captain Fowler. Body of a young woman found round the back of Smiths. Been there a few days."

No luck asking Maggie to do the three remaining interviews then. "Hackett upstairs?"

"He's in his turret eating a burrito. Said he wasn't to be disturbed. I'll let you know when Trandahl arrives."

As Malin climbed the stairs to her office she was still trying to figure out why, according to Hackett, Rachael had been found only yards from the car. Her Facebook page, which showed holidays, picnics and backyard BBQs, never showed any shots of a white Crown Vic.

Sam Petit's background was nothing spectacular. Born and raised in Albuquerque, had an accumulation of old cars which he regularly restored. Mostly antiques with a few sedans thrown in. But what connection he had with Trandahl was a mystery.

Malin stared over at Temeke's desk. Trashed with open files extending as far as the small space on the corner where he usually put his feet. Keyboard stained with coffee spatter and crumbs, and a piggy bank spilling a pile of quarters from its guts.

Her computer showed ten emails, the most important of which was from the media compliance department. Mac's report held no surprises.

Dai Trandahl had been checking out exotic dancers in his spare time, mostly late at night as you would expect. Malin counted fifty instant messages and emails to several women, some of whom had answered in response to setting up meetings and others to negotiating a price for select services over the phone.

But Dai didn't appear interested enough to give out his number. He was interested in offering serious cash to anyone who could help him find a girl called Ella.

Ella Gibson. The dead girl. Now, why would Dai Trandahl pass up hundreds of chicks just to get to her?

The emails weren't what you would call sexual either. A short chain sent two days ago sparked Malin's curiosity.

Trandahl asked a girl name Jewel to help him find Ella. Apparently, he had an envelope of cash for her and wondered where he could send it. Jewel's response was more than hasty.

Give it to me and I'll give it to her. Or you can remember me in your will…☺

Trandahl: How much?

Jewel: Two hundred. Take it or leave it. Meet me at the store. Half an hour. South side.

A plume of fear shot up Malin's spine. Was this the same victim they had found this morning outside Smiths? There was nothing but loading bays on the south side. No cars. No witnesses.

She dialed Sarge's number and before she could ask him for the victim's name she knew what he would say.

TWENTY-SIX

It was five-fifteen on Friday morning and Dispatch was hopping.

A gynecologist living on Juniper Hill Road in the northeast heights was leaving for a Friday morning shift at the hospital when he found a man trying to break into his shiny new Audi A7, which was idling in the driveway.

As far as the doctor could make out, he had a chin full of stubble and thick dark hair, kind of flipped over one eye like it was styled that way. There was some type of firearm jammed in his waistband. The doctor thought it was too dangerous to chase the man up Tramway Road where he then hiked north along Sandia Heights Drive.

Temeke shook his head. How many times had he warned citizens on live TV *not* to leave their sodding cars unattended and warming up in the driveway?

He continued to listen to the suspect report on the radio. White male, five ten, one hundred and seventy-five pounds. Possibly armed and dangerous.

An unrelated incident? Or a coincidence?

Temeke watched a slip of sunlight as it haloed the crest of the Sandia Mountains before creeping down the crevices like molten lava. The grunt of a K-9 behind him caused him to turn. Mauser was pulling on a long leash, tail wagging as if the cul-de-sac of houses was a bowl of food.

Commander Ashton approached the perimeter of the subdivision from the southwest side, where freshly turned soil met scrubland. His eyes scoured the façade of a single storey house with a *Sold* sign swinging from a white gibbet.

No blinds on the windows and builder's schematic drawings still taped to the glass. A deck, enclosed by a railing, extended all the way to the back of the house and steps provided access to the woods behind.

A fir tree stood at the boundary of the neighboring property, a good nine-footer with a deep gouge about three feet up from the base of the trunk. Someone had reversed into it. There were plenty of tire marks to suggest the presence of backhoes and other excavating equipment since, according to dispatch, the property was still empty.

Temeke could hear the faint crackle of officers' radios even though they had been turned low, and he spotted the commander crouching beside a narrow trough of water where partial footprints were visible, sole eroding into the mud.

More hand signals, more barking and then everything went eerily quiet.

Turning his attention to an area of scrub running about fifteen feet from the back of the house, he could see a visible trail cutting through the trees and winding upward toward boulders and scree.

"You do realize a man with pathological issues might be immune to fatigue," Midgely whispered, as she cut through a swath of long grass behind him. "And possibly for long lengths of time."

"True. But harder if he's transporting a living, breathing ten-year-old."

"Could be someone with a military background."

"Aren't they all? In any case, he's not bloody superman."

"You hope," she said.

Temeke knew what Midgely was getting at. A child at the mercy of a man suffering unpredictable mood swings was like underestimating the length of chain by which a rabid dog was tied.

It occurred to Temeke as he stood there that all directions would have looked the same from a child's vantage point and trying to get home at night might be just as hopeless on foot as it would during the day. While part of the search had widened, sending teams off into broader circles, he chose to stay close to the commander who was now moving toward the rear of the house.

The glass in the sliding door had been smashed and a dowel that had been placed in the door track, discarded few feet away. Beside a pile of lumber was a plaid blanket, one corner snagged around an exposed nail. Temeke matched it to the blanket Trandahl had described in Hannah's room. Or one just like it.

Mauser would be able to detect skin particles deposited on the material and any fear scents suspended in the surrounding air. The fact that the dog crouched, nose pointing at the open door, was the reward they had all been waiting for.

Commander Ashton signaled to his men and two officers inched around the back of the house, three more fell in behind. Angling sideways, he pressed his back against the wall, paused, then lurched around the door frame, gun out in front.

Temeke took his cue and followed them in, Midgely at his right shoulder. The interior was empty; exposed floorboards covered with a litter of leaves and two flattened water bottles. There was a dank odor of sweat. At first he thought he had imagined it but no, there it was again—an invisible tendril that somehow managed to hover under his nose, urging him that someone had just left.

He tried to make an appraisal of the possibilities while at the same time struggling with the cold animal of fear. The man they were looking for was hydrated and well fueled. He hoped Hannah was too. It was something he couldn't dwell on because if he lost his head, there would be no Hannah at all.

Footsteps clambered against the floorboards upstairs and the words *clear* rung out as the officers searched each room.

Cuffing the sweat from his face, he tried to take in the sitting room, dining area and kitchen; new appliances gleaming in a shaft of sunlight.

"Bet he told Hannah he'd got the perfect campsite in the middle of nowhere," he said to Midgely, peering through the window at the trees. "Although I doubt they're setting up tent and eating beans by the campfire."

"She might have run away, sir. They do sometimes."

He could hear the optimism in the word *sometimes* but it sounded too remote to believe.

He might as well admit it. The odds of finding Hannah were getting slimmer and slimmer. She could be walking around on a disoriented path where even the slightest deviation would cost her hours of thirst in the burning sun.

If she was with the man the doctor claimed he saw, she might have no chance at all.

TWENTY-SEVEN

Malin said her goodbyes to the mayor, whose face blazed with anger. He was clearly unhinged by the news of Rachael's death and worse, outraged by Hackett's refusal to let him in on Trandahl's interview.

If it hadn't been for the reinforced door, the mayor would have barged in, mouthing off how the police had royally botched this whole thing. How he'd seen more effort in the Darcy Oliver case.

Malin spread her hands and raised an eyebrow.

"Darcy Oliver?" he repeated.

She shook her head: no bell.

"My damn dog!"

Of course, your damn dog, she thought, remembering how a search party of fifteen police officers had been called in over six weeks ago to look for the damn pooch, which, if she recalled, had waddled over to a damn neighbor's house for another damn donut.

Malin closed the door behind the mayor and recorded the time as seven-fifteen on Friday morning. Passed the tissue box across the table to Trandahl and watched him scrunch the last few tissues she'd given him and drop them into the trash.

"How… how did she die?" he asked again.

"She was shot. I'm sorry—"

"She can't be… Why? Who would do a thing like that?"

"That's what we're here to find out."

His throat held back something between a sob and a shout, and she can't have been more than a blur through his tears. "Are you sure? Are you really sure it's her?"

"Dr. Vasillion, our forensic pathologist called to confirm the remains matched a dental X-ray for Rachael."

"I don't understand," Trandahl said, scrubbing his nose with another tissue. "Is this a serial killer? Because there was a woman who was shot in the back of the head in her own home and another found behind a grocery store yesterday. I saw it on the news."

"We're not sure they're related," Malin said. "The woman found behind the grocery store had a history of drug abuse and the woman found in dead in her home had a similar background. Since we don't have the benefit of questioning them it's a moot point. What I would like to clear up is an email we found on your computer addressed to one of the deceased women. Jewel Hansen? Ring any bells?"

"Why would it ring any bells? I don't know anyone called Jewel Hansen."

"Then why is there a letter to her on your computer?"

"I dunno. I've never heard of her, OK?" He shook his head and rubbed his eyes. "Listen, I can't tell Rachael's mom. I'm sorry, I just can't do it."

That was quick change of subject, thought Malin. How he could do that without flinching was award-worthy.

"The medical examiner will visit her in person." Malin tried to sound sympathetic but her patience was beginning to fray.

She then passed him a plastic bag sealed with yellow evidence tape, initialed and labeled *Wrist Watch*. "Do you recognize this?"

He nodded, went a pale shade of gray. "I gave it her last Christmas."

The look of sheer horror on his face gave Malin a perverse wedge of hope that Trandahl would finally come clean.

"Did Rachael ever use drugs?" she asked.

"No."

"Smoke anything?"

"No. Listen, I don't want to sound shitty or anything but I don't see how this is relevant."

"It is relevant, Dai. All my questions are relevant. If she had done drugs there might have been a connection to the other women. So let me ask you this. Did Rachael ever mention being scared for her life?"

"No."

"If Rachael didn't have any enemies then what do you think happened?"

"Someone must have taken her... I-I don't know. I wasn't there."

"You knew her friends, her work colleagues. Anyone have a grudge against her?"

"I think she would have told me."

"Do you know anyone who owns a white Crown Vic?" Malin showed him a few 1996 and 1997 models on her iPad.

Again, Trandahl shook his head and each gasp seemed to tear down his throat. His face was beginning to look like rain on a dusty window pane.

"Any idea *why* the Peak Tram?" she asked, waiting a few seconds for a response that never came. "Someone decided that was a good place to leave her. It begs the question was Rachael killed because she could identify her attacker. Or was it someone she knew? When you think about it, maybe this someone knew the Peak Tram was Rachael's favorite place."

Trandahl rubbed his temples. "She won't ride the Peak Tram. She hates heights."

"Perhaps she enjoyed the view. A lot of people go up there and park, especially at night."

He didn't seem too excited about that either.

"Hannah's cell phone was found in the car," she said. "Maybe the kidnapper allowed her to take it. Shows some kind of compassion, don't you think? Yet the same compassion wasn't extended to Rachael. Looks personal."

Trandahl looked at her for a long moment and then wiped a finger under his left eye. "Do you think Hannah's still alive? Do you think there's a chance he'll spare her?"

"Anything's possible. But you need to understand we really don't know."

"No, no, I realized that but I want to get a picture of this guy." A hissing breath through clenched teeth. "Who he is… What he wants."

"When you went upstairs to Hannah's room, did you notice anything missing?" She saw him shake his head. "Let me jog your memory. A blanket perhaps?"

Trandahl eyed the ceiling for a good few seconds and then nodded. "Plaid… beige, I think. Why?"

"They found one just like it in an empty house close to where they found your wife. I would say that's very positive." Malin wrapped her hands together.

She tried to still the silent electrical storm in her head, the voice that told her Trandahl had no idea where Hannah was, let alone had anything to do with his wife's death. Repeated sighs and a permanent frown told her he was desperate and she finally gave into the nagging dread that she was wasting valuable time.

"I want to go home," Trandahl said. "I'd like to be alone."

In Malin's mind, his request was perfectly reasonable. Who wouldn't want to have time on their own to grieve a murdered spouse? But home? Where all the blood was?

FBI agent, Stu Anderson, was already half-way through the door before she could respond. He briefly introduced himself to Trandahl before beckoning her outside.

"Might be a good time to take a break," he whispered, making way for Hackett and Lieutenant Alvarez. "I want to go over the websites Trandahl's been visiting. There are pornographic items on his laptop, so a polygraph test would be a good idea. We'll take over from here."

Malin felt beaten, but was determined not to show it. She took his pat on her shoulder as a paternal dismissal. At least he didn't grab her by the back of her shirt and drag her out into the hallway.

She looked down at her belt to check an incoming text. Dr. Vasillion wanted to walk her through Rachael Trandahl's autopsy in ten minutes. Just enough time to grab a coffee and call Temeke.

She walked to the cafeteria and found Captain Fowler stuffing his face with a muffin and flicking through Time Magazine.

"So, how's it going?" he sized her up with a practiced look.

"Peachy."

"Yeah, that's what I heard. So Trandahl confessed and you got the rest of the day off."

"Wouldn't that be a first?"

"Did he ask for an attorney?"

"Waived his rights. Said he had nothing to hide."

Captain Fowler leaned back in his chair and narrowed his eyes. Looked like he wanted to bring her down like a wounded wildebeest. "Probably making stuff up."

"Suspension of disbelief?"

"Nah. Pathological liar. So, where's your partner?"

Malin wondered why Fowler had used the words *pathological liar* and *your partner* in the same sentence. For some uncanny reason it was all she could do to stop smiling. What was it Temeke always said about Fowler?

He's like a hemorrhoid. Pain in the butt when he comes down those stairs and a relief when he goes back up again.

"He's with the search party," she said. "Has been all night. Lucky he found Rachael when he did. She'd have been hard to recognize with all those wild animals up there."

"Dang, you're a joy to talk to."

"It's hard seeing stuff like that. A woman all bloody and battered and left to rot like a piece of trash."

"How did Trandahl take the news?"

"Pretty bad. But it's only going to get worse when Stu goes over all that internet porn. He's not going to stop until he gets a confession."

"What's the betting they find semen under the computer desk? He'll be asking for a lawyer then."

Malin walked toward the door and pressed a hand against the frame. "I'll send someone over the mayor's house to do a welfare check in case Trandahl harms himself."

"He needs to man up. Stop blaming the world for all his problems and stop pointing the finger at some guy in the neighborhood who was never there. They all do that."

"Do you think he's guilty?" she asked.

"It's hard not to say yes. He's not going to like the rules and regulations of the penal system. He's not going to like close management. But that's where he's going. Then he'll end up on *The Row* and get a TV and good food. He'll feel like a real man then."

"I hope you're wrong."

"Nah, I'm never wrong." It was hard to take Fowler seriously with blueberries in his teeth. "Temeke say anything about a promotion? Anything about Suzi?"

Malin shook her head.

"How much are you earning now?"

"It's a good pay scale, sir. Can't complain." Smug bastard, she thought as she let him stumble over that visual.

"Ballpark figure?"

"You know I can't tell you that."

Fowler leaned forward and angled his head. "Looked at your stats recently? I have. Not exactly *peachy*."

Liar, she thought.

They were peachier than they had ever been. Five high profile cases solved in less than a year? He had to be out of his gourd.

Had Temeke signed off on a document confirming that they would be taking over Suzi Cornwell's unsolved cases? It was the only thing that would have made Fowler mad.

She grinned. It was too good to be true.

Fowler no longer had any hold over her. He was about as influential as a layer of dust on a city street.

TWENTY-EIGHT

She went in search of a quiet place and wedged herself in Temeke's squeaky chair. Half-closed blinds blotted out most of the morning sun and the light that filtered through the slats was enough to see by.

Jotted on a pad was a diagram of the crime scene and detailed notes. She glanced over the most salient of these.

Ella Gibson: 5 ft 9 ins, blood lividity consistent with position. Men's suits in closet. Get size. Ask Mac about most recent web searches on Ella's computer.

Missing woman: Jewel Hansen. Regular drug deal? Or one-off?

Interview store manager - Josh Childers.

Malin brushed the files aside and put up her feet on Temeke's desk. She dialed his number. His breath sounded ragged over the phone.

"Having a break, Marl?" he asked.

"Yeah. You?"

"We all took five. I'm on my fourth protein bar. Midgely's on her twelfth."

Malin felt the bubble of a laugh in her throat which quickly subsided with the onset of her frustration.

"I'm not getting anywhere with Trandahl, sir. What's worse, I keep going back to the beginning and asking myself why would he kill his wife *and* daughter? All I can come up with is he met someone online. Someone who didn't want the responsibility of a kid."

"Would you consider Trandahl a good catch?"

"He's a good-looking guy."

There was a pause. "And Rachael?"

"I reckon she could turn a few heads. Thing is, the neighborhood is safe. Mainly property crimes and not violent crimes, which means the victim was likely targeted."

"If you put Rachael in a continuum of risk, what do you think elevated that risk?"

"She drove to school at the same time every day. Stayed there, what, four hours? Probably went shopping afterwards and then came home. Simple schedule. Easy to stalk."

"Were there patterns in the attack? Any signature aspects?"

"Blood stain in the bedroom. On the bed and carpet. We don't know if it was sexual in nature. At least not yet." Malin recalled the nature of the bedroom and jewelry on the floor. "I'd put the criminal in an organized category. No body, no weapon and very little evidence to tell us why there was a pool of blood on the bed. The scene appeared staged."

"So the perpetrator's educated. Socially and sexually competent. Lives with a partner," Temeke said. "May have suffered harsh discipline as a child. There's going to be situational stress in his life or at least something that triggers it. So he may have a variable temperament and we know he's mobile. We also suspect he is fully aware of the media."

"You say *he*."

"How much does Rachael Trandahl weigh?"

Malin let her mind slip back to the photograph of Rachael in the hall. The one with the pale blue dress that embraced her generous curves. "One-forty-five?"

"She was carried to a car, Marl. She didn't walk. He had to have been reasonably strong," he added. "It was quick because according to witness statements Rachael's car wasn't seen leaving the house that morning. The perpetrator had to have been familiar with the house and the road behind it. We also know he wrapped her up in something. The hall carpet's missing and so is Hannah's blanket."

Malin made a note to bring that up with Trandahl. Although in retrospect, she wondered why Trandahl hadn't mentioned it.

"Rapists and burglars aren't known to transport their victims," Temeke said. "Bodies need to be bagged. Consider the time it would take. The risk rises with every second. So what does that tell you?"

"A rookie killer, sir. Didn't think. Didn't care. Shedding his DNA and saliva all over the house. There's gonna be a ton of trace evidence in that bedroom."

"We're both agreed that Rachael was a low risk victim. That tells us it was a personalized attack. The bedroom suggests an intimate partner killer and the blood was on the victim's side of the bed. Whoever did it knew his way around the home. No sign of a break-in or a struggle. The blood spatter wasn't consistent with blunt force trauma and we know now she was shot at close range. One of the pillows was missing, perhaps the one used to cover her face."

Meticulously planned, Malin thought. "When you say she was targeted, it can't have been a drug hit. According to Trandahl she wasn't using."

"And a kidnapper wouldn't want Rachael dead, Marl. He'd want her on display so we can see he's serious. Do me a favor? Go to my house. You know where the key is. Forward the email from Hackett about Midgely's transfer. I can't open the damn thing on my phone. The password to my laptop is BX15KXT. License plate of my old *Panda* in the UK. That's a police unit to you. And take your sodding feet off my desk."

"On my way." Malin chuckled and hung up.

She let her eyes glaze over the window, refocusing to the green outside. As for Trandahl, all red flags pointed to him, yet she had no real leads this early in the case. Sometimes perpetrators screwed up. They stole things or sold things. She'd get a tail on him and install video equipment near his residence if she had to.

If he did anything wacky—for instance, sell his house—she'd get a warrant to search the new one. Probably do it when he was at work and stick the warrant on his pillow. Search and seizure usually took a few hours, less if you were quick, and anything stolen would be taken down to a storage locker and listed by the evidence custodian. She felt better already.

Her phone did a counterturn on Temeke's blotter and the neon beam hit the ceiling.

Dr. Vasillion. Silver hair, lean and elegant. So out of place with what he did.

TWENTY-NINE

Malin took a detour to OMI first before driving to Temeke's house. She had to wait fifteen minutes for the doctor. He was taking a shower.

Her first visit to the Office of the Medical Investigator had been during the Eriksen case almost nine months ago. Row upon row of autopsy stations, equipped with the most up-to-date features. Clean and bright, it could have passed for a gourmet kitchen, except for doctors wearing face masks, shoe covers, aprons and caps, and pulling bodies onto sheet-line gurneys before rolling them into a cooler. Each work station was meticulously hosed, floors mopped, instruments cleaned and tubes of blood and vitreous fluids placed into a refrigerator.

Dr. Vasillion, squeaky-clean and smelling strongly of antibacterial soap, took her to his office. A large touch-screen computer displayed a graph of secretor types, antigens and the letters A, B and O. Malin had no idea what it all meant.

"Nice offices," she said, aware that she said it every time.

"The quality of the facility matches the quality of work," Dr. Vasillion said, reading her roving gaze. "The victim's clothing, in case you were wondering, is kept in a drying cabinet. They'll be packaged and sent to the labs."

She took the seat in front of his desk. "How big is this place?"

"Sixty thousand square feet, which includes storage for bodies as well as faculty, residents and fellows."

Enough space for the living and the dead, she thought.

"I can give you a tour sometime."

"I'd like that."

"Our MRIs and CT scans do virtual autopsies in real time. Knives are almost becoming a thing of the past."

"You're kidding."

"It cuts down delays." His face crumpled into a smile, mouse clicking frantically. "Determines cause of death in about thirty minutes. Shall we begin?"

He swiveled the computer to where she could see it and pulled up Ella Gibson's file. "I have medical histories and records for Rachael Trandahl but sadly not much for Ella Gibson."

Malin scooted her chair along the edge of the desk and leaned over a little to get a better look. No more attaching an MR film to a light box. Ella's skull was now displayed on his monitor.

"For Ella Gibson, two gunshot wounds to the head. I've got a rush on the ballistics report but having done a brief examination of the fragments I'd say it was fired from a handgun. Probably a nine mil or similar. You can see here two bullets fractured the skull within millimeters from each other causing massive hemorrhaging to the brain. Contusions on her face were likely the result of falling forward after being fatally struck."

"Is that her body weight?" Malin pointed to a number on the side of the screen.

"One hundred pounds? Yes. At five feet, nine inches, she was undernourished. Stomach contents reveal her last meal was a cup of lasagna and half a glass of wine. Tox report states her blood alcohol level was point-two. Her livor mortis and rigor mortis suggests she died twelve to fourteen hours after she had eaten that last meal. Manner of death: homicide."

Malin wondered what kind of woman Ella was, stitching together a patchwork of escort jobs only to wind up a junkie. With better money management, she could have been a millionaire.

"Was she raped?"

"No." He swiped the screen to bring up Rachael Trandahl's details.

"Trandahl also suffered two gunshot wounds to the head. Possibly, a nine millimeter. First bullet entered the victim's left eye, fracturing her skull, before coming to rest in the muscles at the side of her head. Here you can see how a second bullet entered the right side of the victim's head, causing skull fractures and injuring multiple features of her brain. You're talking a couple tenths of a second between impacts."

She remembered Dr. Vasillion telling her on a previous case that where a 115-grain jacketed hollow-point cartridge had been fired, it likely traveled at around 1,250 feet per second, hitting the target with about 399 joules of energy.

"Were both wounds instantly fatal?" she asked.

"If she had been standing, which she wasn't, she would have dropped like a sack of rocks." Dr. Vasillion swiped through a series of numbers.

"Would you say it was the same killer?"

"Off the record, and given the ballistics report—I would say you're looking at the same gun."

"Any defensive wounds?"

"None. But we did find fibers. Red, black and white. Mainly those adhering to the wounds on her body and hair. These appear to be wool and consistent with a carpet."

"No point asking if she was raped?"

He shook his head. "Vaginal swab revealed no signs of semen. But she was pregnant. About nine weeks. I'll call the husband and let him know."

Malin tipped her head forward to allow for a swallow and quickly straightened. It was news she wasn't expecting. News she was grateful not to have to pass on to Trandahl herself.

"Rachael Trandahl appeared fit. Didn't drink much and certainly didn't smoke. Good heart, good diet. Organs in good shape. Due to stomach contents, livor and rigor," he said, "I'd estimate time of death between seven and eight in the morning. Manner of death: homicide."

"Thanks, doc, I appreciate it."

"There is something else. The blood on the bottom of Rachael's shoe belongs to Ella Gibson."

Malin felt like she was in a fog. The vicious attack on Ella Gibson was connected by a simple footprint?

"I'll need to talk to family members and witnesses," he said. "Then I'll file the death certificate."

He swiveled the monitor back toward him, tapped out a few notes and then leaned back in his chair.

"I'm leaving early this afternoon." He loosened his tie. "So I'll email you both reports tomorrow, if that's OK?"

"Going somewhere nice?" she asked, not knowing quite why she said it.

"Yes and no. Taking time off to help Jen move out. We decided to call it quits."

"Oh…" *Happy day.* "I'm sorry to hear that."

"Probably didn't do anyone any favors. Truth is, I'm happy settling for TV as conversation and Friday nights are a bottle of wine and a take-out meal. Not quite Jen's style. Anyway, she'll be fine. I understand she wants to try and rekindle things with her ex."

Malin felt light-headed and she could hardly swallow. "Her ex?"

"Yeah. Matt Black, the CSI guy. Well, they were close to being engaged before I came along. Anyway, I'll be back tomorrow. Let me know if there's anything else you need."

The parking lot gave her a sip of fresh air and slumping into her car, she was left with an ear full of silence. Long enough for her decide she and Matt never quite had the same rhythm. Never really clicked.

Then the tears came.

THIRTY

Temeke watched as volunteers, wearing backpacks and orange hi-viz vests, assembled first aid kits beneath the constant *whop, whop, whop* of a helicopter.

The outer perimeter of the search had trickled down as far as Paramount Estates and Eagle Rock. Witnesses claimed seeing a man and a little girl walking on a strip of pasture sandwiched between Elena Drive and Tramway Road.

Small business owners had closed down for the day in order to join in the search, downing bitter coffee and tearing into donated boxes of freshly baked donuts. Some were parents of previous cases of missing children—people not afraid to cover some of the most rugged terrain in New Mexico—and jazzed enough to stay the course.

The temperature had risen to 100 degrees, winds gusting as the air continued to heat up during the morning.

Midgely had been knocking on nearby doors to get owner permission to make searches on private property. Temeke had been slugging on a near empty water canteen, eyes peeled on the lower saddle of the Sandias as he navigated his way through grasses and cane cholla.

His radio crackled with static; Midgely's voice muttering something about a man jumping over a back wall of a nearby property. He looked down the road and found Midgely running toward him, thumb jabbing the air.

"Owner of that monster house asked if I could take a look around her kitchen. She'd been baking earlier, a few loaves of bread and a dozen muffins. Left them on a cooling rack for an hour and when she came back they were gone. Odd in light of a kidnapper on the loose."

Temeke had to agree.

"Judging by all the paraphernalia stuck to the fridge, I'd say she likes dogs and Cracker Barrel restaurants. Her wallet's open on the kitchen table. New Mexico driver license. Carol Carter. Date of birth 06-09-85. Just in case that's of any interest."

Why did little buzzes of intuition whisper in Temeke's ear every time Midgely barged her way into anything? He could see in her face all the intrusiveness and curiosity that had once been his. All of it turning to anger and frustration the more seasoned she became.

"Any parking in the back yard?" he asked.

"No one would be able to get a low clearance vehicle behind her house with all those trees. But there's a path that leads to a small scree field, probably the lower section of La Luz Trail. I made sure to tell the captain."

Temeke could feel his bladder twitch and held up a hand. Leaning his rifle against a tree, he chose a thicket of ponderosa near a large boulder to tend to business.

"Where's the commander?" he shouted.

"Way up there."

He could see Midgely between the branches, finger pointing in the direction of a track that weaved between the pine trees, rising above the canyon on the hillside.

Officers peering through binoculars and K-9s chuffing in the dirt, ears pricked and eyes keen.

"See anything else behind that house?" he asked.

"A few bones littered about by the dumpster, and before you ask, the medical team thought it was a roast chicken."

"Was the soil disturbed?"

"There's bear and cougar tracks everywhere. I reckon they've been feasting on her trash for months."

Slinging his rifle over his shoulder, Temeke wandered back toward her. He could hear voices in the distance: an officer talking about getting more water from the mobile command center and another expelling a rattling breath before hoofing it to the road. Looked like one of the Sandia rangers.

"You know what I've been thinking?" Midgely said as they headed uphill.

"If it's something juicy, I'm all ears."

"If the kidnapper took Carol Carter's bread and muffins, it's possible he's looking after Hannah. Making sure she's well fed."

"I hope you're right, Midge. Because it doesn't leave me with much confidence."

"If this man's a threat, don't you think he'd have popped off a few rounds from his lofty roost?"

"You think he's gone up as far as the crest?"

"Best to take precautions."

Temeke wanted to reassure himself that Hannah was safe, that her mother's killer had given up on his mission. That the danger had passed. But there was no escaping the glaring fact that she was a witness and that made her far from safe. His head was filled with random thoughts. Hannah. Serena. Home. Then somehow to Malin.

He missed Malin if he was honest. How they both preferred silence when they worked the field; not that he didn't appreciate Midgely's free-spoken yapping—but Malin had that inner strength he admired.

He remembered when she first came to Northwest Area Command and how he'd thrown a few shitty comments her way. If only he could turn back time, but the damage was already done. She'd never flinched, never complained and in no time at all, she'd made it in the *boys' club*. For Malin, the process of learning the ropes seemed to have happened so fast, she had already become one of their own. Her presence in his thoughts was like a string of Christmas lights. He was moved by her.

Looking down at the Peak Tram parking lot, he could see a circus of Eye Witness News Vans ascending the mountainside toward the first tier of officers and volunteers. He knew they were hoping for a story, something to feed the frenzy of impatient citizens.

He followed Midgely along a narrow path that threaded under a canopy of conifers, eyes drawn to her sidearm. She was packing a good deal of heat, while her mouth flapped on about how law enforcement should be rewarded with a barbeque when they reached the summit. It was a good twenty minute walk before one side became a sheer drop, descending through boulders and grass and clusters of prickly pear.

He was conscious of his sweat-stained shirt and the glaze that was forming under his baseball cap. He flicked it off briefly and wiped his skin with his cuff.

The phone lit up on his belt and he was glad to see it was Malin.

"Morning," she said. "How's it going?"

"OK." Temeke felt his face tense. There was something in the air he couldn't define. A familiar scent that hovered stubbornly beneath his nose. "Just done a few knock-and-talks. Now headed uphill."

"Hackett wants us to get a warrant to search the Cerro Colorado Landfill."

"It's a bit early, isn't it?" Temeke was already steeling himself against the stench and the thought of poking through a hundred tons of dirty diapers. None of it did much to dispel the queasy feeling in his stomach. "We may still find her, Marl."

"Hackett's assistant showed me the video of Rachael at the gas station. So I did a little digging. About three years ago, the manager was arrested for breaking into his ex-girlfriend's house. Didn't take the breakup too well. There was a restraining order and two violations. Then all went quiet. You don't think he wanted to know Rachael a little better than she wanted to know him?"

Temeke recalled the store video, angled down toward the subject as he stood a few feet behind Rachael to tape her phone conversation. The resolution wasn't too great but he'd recognize the manager if he saw him again.

"I'd like to talk to him if that's OK with you," she said.

"Preferably at the convenience store, Marl. You don't want him bolting."

"What bothers me is that Rachael sounded scared on the tape."

"Forensics have Rachael's phone records, right?"

"Yep. All her contacts are labelled with names except one. She called that number three times on Wednesday and the last tower to bounce the signal was on Coors Boulevard. Since then, no signal, no hits. Apparently, she was calling a burner."

"I guess we can definitely rule out a close friend." Temeke stumbled over another tree root. "If she was being threatened, it might explain why she had a gun."

The landscape darkened suddenly as a cloud blotted out the sun. Temeke ducked under a low hanging branch and then paused. Rifle lowered, he glanced downhill again at a crush of reporters in the parking lot with crews and booms. Others carried little more than a smartphone equipped with Ustream and some kind of video editing suite. They were all there, waiting to weigh in on the latest updates.

"Do me a favor, Marl. There's a gynecologist up here at number fifteen Juniper Hill Road. He saw a guy trying to break into his nice new car around seven this morning. See if you can get him a photo array. Failing that, a forensic artist. Anything to narrow down the options."

"Will do. I'll make a few calls on my way to your house."

"Don't take any shit from the cat. He gets one scoop. *One*."

"See you tonight," she said.

"I look forward to it."

There was an eerie silence after she hung up. Temeke gazed west across the Rio Grande to the horizon where a haze hovered over three small volcanoes. Looking upwards, he scanned the crawling cables of the Peak Tram that run up the western face of the mountain and at Midgely's silhouette as she powered along the trail.

It occurred to him that the man the gynecologist saw might have been a known carjacker and if so, his mug shot would already be in the database. The downside was that the man might not have anything to do with Hannah's disappearance.

As he continued to climb, he refreshed a mental image of Rachael Trandahl's body, head smeared with blood. The only evidence they had of a gun was the empty box in Rachael's bedroom. The bad news was… if the bullet had been fired from a nine mil it was safe to assume there were several thousand like it in Albuquerque.

The dumpsters outside the house had been examined and luminoled. All came up negative for blood. If Trandahl was trying to hide something, wouldn't he be sneaking back into his house at night rather than passed out in the mayor's spare bedroom?

An eagle took flight from the apex of a pine tree, a wild flurry of wings soaring over spruce and scrub oak. It circled in front of one of the granite spires and was gone.

Although Temeke knew every snaking trail and every crevice, today he didn't have the same deep sense of peace.

THIRTY-ONE

Malin looked up at the wall clock. Nine-fifteen. She called the Porsche dealership about the car delivery Trandahl had mentioned and was told there was no requisition for a car to be delivered or, for that matter, a driver to bring Trandahl back to the office Thursday afternoon.

However they did confirm that Trandahl rode a bike into work. Every day.

Malin called Trandahl and got him on the second ring.

"This car you said you delivered during your lunch hour to the heights," she asked. "Just so I understand this correctly, you had a window of what... about an hour and a half? Was this a favor for a friend?"

She could hear him huffing breath and moving about. He was clearly thinking about it. "OK, so I didn't deliver a car. I guess you could call it an extended lunch hour."

"So what did you do?"

"I went to the bank because my wife had taken out a shit-load of cash recently. Over a thousand dollars. I asked the manager if she'd given a reason. He said he didn't ask."

"You have a joint bank account?"

"Yeah." Dai sighed again. "As far as I know, we don't owe anyone that kind of money. I assumed she'd tell me in her own time but she didn't."

"And you didn't think that was important to tell me?" His silence had already put his statement at risk.

"Before you go," he murmured, "the doctor called. He said Rachael was pregnant… She never told me."

"I'm sorry."

"Why wouldn't she tell me? She was my wife. I hope the money wasn't to terminate it. Anyway, I asked for a paternity test."

Malin heard him hang up. He must have been shitting it by now.

She called the forensic artist and asked to meet her at number fifteen Juniper Hill Road at ten thirty. If the photographs she had on her iPad failed to throw any light on the man the doctor saw, it seemed the only option.

She also left a message for Kate Harroway at the bank. Kate was in meetings until four, at least that's what her voicemail announced. As for Dowie, he was on a hunting trip with a few of his friends. Wouldn't be back until next Thursday.

Malin found the doctor outside an adobe house, made all the more orange by the sunshine. He was checking his watch as she pulled into the driveway. It was gone ten thirty. No sign of the forensic artist.

He held out a hand. "May I ask how long this is going to take?"

"Ten… twenty minutes." *More if you continue to use that smart-ass tone.*

"And you are? I don't believe we've met."

"Detective Santiago."

"Doctor Gordon." His tone turned grand. Probably to match the Ph.D. he wanted to tell her he had.

"I hope I'm not late," she said, offering her badge.

"Oh, no, not at all. Listen, I really don't have much time."

No one ever does. "I have some photos I'd like you to see. It'll only take a moment."

He walked her under a mission bell that hung over the arch, leading to a cloistered courtyard. A bee hovered lazily over a mosaic-tiled fountain, almost brushing past her cheek as they entered the kitchen.

Neat and confident, the doctor had a nipped in waist, white shirt and black pants. Quite fit, she thought, staring at thick graying hair clipped close to the scalp and spectacles. She'd seen so many men wearing them. Must have been all the rage.

"The neighbors," he began with a nervous laugh. "I can't remember the last time the police dropped by. A whiff of scandal and… well, it's toast."

"We don't usually just *drop by*, sir." Malin knew exactly what he was trying to say but she wasn't going to hurry it up on account of his embarrassment. "You're a witness in an ongoing investigation. What could be more exciting than that?"

"Yes, yes, of course." He gave her a look as if he was trying to determine if she was messing with him or being straight-face serious.

She gave the sitting room a once-over. Books scattered on the couch, pillows dented and strewn about the floor. No wife. Couldn't be. "Been here long?"

"Seven years."

"Nice house." At least it would have been if he cleaned it.

He gestured to the couch and sat next to her. Kept shaking his head at the mugshots on the iPad and muttering that the man he'd seen trying to break into his car looked nothing like these. Not as run down or as whiskered.

"The beard," he said, patting his own chin, "was cut close to the face with a few streaks of gray. He didn't have that homeless look about him. Seemed more like he *had* to be there rather than wanted to be."

"You said in your earlier report that he had a gun?"

"Yes, tucked in his pants. Looked almost apologetic when he saw me and then took off up the hill. I really can't tell you anymore. Can't even remember what he was wearing." Dr. Gordon took off his glasses and rubbed his eyes. "Jeans... dark colored shirt, something like that. No hat."

"Was he alone?"

"Oh, yeah."

"Anything unusual about him?"

"Cleared the gap between my house and the turn off to Sandia Heights Drive in less than ten seconds. I've done it many times. But not that fast."

"So no limp, no strange walk, nothing that would easily identify him."

"Yes, there was something. The right side of his face drooped a little. Could have been Bell's palsy."

Something a doctor would notice and may have accounted for that *apologetic* look. "That's very helpful. Thank you."

Malin dispensed with questions about the doctor's career, family and friends. She wanted to leave that to the forensic artist, whose car was just pulling in. The sound of the doorbell bought a strange mix of anticipation and relief.

Malin said her goodbyes and inched out of the front door. She shielded her face from the sunlight, which shimmered through an arc of water from the sprinklers.

Driving downhill toward the gas station, she tried hard to ignore a headache. Interviews always set her on edge. You never knew if a witness lived alone or the house was full of family members, either cloistered away in their own rooms or brandishing a knife in a dark corner. She banished the vision.

Parking under the canopy of the Chevron gas station, she ran a background check on Joshua R. Childers. Apart from the restraining order and two violations, he'd been charged with a misdemeanor for possession of marijuana.

She felt oddly jumpy as she made her way to the store, patted the gun in her belt when she heard footsteps behind her.

"Whoa, detective. Didn't mean to startle you."

"Josh Childers?" Malin asked, recognizing the spiky blond hair.

"That's me. Is there a problem?" Then he inclined his head. "Wait, is this about Rachael Trandahl?"

"Yes, sir, it is."

"It's all over the news. I can't believe she's gone."

"I'm just talking to people who knew her."

He led the way to a small stock room at the back of the store and offered her a seat.

"I knew her a little. She came to fill up here once a week. Real friendly."

There was a hazy tone in his voice, the suggestion of yearning. Malin recognized it all too well. She also noticed dark circles under his eyes, whether from lack of sleep or the jaundiced shadows of drug abuse, she couldn't decide. Might have been a looker in his teens, only he'd been robbed of it all.

"Is there anything else you can tell me about her?"

"No. I mean, not personal things. She was one of my regulars. Never paid at the pump. Always came inside. She was being…" He paused and then gave her a look. "Threatened."

"Who was threatening her?"

"I don't know. But she told me she'd been getting weird calls. Death threats. She got a text once when she was in the store, something about a coincidence and how everything's connected. She asked me if I knew what it meant. I had no idea. But that's how we got talking."

Rachael must have felt comfortable with Josh to tell him her problems. Malin could see why. He was chatty. Easy-going. Probably a good salesman.

"This your video equipment?" she asked, looking at a surveillance DVR and a live camera display monitor.

"Yep," Josh said, taking a seat beside her. "Actual footage is recorded of the fill-up area outside. We can make sure employees are doing their job and no one's robbing the place. There's a spot monitor over the door. Plug and play. More of a deterrent when customers can see themselves live. There's a camera mounted on the ceiling behind the cash register and one in the corridor to the bathrooms. Plenty more outside since the pumps are a hotspot for crime."

"Can you see license plates outside?"

"Oh, yeah. We don't often see someone filling up and driving off without paying, but when we do we've got it all on tape."

"When did you last see Rachael?"

"Sometime around four on Wednesday afternoon. She'd been crying."

"And you could tell that how?"

"Her eyes were red and wet." He gave Malin a *duh* look, but the truth was he had to have been pretty close.

"Can you tell me what happened next?"

"She paid for the gas, bought a couple of bottles of water, I think. Told me she wasn't feeling good."

"Sick or what?"

"Depressed is what I understood. I told her she looked nice. Well, she did look nice. All dressed up. Anyway, I asked her if she'd had any more phone threats. She said no. Didn't wanna to talk. It wasn't like her. She always talked. After she'd finished paying, I followed her to the back of the store. Wanted to ask if she was OK but she started talking to someone on the phone. I don't really remember much of what she said."

"But you taped it."

"Right. I made a copy of the tape and gave it a Mr. Hackett. One of yours?"

"Commander Hackett. Yes."

"She was talking about her husband being suspicious," Josh said, scratching his head. "That she didn't sign up for it. Not sure what she meant by *it*. Then something about not drinking."

"Do you get the feeling this person was a man or a woman?"

"Thought I heard a man's voice but couldn't be sure."

Malin looked over at the TV monitor. "No CCTV on the south side?"

"Afraid not."

Pity, Malin thought, they would have seen what direction Rachael took after she left the store. "Do you remember what car she was driving?"

"Red Toyota Highlander. Matched her dress."

"Did you like her?" Malin asked.

Josh looked at the ground, ran his tongue along his bottom lip and then looked back up. "What do you mean *like her*?"

"You know. Find her attractive?"

"Who wouldn't? She had a nice way about her. Sometimes you can't define that in a woman. Sometimes it just *is*."

"So you didn't ask her out?"

"No." He laughed at that. "Do you always wear your hair like that?"

"Like what?"

"In a bun?"

"Yep." Malin shrugged.

"Don't like me asking personal questions?"

"It's usually my prerogative to ask the questions."

"I suppose. But it's more fun this way. Besides, you know all about me."

"Yes." Malin had no idea about him. Background checks never delved into psychology.

"You think I was the one sending death threats?" he asked.

"Didn't cross my mind."

"No, I don't suppose it did."

"You do recreational drugs?"

Josh visibly reddened and shook his head.

"It's not why I'm here," Malin said, eyes glazing over shelves of 7-Up and cigarettes. She had a fleeting feeling he wasn't telling the truth. "I just wanted to know how well you knew—"

"Let me be honest. When you asked me about Rachael I wanted to tell you she's the type of woman I'd love to know better and yes, that means intimately. And now… now some bastard's gone and blown her head off. So I've got no chance."

Malin gave him a distracted smile. "She was married."

"Yeah, well… there you go."

"Did she ever buy alcohol from here?"

"No, never bought any grog. Only bottles of water and sometimes juice for the kid."

"But she didn't buy any juice that day?"

"No, I don't think so."

So he had no reason to card Rachael at any time. Wouldn't have known her address. And Hannah may not have been in the car.

"Are you saying Rachael had a drinking problem?" he asked. "That she shouldn't have been driving?"

"I was just curious, that's all."

Drinking always had something to do with something, Malin thought. But in this case, it had nothing to do with anything.

She stuck out her hand. "Thanks for taking the time. I appreciate it."

She flinched, with that crawly sensation in the pit of her stomach from the encounter. Not someone she'd ever want to be alone with again.

Her mind was a riot of information. *Rachael and Ella... two women shot at blank range. Similar style shootings and within two days of each other. Then a child—a viable witness—goes missing. Where did Trandahl fit in this picture?*

As she drove out of the gas station, she thought about Childers, how he might have looked ten years ago. Cute surfer looks maybe, but definitely not Rachael's type.

Yet he had been crushing on her.

THIRTY-TWO

Walking, walking, walking. What time was it?
Sunup, he said. That's what.
Where were they going anyway?
He kept showing her his hand and telling her not to bite him again. She'd drawn blood and now he was whining about a tetanus shot.
"You're a ladeeee. And ladeeees don't bite!"
Well, this one does, she thought, running her tongue over the back of her teeth, which were crammed with blueberries from the muffins.
There was silence for a while as they chomped on bread. It felt good to eat.
She looked down at her shoes as they walked. Her matchstick legs stuck out below the turn-ups of her jeans. Dad always said there was too much light between them, and that they reminded him of Gru in Despicable Me.
"What's on your mind?" he asked, catching the downward tilt of her head.
"Nothing."

She could tell he wanted to know what nothing was and felt the grip on her arm tightening. There would be bruises if he didn't stop it. Then he'd be sorry.

His voice changed like he was trying to be polite. Said she was a Spartan which she guessed meant tough, like the soldiers in ancient Greece.

He said his name was Lee. She wondered how you spelled it because there was a L-E-I-G-H at school. Only that was a girl.

He kept saying her mom was waiting at the camp site and he kept pulling her along the trail, sometimes telling her which way and sometimes quiet like he didn't care.

He'd help her over boulders and creeks, and there were times when he kept sighing. Especially when she asked about her mom.

"You ask too many damn questions." He stopped to catch his breath. "Stop talking and just walk, OK?"

"I saw the blood. I heard—"

"You've got a wild imagination, girl. She fell and hit her head. End of."

She felt the sob in her throat, tried to keep it down. "You were yelling at her. Don't tell me you weren't."

"I was yelling at the dogs... coyote, whatever the heck it was. Why do we have to talk about her?" he said, sighing again.

She wondered if she'd got it all wrong. If what she saw was just a dream. But she felt all sorry and sick and wanted to run back the way they'd come. There'd be an opportunity soon enough.

"She's up there." He pointed again to the crags.

Something didn't seem right about the up here, down there *thing. If Mom was lying in a rug, how could she be up there and walking like nothing was wrong?*

"Do you have a phone?" she asked.

"What's a phone got to do with anything?"

"I want to call my dad. Mom's hurt. He should know."

"What are you after? A full-blown doctor's report? Heck should I know?"

"We shouldn't have left her on her own."

"And you care why exactly? She wasn't nice to you. How come she always called you little girl? *It's not like you don't have a name?"*

It was a good question, only she didn't know how to answer it. Her mom had a way of talking that even she found unnerving. Made her feel like a beggar child.

"Maybe they switched babies on her at the hospital," he said. "My, I'd be pissed if they did that to me."

"What do you mean switched babies?"

He shrugged. "Maybe you're not her kid. Maybe you're someone else's because you don't look much like her."

"I look like my dad."

"Ah, well that explains it. I happen to like your name," he said. "Means handmaid of the gods.*"*

She didn't like the handmaid part, but the gods bit sounded good. If she was anything of the gods wouldn't she have magic powers? Because they'd come in real handy about now.

"All people have names. It's respectful to use them," he said.

He was right. She'd never heard other mother's calling their daughters little girl.

"I shouldn't say this," he said, "but your mom had problems."

"What problems?"

He stopped for a moment and wiped the hair off his forehead. Tried to smile, but one side of his mouth came out like a lopsided sneer. It was the first time she'd noticed it.

"How old are you?"

"Ten."

"Not old enough, then."

"Old enough for what?"

"To keep your mouth shut. Because it's a secret and if you can keep one, I'll trust you."

She nodded rapidly.

"Do you know what loyalty means?"

She nodded again. That was an easy one. Her dad taught her loyalty. Once friends, always friends.

"Well, it's hard to do. Especially when you like a few girls at once. But your mom, she wanted to be best friends. My only friend. But there was another girl… someone I liked better. Make sense?"

It kinda did.

"So you see, I had to do something. I had to make it stop." *He kept looking around and frowning.* *"I told her… I said I couldn't see her anymore."*

"Why?"

"Because I couldn't. Your mom didn't like me liking someone else. That's all you need to know."

He told her to be quiet. Angled his head, eyes flicking this way and that.

"What?" she asked.

"Dogs… coyotes. They can smell us up here. If we can get to higher ground, we'll be OK."

She heard a few barks and howls and decided higher ground sounded good.

"There's a pack of them. Could take us down in seconds."

He was scared. She knew it. If he was her age he'd be hiding behind his hands. Coyotes… she didn't know much about them except that they were related to wolves and just as mean. She had a dog once, a Chow. He barked all the time and Mom left the back door open and out he shot. Never came back after that.

But she knew things about dogs. And other things.

It was probably a good time to share them.

"Even when dogs are afraid they still bark," she said. "It's a warning to other dogs. A pack thing. There's probably more up there."

Lee gave her a funny look and pushed her on. Then he tilted his head at the sky and said he saw a rescue flare.

She wasn't sure what that looked like so he explained.

"That's not a rescue flare," she said. "It's a shooting star. Something wrong with your eyes? There is something wrong. I can tell. Especially when you smoke all that stuff in your pipe."

He looked down at her briefly and then back up again. He totally wasn't smiling. All he could manage was a sneer.

Then the whole world went quiet.

It was just her and him.

And no one else.

THIRTY-THREE

Temeke look up at the crags. At 10,678 feet in elevation, the sheer height of the mountain was breathtaking. *Bien Mur*, or *Big Mountain* as the Sandia Pueblo Indians called it was a steep and rugged climb. By day, gunmetal crags poked through a thin layer of conifers and by night, the reddish-pink hue of a watermelon. It was a hike he often did alone.

It was eleven-thirty when Temeke got two calls. He parked himself on a tree stump bordering the trail and told Midgely to take a breather.

One call was from Commander Hackett asking Temeke to go home and get some rest, which he ignored. The second was from the labs confirming the blood on Rachael's legs had no existing forensic profile. CODIS had not been able to spit back a name.

He tipped his head back to drain another bottle of water and studied Midgely out of the corner of his eye. She was swiping through her phone again, and with as many hours as she'd been gawping at the news, it was no surprise she carried two portable chargers.

"Looks like finding Rachael's body has been a big boost to the case," Midgely said, angling her phone away from the sunlight. "The *Journal*'s running a retrospective on Dai Trandahl. Someone must have slipped up and released protected information."

"I hope it was worth the risk."

"They're saying this case is a number one priority, sir. Well, it would be with a missing kid. National television networks are sending photographers here. They want Trandahl to do a live segment."

"Agent Stu Anderson conducted a polygraph test with Trandahl yesterday and then subjected him to a post-test interrogation. All recorded via live video," Temeke said. "He hasn't confessed. Not as far as I know."

"Do you think he did it?" Midgely asked.

"With no murder weapon or fingerprints to tie him to the scene, it's not a slam dunk for the DA. At this point, it's down to circumstantial evidence. But you know what they say. If the nut won't crack..."

"Yeah, yeah, get a hammer. Did he admit to doing pornography?"

"Trandahl hasn't admitted to anything. When it goes to trial, you can guarantee his attorney will probably say porn is irrelevant to the case and violates his constitutional rights. Bad character and all that."

"But it's a motive."

"Not necessarily for murder."

"I won't be able to sleep tonight, sir. Can't stop seeing Rachael's face. All bloody and battered... and the kid, only ten years old."

"I still see flyers on my desk from years ago, love. Old cases, cold cases. It never goes away. You always feel that wave of nausea when you can't get justice for them. Nobody ever said police work was easy." Temeke patted Midgely on the shoulder. "Why don't you go on ahead? I'll catch up in a few."

She nodded and gave a stiff smile. He could see she was reluctant, and then was off in that determined stride of hers.

He needed to be alone. Wanted to jog uphill to dispel the whispers in his mind. Some of them guilt, some of them defeat. They came and went throughout the years, reminding him of his frailty.

He could hear the tumble of rocks each time he climbed and the mournful exhalation of wind through the pine trees. There was something up there and although he had deviated from procedure and left Midgely to go on ahead, he was sure his intuition was sound.

It was a beautiful day. No wind. The higher he climbed, juniper faded to piñon and piñon to ponderosa. Energized by the cooler air, he realized there was much that was beautiful about Albuquerque. Adobe browns that turned Titian red at sunset, the smell of sage, the big blue skies. But a day like this turned all that to despair and suddenly it was all very clear.

He was tired of the filth, the darkness of an alley where madness oozed out of the drains. No matter how many meth houses law enforcement exposed, there'd always be others springing out of the cracks. Strong chemical smells and gun caches. Explosives even.

Young teenagers disappeared and were found months later abandoned in a dried up arroyo. They were placed in cold storage and toe tagged with a generic name until the real one could be found. If anyone was going to stand for the missing kids it was him.

He stopped and took in the sights. How far was the debris field to the TWA crash site?

Not far, he thought, although he had never taken this route. Images of the crash whirred in his head and then dissolved as he paused to listen. He found it hard to focus, something at the border of his subconscious nudging its way to the surface.

On the way up, it occurred to Temeke that Malin was a long way off. Approximately thirteen miles away and not by his side as she had once been. Rookies didn't need hand-holding, not once they'd settled in and got the swing of things.

He'd taught her to think outside the box. When looking for felons, it was important to take all the probabilities and statistics that make up a complex human being in order to assemble a criminal profile. No one scored a bullseye every time, but Malin was sodding close.

He dialed her number. "How's it going?"

"Four things," she said, getting straight to the point. "Trandahl invented a story about a long lunch hour he had yesterday afternoon, which Porsche couldn't verify. He finally admitted to visiting his bank manager at Mountain Financial because Rachael withdrew a large sum of money. Apparently the manager couldn't tell him why she'd made the withdrawal. Well, he wouldn't, would he? A thousand bucks is a lot of money."

"Not if she was planning on leaving him."

"Dr. V said there was no indication of sexual assault with either of the victims," she said. "But Rachael was pregnant."

"How far along?"

"Nine weeks."

"Blimey. That must have been tough to stomach."

"Yeah. Well, I was thinking, you remember the cold case Hackett wanted us to look at? Andrea Irwin and Maria Velasquez? Both attacks took place in the foothills. One in June and one in August of 2004. Andrea met her assailant in the mall parking lot and Maria met hers outside Walmart. Similar scenario. Security footage reveals a white sedan. Both assaults didn't occur at the time of the initial meeting, but sometime later on in the vicinity of Tramway. Rape kits were collected and held in custody but they weren't tested. Something about inadequate funding and the fact that Velasquez and Irwin were earning money from meeting men online. So, no point trying to find DNA in the CODIS database. But when I submitted details from both cases into ViCAP, I found two more instances with a similar MO. Both in Colorado in 2006."

"Same age? Same victim pool?"

"Married women, thirty-five to forty with profiles on various dating websites," she said. "The man was described as tall with a close-cut beard and drove a white sedan. Both victims' husbands were questioned at the time and alibis were sound. Neither had criminal records. *And* they had no idea their wives were seeking men online for sex."

"You're right about the similarities. Rachael Trandahl, Ella Gibson, Jewel Hansen; an innocent date turned violent. So nothing since?"

"Two more in Camelback Mountain, Arizona. One in 2008 and the other in 2010. I'll keep checking, sir." Malin went quiet for a moment. "I met the gynecologist on Juniper Hill Road. He reckoned the man he saw had Bell's palsy. He also mentioned the guy was fit."

"And Josh Childers?"

"Something weird about him if you ask me. I think he probably hit on to Rachael a few times. Maybe spooked her out a bit."

"Dozy bastard."

"That's all I have for now, sir."

"Thank you," he said. "For everything."

"You're welcome."

He smiled after she hung up, eyes riveted to a light covering of pine needles underfoot.

He wondered how many yards Midge had on him on the lower path, whether she was sitting on a boulder up ahead and peeling the wrapper off another protein bar.

He was too wound up to eat and his eyes ranged back and forth over the limestone ledges where the purple heads of alumroot nodded in the breeze. Lack of sleep and stress made him feel light-headed. Either that or it was the altitude. His dad always said walking's shit for the knees. He was right.

What if this guy wasn't up here at all? What if they had all been following a false trail?

He noticed a slight crunching underfoot and put it down to dried twigs and the spread of last year's leaves. He needed to be quieter. Behind him, the view plunged precipitously—a twenty-four hundred foot drop to Tramway—and ahead, a narrow trail almost overgrown with trees. The steep incline was heavy going, compounded with the fact that he'd had a bad feeling all morning. Call it spider sense, but there was something odd about the sights and smells. He had to keep reminding himself he wasn't out for a hike, but searching for a missing child. *Assume nothing.*

He moved onward at a clip, trying to burn off the anxiety but not quite succeeding. The August air couldn't rid him of the tension he felt and once he reached a clearing, where the ground leveled off for a short time, he saw footprints etched into the mud. A small pair, skidding slightly to one side as if propelled forward against their will. Then a larger pair behind. He didn't want to draw attention to himself and pausing under a tree, he listened.

There in the silence, he heard a twig snap. Then a cough.

THIRTY-FOUR

Temeke would remember every detail of that moment. The sun on the back of his neck, a layer of sand that furred the rocks and the gleam of quartz everywhere. But as he turned at the sound, he could tell even from a distance that the man had already seen him, quaking at the gun he held.

Temeke pegged him at mid-thirties and tanned as a Tanoan golfer. He was topless, having abandoned his shirt somewhere along the trail, and his eyes were wide as if he'd just taken a hit.

Crack? Possibly.

There was something otherworldly about him; scruffy hair and a three-day stubble, but he was certainly no slacker. By his stance, he was ready to bolt at the slightest hint of an altercation. He appeared to be alone.

"Stop! Police!" Temeke shouted.

The man lurched in response and bolted downhill. Temeke had already made the decision not to shoot but to track instead. If he knew where Hannah was, Temeke wanted his guy fit and talking.

Using his radio, Temeke alerted his team to a possible

suspect and confirmed his position. Whether the suspect was armed or not remained to be seen but he matched the description the witness had given from a sighting on Juniper Hill Road.

Temeke couldn't match the man's stride, not with his rifle out in front. Although the trail was littered with rocks and boulders, the suspect wound through the undergrowth like an athlete. He seemed to be sprinting for a thick row of trees as if hoping for cover.

Temeke knew he'd have to think of something to draw him out. All he could hear was feet pounding the dirt and breath coming in ragged gasps.

His feet. His breath.

The thought of Hannah lying in a shallow grave somewhere threatened to drain his energy and he jogged hard, didn't want to lose him in case he doubled back and came at him from a higher vantage point.

Where was the suspect's shirt? If it had been abandoned north of here it might have explained why the K-9 unit had been drawn to that area. Temeke knew there were law enforcement agencies stationed to the south, leaving this central stretch of wilderness, for the most part, unmanned. Apart from the intermittent drone of a distant helicopter, which appeared to be circling back from Placitas, the woodland around him was silent.

He could feel the sweat on his forehead, feet slowed by the uneven terrain, and the rifle became a dead weight on his shoulder. Sucking warm air into his lungs, Temeke approached a large boulder. Keeping within two feet of it, he moved slowly around, hoping to softball his approach.

There was no sign him.

Probably weaving through the trees or crouched behind a thick piñon to catch his breath. Either way, Temeke felt as if he was being played.

Then thudding footsteps, wide strides that confirmed what Temeke dreaded the most. The man was now heading uphill.

Temeke followed slowly, brushing against low branches almost creeping up the slope when every part of him was screaming to go faster. He could hear panting, hoarse and loud and snapping twigs. Closer this time.

Temeke stooped behind a pine tree and listened, letting his eyes adjust to the shade. He was suddenly aware of the weight of his backpack but tossing it wasn't an option.

He took small sips of air and tried to reorient himself.

To an outsider, the natural features of the mountains would have merged into one. Where everywhere looks the same. Brown and dead in the shade, and a muted green in the sunlight where recent rainfall had brought life to the land.

Snapping twigs… the swish of branches… the thud of a nearby rock.

Was he leaving markers or trying to confuse Temeke? It was possible he was hurling rocks in every direction just to pull him off the scent. If Temeke could see where they fell he might have been able to trace them back to the source. But the sounds were sporadic and echoed against the crags, and he couldn't distinguish where they came from.

Then silence. Just the clatter of his heart and he couldn't see anything either.

The suspect must have stopped too.

Temeke waited almost twenty seconds. There it was again—a dull thud.

This time the delay to echo was about a tenth of a second. It was possible the suspect was about fifty feet from the cliff face and instead of heading west, he had turned back and was now running directly toward it.

That told Temeke two things. One: there was something up there the suspect considered worth returning to before making his escape and two: he was heading directly toward the TWA crash site.

Temeke heard the occasional cough, signs that the man was tiring. He squinted through the trees, shoulders aching and conscious of a pinched nerve in the back of his neck. Inclining his ear toward the crags, he was mindful of barking dogs in the distance and the quiet progress of law enforcement as officers approached from both north and south.

Temeke followed another sound. A breath so slight, it could have been the breeze through the pine trees. Heel to toe, he moved silently, tracking east for thirty seconds and then picking up a trail heading sharp south.

Then Temeke saw him about fifteen feet to his right. A large bumbling figure, weaving through the trees, handgun nestled in his waistband. He was muttering to himself, then he paused just as Temeke was doing.

Temeke took in the surrounding area, studying the slopes, hoping to find an opportunity to get to higher ground. But the dry foliage underfoot would break his cover and give the suspect a clear shot.

Bringing the rifle to his cheek, he pushed his support hand forward on the forestock and peered through the scope. The suspect was shaking slightly, hand snaking around his back to tap the gun in his belt. Then in one fluid movement, he drew the gun, eyes sweeping the area in a circular motion. He kept turning, one hand occasionally raised to wipe the sweat off his face.

He couldn't see shit.

Temeke took a breath and held it. His scalp began to tingle beneath his cap and he realized this sudden gesture was to lure Temeke out of his hiding place. To take a shot. He could almost read the suspect's mind. He had to be telling himself that the sound of barking was far enough away to give him the lead he needed.

He was wrong.

The units were already tracking, moving silently through the trees and inching through the underbrush at a gradual pace.

Temeke looked up at the tramway cables and reckoned there was still about a quarter of mile to go before seeing any debris from the plane.

Suddenly a sharp crack. Then another.

Temeke fell to the ground, belly crawling in the dirt. He rolled off the track with three rapid turns, while trying to take inventory of damage and hits.

Nothing.

Then two more gunshots lit up the canyon.

Killing cops was obviously a line this man shouldn't have been crossing and what he was aiming at was anyone's guess. Bullets pinged off trees about ten yards from where Temeke was lying. It was close. But not close enough.

He would have returned fire, but the thought of Hannah put a stop to any reasonable procedure.

Then the man lowered the gun and replaced it in his waistband. He was walking faster now, away from Temeke with no idea he was being followed.

Temeke stood, lowered his rifle and matched each footfall. He wondered briefly if the man was capable of rational thinking, but he couldn't assume he wasn't. So he settled behind him at a distance, choosing the same meandering route as if the suspect might have lost his bearings.

Temeke could hear other sounds now over the muffled hush of the forest. He figured two more minutes at most before a K-9 would alert on the spot and then lunge out of the trees with his handler in tow.

But the suspect seemed to be walking without thinking, mesmerized perhaps by the glint of the sun against the crags, the slapping of sapling branches against his thighs. Then something jolted him out of his trance, a skittering sound like claws on bark. His chin shot upward.

A squirrel raced up a tree toward the fulcrum of two

branches, dislodging a large fir cone along the way. It bounced from branch to branch, coming to land three feet from the suspect's foot.

Temeke could hear the loud exhalation of breath, where the suspect had fallen prey to a false sense of confidence as he became more attuned to the sounds of the trees.

It was likely he'd trudge onward on autopilot, thinking the topography was the same. Blue sky above and trees all around and there was nothing up here except squirrels.

Several times the man lost his footing, stumbling over rocks and roots and then he veered sharply into a thicket of juniper and large rounded boulders. But he was running from something.

Temeke raised the rifle, eyes trying to lock in on a target. He checked the backstop and beyond.

Nothing.

It was seven long seconds before he heard something. The click of a pebble as it vaulted downhill.

Then up ahead something moved. Two shapes magnified in the scope with their backs toward him. If he wasn't mistaken one was small, childlike.

Then they were gone.

Temeke crept up the steep path to where he had seen them. The daylight was muted, barely a bar of sun through the canopy of trees. The place felt hollow and uninviting, and he was aware of something besides the whistle of wind along the cables of the Peak Tram.

He knew that ancient feeling. An early warning. A presence where you least expected one.

He surveyed the dirt, looking for tracks or any signs of broken branches and crushed grass.

Then the sudden crunch of detritus.

He paused. It paused.

Heard a heavy tread at nine o'clock. Raising his gun, he began to turn and would have centered the crosshairs and squeezed the trigger.

But today, a hard knot of fear caused him to freeze before he heard the loud crack of gunfire.

THIRTY-FIVE

She heard the sounds before Lee did. Radios and stuff. Like there was a whole pile of people down there having a party. But she kept slipping in and out of a haze and wondered if she was dreaming.

"Is there any water?" she asked.

Lee gave her a bottle. "Keep drinking and don't get dehydrated."

"What's that gun for? You gonna kill someone?"

"I'm not gonna kill anyone. But if you must know there's bad guys out here pretending to be cops and dogs too. The dogs... they do awful things. Killed my baby brother."

"How?" She wasn't sure she really wanted to know but the question just popped out of her mouth. "How did they kill him?"

"Four of them. Held him down and..." Lee shook his head, eyes red and wet. "When my dad came home it was too late. Locked me in the basement for letting it happen."

"But it wasn't your fault."

"No. But he tied a belt around my neck and attached one end of it to a pipe. I bit my way out. Took three days, sixteen hours and forty-five minutes."

She couldn't quite imagine being in a basement and chewing your way out of a belt. Didn't really know what to say about it. *"I hate dogs too. Got bitten when I was four."*

"Yeah. They'll do that to you."

What she really wanted to know was what had happened to her mom.

"How do you know my mom?"

"We've been friends for a while. Few years."

"Why did you shoot her?" She knew it wasn't balloons they were popping in the bedroom.

He didn't say anything. Just gripped her arm even tighter and told her to hurry up because he wanted to get to Camp 260 before it got dark.

"Shouldn't we call Dad? Or the police?

"Police won't help," he said, rifle slung across his chest like he was some superhero. *"They don't come up as far as this. Only hunters and homeless."*

Her foot struck against a rock, where it hurtled over a steep ledge. Bump, bump, bump, down the hill it went. She tried it again. There were plenty of rocks to kick. She'd been doing it all the way up.

Lee didn't tell her to stop. Didn't seem to hear it. Just went on muttering stuff, free hand slipping around his back and slotting the handgun in and out of his belt like he'd got an idea one minute and then changed it the next.

Then he'd clamp that same hand around the big rifle to stop it bouncing around on his chest. Serve him right for having so many guns.

She thought of running away. But she'd already done that twice and he'd yanked her back by the scruff of the neck and told her she was implicated, whatever that *meant. Because her fingerprints were on the gun like she'd gone and shot her mom.*

"If you keep doing that, I'll shoot you in the knee," he said. "Know how painful that is?"

"No." His voice made her shiver.

"Well, let's just say it's about as painful as chopping off a finger."

He had a knife and he'd threatened her with that too. She didn't much care for pain, wouldn't like the sound of knife grinding against bone.

The closest she'd come to it was when she was cutting a piece of cooked chicken on the chopping board. Never felt it until the knife went through the upper joint of her index finger. A sharp sting and then the blood. She knew chicken didn't bleed like that.

Last time he'd used that knife was in that empty house after breakfast. Used it to pry the lid off a can he kept in his backpack. There were a few rocks in it, some yellow, some white and a sooty glass tube. He held a lighter underneath and began smoking it. Different kind of vaping, he'd said. But it scared her.

Then he reached into his pocket. Pulled out a lighter and a cigarette. Or the remains of one. Sucked in a cloud of smoke and huffed it back out again.

He saw her looking and told her smoking was for medical reasons. Opened up his mind. Said he could smell things a mile away and see things in the dark.

"I'm more dog than dog." Then his lips twisted back in a snarl and he started laughing.

"Where is this stupid camp anyway?" she asked.

"Not far. You'll like it when you see it. Full of history and ghosts."

"I don't like ghosts."

"Well, you'll like these ones. Captain Ivan and co-pilot James. Good people. So you can stop crying like a baby."

"I'm not crying," she said, knowing the ghosts weren't the type to spook her and float three feet off the ground. She didn't believe in them anyway.

"I heard you crying at breakfast. Allergic to eggs or what?" He tried to push the hair out of his eyes, only it kept flopping back down again.

"No. I like eggs."

"Well, what then?"

She was embarrassed to say but she couldn't hold it in any longer. "I need to pee."

"Plenty of trees, girl. Just take your pick."

She took her pick, chose a bushy evergreen to hide behind. Her eyes were watering again, vision fading in and out. Had he put something in the water? She pulled down her jeans and sprinkled the grass a little.

"I can see your head," he said. "Gun can see it too."

It was hard to go when all he did was yack on about how brains looked when they weren't in a skull. She hauled up her jeans and watched him through the branches.

Then quick as a wink, he was right there, hand on her wrist, heaving and tugging. He was twitchy now like he'd heard a sound or something. Finger against his lips and then hand patting the air.

She crouched.

He took both her hands, wrapped her fingers around the gun. Told her to point it at the bad guy in the black zipper pants. The one out there on the path with his back to her. Because the dogs were coming and there was nothing he could do to stop them.

"If you don't shoot first, he'll shoot you," he whispered. "When he turns, you pull that trigger. Keep your finger on it until he's down, you got that?"

She nodded. She'd got it.

THIRTY-SIX

Malin looked down at her notes. She had interviews with Beverly Herrera in the substation, Naomi Michaels via phone and Emma Burnett in the gym.

As for Kate Harroway, Malin was hoping to meet her at work. Kill two birds with one stone, so to speak.

Malin did a brief background check on each before Beverly Herrera arrived. Malin saw a tall woman, shoulder length dark hair and a hard-to-read face. If she hadn't been born and bred in New Mexico, Malin would have assumed she was foreign.

She didn't gesture much, nor could Malin see her teeth when she was talking. It reminded her of Temeke, where a continuous stream of sounds came through a barely open mouth.

"How long have you known Rachael?" Malin asked.

"About ten years. We worked in the finance department at Sandia Insurance before she moved to the bank."

"Would you say you were close?"

"Yeah. Our kids are about the same age. We'd go out after work and I'd babysit for her sometimes."

"Did she have depression?"

"She definitely had something. Took medication and it wiped her out sometimes. Couldn't even get out of bed. So I'd take Hannah whenever I could."

Malin made a mental note. Beverley had already climbed fifty rungs on the *compassion* ladder. "So what went wrong?"

"I started noticing it about two months ago. She was withdrawn. Didn't want to go out to lunch or meet after work at the wine bar. Then I saw the bruises. On her arm. I noticed because she'd always worn sheath dresses to work before, or sleeveless tops. She wore cardigans after that."

"Did she say how she got them?"

"It was about a month ago when she and Dai went out to dinner. She didn't ask me to babysit. I don't know who did. But when I asked her how it went, she told me he was seeing someone else. I mean, how stupid to take her out in public and then blast her with his infidelities. She said she screamed. Who wouldn't? Then he forced her into the car because she was threatening him in the street. I know you want to know exactly when this was but I don't remember. So I'll tell what I do know and that is I thought I could tell a person just by looking at them. Thought he was solid. Well, I was wrong."

"It's easy to say in hindsight."

"No, really. I liked him. Had no idea he had such a dark side. If you can do those kinds of things to a woman behind closed doors what does it make you? He must have enjoyed the torture. Because it was torture and yet she had to be very *thankful*, if you know what I mean."

"No, I don't know what you mean."

"She had to promise him she'd do anything he wanted otherwise it was over. She didn't elaborate. I assumed it meant the pleasure was all his. I do know that she wasn't allowed to complain about these other women. She had to accept it. I can't imagine how she put up with it. But that's when I saw this… rapid decline. I don't think her work suffered. She would have told me. But I noticed. You do when it's your friend."

"What else changed?"

"She'd have these red eyes and shrug it off. Say it was allergies. She said if things got bad between them he'd blame her and say she made him do it."

"Do what?"

"Hit her, I guess. Then he told her he didn't want to see her anymore. That was…" Beverly calculated on her fingers. "Eight days ago. Didn't want her coming over to see him at work because it was embarrassing. It gets worse. We went to the park together with our kids for a picnic last weekend. Rachael wasn't nice to Hannah. It was the little things. Not listening to her, not responding to her needs. Then it was the big things. Disciplining her for not putting the paper plates in the trash or not tying her shoelaces properly. It went on and on. I had to tell Rachael to stop."

Malin was beginning to get the picture. For the sake of simplicity, Rachael was being bullied by her husband and in turn neglected Hannah. Malin had seen the pattern before. The unraveling of precious bonds and the wasting away of self-esteem. Because Rachael had been degraded and dumped in plain view. Cruelty wasn't necessarily the overriding motive. Control was.

"If Rachael disagreed with him, she was criticized. It was his word or zip," Beverly said. "We mustn't forget the bastard was as infallible as the Pope."

"Did she mention other women he was seeing?"

"There was one he kept comparing her to. So Rachael looked her up on the internet. Facebook, I think. She found out her address and followed her to the mall. I didn't like the sound of it. She bought a dress exactly like hers… this other woman that is. Wore it to work one day and went to visit him for lunch. Might have made him mad."

Malin's frown incited Beverly to explain.

"Well, he hadn't invited her for lunch. She just showed up."

"Did Rachael ever meet this other woman?"

"Hell, no! Rachael would have told me if they had."

"Did she happen to mention a name?"

Beverly shook her head. "That's the thing with her. She always used to tell me everything. But then… she didn't. So I did something. I confronted Dai. Screamed at him like he was a pervert. But it was the weirdest thing. He had no idea what I was talking about. Kept shaking his head. Asking me if I was sure that's what Rachael had said. So I asked him about the bruises. Surely, he'd seen those? He said he hadn't. Because they don't sleep together any more. Don't even use the same bathroom."

After a few more questions, Malin thanked Beverly. She was left with two questions. Did Dai have two faces? One for the public and another for his wife?

Or did Rachael?

The phone interview with Naomi Michaels was brief. Naomi had worked at Porsche for six years. With no upward progression at the time, she resigned and found an assistant manager position with American Toyota. Just a hop across the street. She was very much married. Very much the faithful wife. With words like *bless you*, *inappropriate* and *unbiblical*, it was clear which side of the veil she was on.

Naomi couldn't offer much except that Dai Trandahl was polite at work. They had talked in the cafeteria sometimes. About their spouses and children.

No, she didn't recall Dai ever saying anything bad about Rachael or Hannah for that matter. He was the model of gratitude. Except for his mother-in-law who was, as Naomi remembered it and could barely say in a whisper, *the bitch from hell*.

She said how sorry she was about Rachael. That she'd been praying for Dai through it all.

Malin thanked her. Didn't see much use in asking any more questions.

THIRTY-SEVEN

Malin pulled into White's Gym half an hour early. A large building made entirely of glass with a row of adjustable benches in the front window.

She nodded at the girl on the front desk and opened her jacket to reveal the badge on her belt. "Detective Santiago to see Emma Burnett."

She hated lanyard IDs. It was like wearing a long necklace that invariably got caught on the corner of the desk every time she bent down.

"I'm a little early," Malin said.

"No, you're fine," the girl said, patting the air. "Take a seat and I'll find her."

Find her… It was a big place, Malin thought. There was a large running track on the ground floor which ran around the perimeter and above it, a gallery of aerobic and jazzercise rooms.

She didn't have to wait long.

Yoga pants and a red t-shirt with the gym logo curving across an ample chest. Emma was lean and extremely fit. One look at her red hair parted down the middle and a cheeky smile and Malin got the impression she was open and, hopefully, honest.

"Can I offer you some water?"

Malin nodded at the bottle Emma handed her.

"I read something about you and your partner," Emma said sitting down beside her. "A brutal homicide… well, several actually, last year. Nine little girls. Must have been awful."

"I'm flattered you researched us."

"I wanted to be familiar with you before you came here. Looks like you both work with kids. That means you've got compassion. Not that the police officers don't… well, you're a detective. Maybe that's the difference."

No difference, Malin wanted to say, but the girl was digging herself deeper, reddening and stuttering. There was something about her choice of words. A turn of phrase. The angle of her head. She seemed to be a solid witness.

"I admit I don't pay much attention to the news," Emma said, "but I did see the article in the *Journal* about Rachael Trandahl. I can't believe someone would do a thing like that."

"So far no witnesses have come forward with convincing information. That's because, we assume, that she was targeted rather being random."

"So he knew her?" Eyes locking with Marlin's as if she was assessing her. "The killer."

Why did everyone always assume killers were male? "Possibly. At least it's beginning to look that way."

"That's why you're here isn't it? To talk about Dai."

Dai. She called him Dai. "How well did you know Mr. Trandahl?"

Emma took a sip of water and then placed the bottle between her knees. "He comes here about three times a week. Uses the weight room. Sometimes the pool. Nice guy. Friendly, you know?"

"Does he keep himself to himself?"

"For the most part. But he's helpful when you need something. He's helped me move heavy boxes of protein powder to the storage closet behind the front desk. I've never asked. He always offers."

Malin chugged back the water and put the bottle on the table. Dai was observant or he'd been watching her from the exercise machines. Was he a stalker? Hard to tell.

"Mind if I ask you something personal?"

"Sure."

"Does he flirt?"

"He's not all over you so you have to be all over everywhere else trying to get away from him. That's not his thing. With me, he's been great with relationship advice. We talked a lot about commitment, about how to ask my partner to marry me. When I did, all of a sudden she couldn't deal with being gay any more. He was the only shoulder I could cry on."

Sounded like Emma knew Trandahl better than she was prepared to admit. "Is Dai always so accommodating?"

"There was this lady, late seventies, who used to lift weights upstairs in Senior's Group. She did something to her shoulder. Must have been agony. He waited with her until the ambulance came. He's kind like that."

Malin couldn't quite get a handle on how kind Dai Trandahl was and would have said 'if you say so' if she hadn't been pressing her lips tightly together.

"Everyone likes him here," Emma said.

Malin assumed Emma meant the staff. Judging by the size of the place, *everyone else* would mean several hundred. "Did he ever talk about his wife?"

"*All* the time!" Emma gave a loud sigh. "I don't know if it's important but he said Rachael forgot to pick Hannah up from school a couple of times last week. Just clean forgot. It made him mad."

"How mad?"

Emma had to think about that for a bit. "Mad enough to beat the crap out of her. Oh, I didn't mean it like that. He's a pussycat. Really."

Malin decided to add *blunt* to her mental list of Emma's characteristics. "It's not unusual for someone to appear easy going on the surface and be something completely different underneath."

"Dai's not… he's not like that. Look, he and I went out for lunch, a few times actually. He was shit-scared."

"Why?"

"He found a scrap of paper beside the computer. It looked like a password. He said Rachael rarely used the Facebook. Hell, she didn't even have an Instagram account. But here was this password… like she'd used it to sign in for something. At first he thought she was just buying things online. But when he started nosing around—and Dai knows a thing or two about computers—well, it didn't look too healthy."

Malin tilted her head and Emma recognized it as a prompt.

"He started looking through the search history and it looked like she was on Facebook a lot all of a sudden. But she wasn't surfing for men. She was looking for women. One in particular."

Malin suddenly realized they were thinking along parallel lines. "So she was gay?"

"That's what it looked like. Anyway, Dai wanted to show me. That's why we went out."

"Do you remember the name of the woman she was interest in?"

"Ella Gibson." Malin knew what Emma was going to say next. "Of course, he wanted me to contact her. Ask her out. So I did. She said she was flattered but already in a relationship. It was odd because her profile said *single*. Maybe she hadn't gotten around to updating it."

Single was usually the status of an escort, Malin thought, but decided not to elaborate. "And that was the last time you contacted her?"

"Yeah. But there is something else. I remember Dai saying Rachael kept buying new clothes. Having her hair done and going to the spa when their account was almost in the red. She wasn't going out at night because she was always at home when he went to bed. And Hannah would have said something if she wasn't. He thought she must have been meeting someone at lunch."

"As far as you know, did Dai ever mention following her?"

"No. He told me he wanted to but he said it would be a violation of her privacy."

"So in lieu of her rights, he just stayed at home and wagged his tail."

Emma shrugged. "He was scared of her. She could fly off the handle at the slightest thing. By the sounds of it, Hannah got the brunt of it. He dreaded leaving her alone with her mom."

"Did Rachael hit her?"

"Hannah told him she'd slapped her. Shut her in her closet for God knows how long." Emma sucked in her bottom lip and frowned. "I think he was haunted with not knowing. That it may have been going on for some time."

THIRTY-EIGHT

The phone droned in Malin's belt and she almost jumped. "Yep."

A crackle of static. "Malin? It's me."

"Midge? How's it going?"

More static.

"Midge, you're breaking up."

"Not so good. There was an active shooter in the hills. Never thought I'd have to say... Officer down."

Malin's rib cage began to swell with a deep breath and then she let it out slowly. "Who? Who was shot?"

"Temeke. They've taken him to UNM Hospital. I'll see you there."

Malin barely heard the squawk of the radio about spent shells at the scene and how they hadn't caught the guy. She ran code all the way to the UNM Hospital, pulse pounding as she reached for her phone and hit the callback button.

"Please God, don't let it be another end of watch," she said out loud, voice almost squealing through the tears.

She willed Midge to pick up, feeling a surge of impatience when all she heard was voicemail.

Malin wanted to ask her how it had happened. Where had Temeke been shot? How many times? Had he opened fire?

A steady stream of police officers were headed the same way. The rest were still out looking for Hannah Trandahl in the mountains. There had been no more sightings but there was still hope. Malin knew inexperienced climbers often vanished into thin air. Especially children.

Snapping the phone between her hand and the steering wheel, Malin careened through an intersection as cars peeled off either side to let her through. The images of Temeke she conjured in her mind were as bad as they come. A face covered in blood, forward and back spatter over grass and tree. In her head, a burst of gunfire like the ones at the shooting range.

When she arrived, she was told by a nurse that Temeke was still in surgery. He had been struck in the chest, shoulder and hip and, yes, he had been wearing body armor.

Malin's legs were shaky, head buzzing. Slumping on a seat in the waiting room, she leaned her head against the wall. If she could profile the shooter, he wasn't exactly experienced in firearms. Maybe he was drunk, drugged up, failed to aim straight. Either way, she was thankful Temeke's vest had shielded him from a fatal wound and, as for his shoulder, is was no more than a flesh wound.

"You OK?"

There was Midgely stooping over her, pale and hollow-eyed. Malin felt a stab of pity just looking at her.

"Yeah. You?"

Midgely sat down, touched Malin on the arm and lowered her chin. "He was lying on the ground when I found him. Radio was gone and so was his gun. I stayed with him until someone came. Twelve seconds. I counted. Then I ran downhill. Shouted my lungs off but I guess this shooter didn't know jack-shit about rules. I ran into a bunch of deputies who hadn't seen him either. But he won't get past Hardy's dog. That, my friend, means the sonofabitch was heading uphill not down."

"Are you sure?"

"Quite sure." Midgely bent an ear to the *whoop whoop whoop* of sirens outside. "He'll be charged with assault with intent to murder and there'll be a felony firearm charge. Wanna bet the bond will be set at $50,000."

Malin held up a hand. "I can't breathe."

She felt Midgely push her head down between her knees. It was stiflingly hot in the waiting room and it took her a moment to focus on where she was and evaluate her feelings. Slight nausea and dizziness. A good deal of panic.

Temeke's long hours of surveillance and intricate notes kept on each witness were indications to dig deeper. Something she could have followed up earlier on if she hadn't been holed up with Trandahl.

She couldn't hear the nurse talking over the whispers in her mind. A voice relaying Temeke's chance of survival on a scale of one to ten. Malin wondered if a spirit simply rocketed into outer space without a care in the world. Did they ever look back?

"…been asking for you. But he's sleeping now. If you want to sit with him you can."

"What?" Malin looked up at a nurse. "What did you say?"

"The detective, ma'am. He's been asking for you. Well, mumbling really. They say strange things while the anesthetic's wearing off. He's been yacking on about a boy and a sword and something burbling through a wood."

"So, he's OK? He'll be OK?" Malin sprung upwards.

The nurse gave a grin. "He was bleeding badly but it was lucky he was wearing a vest. Had a nasty bump on his head but apart from that, he'll be OK."

Yes, lucky, Malin thought. Although *luck* wasn't a word she liked to use. The universe was orchestrated in tiny detail from beginning to end. It wasn't as if things happened on a whim.

The nurse patted her on the arm. "No radios, if you don't mind. Nice and quiet."

Malin felt the warmth of Midgely's hand on her back and allowed herself to be led to Temeke's room. Lieutenant Alvarez gave up his seat, said he was going outside for a coffee.

Malin stared at Temeke. He was bolstered by a thick pillow and his body was covered by a sheet from the chest down. His wounds were covered in gauze and he was sleeping.

"The nurse said he's heavily sedated," Midgely whispered. "Shot with a nine mil apparently. Doctor says the bullet track in his chest went in at an angle. That tells us Temeke wasn't facing the shooter. Second bullet shaved his shoulder. It's the one in his hip that'll be the hardest to handle. But they want him walking around as soon as he's coherent."

"Thank you."

"For what?"

"For being with him."

Midgely grinned and patted the cell phone in her belt. "I'll keep you posted." Then she was gone.

Malin focused on the monitors; blood pressure, oxygen saturation… what did it all mean? His temperature was at 98.6. That was good, wasn't it? She began to wonder what hers was. Why did they always set hospital room thermostats at twelve below freezing?

His fingers twitched a little. Then his eyelids. But that was all the twitching he did for the next twenty minutes.

Nurses poked around, took vital signs and, for the most part, left him alone.

"Sir, it's me." Malin leaned over the bed, fingers hovering over his arm. "If you can you hear me I want you to know everything's OK. You're gonna be fine. Probably be back to work by the end of the week."

No response. He was too far gone with whatever it was they'd given him. Malin reached into the bedside drawer and found a Bible. It wasn't much use to a non-believer, one who didn't do well driving past a church without remarking on how empty the parking lot was. Bad attendance, he reckoned, due to the threat of being shot up by a lunatic, especially after that awful incident in Texas.

"That's where the shooters gun you down," he'd said. "In a packed place where you can't get out."

Malin read a few verses out loud from the book of Revelation. Horror stories didn't come this close nor did any visual interpretation of a dystopian culture. It was all about love in the darkness. A wake-up call. Something that might have given him hope.

The sound of his voice made her jump. "Did you... did you get..."

Malin leaned over the bed. "No, no. It's OK. You're OK."

Temeke opened his eyes and whispered, "Hannah..."

"We haven't found her yet. Do you remember what happened?"

"My phone."

"Sir?"

He started to cough, wet and phlegmy like a guy drowning in his own lungs. Malin found a cup of water and pressed the straw against his lips. He took a few sips and then tried to whisper something. She couldn't hear what it was, didn't ask him to repeat it. He was already asleep.

Replacing the Bible in the open drawer, she found the phone in a plastic bag. The four digit security code was already burned into her brain. He'd asked her to memorize it over a year ago in case anything happened to him.

The coordinates were still etched into his GPS. N35 10.886' W106 27.594'. Domingo Baca Canyon Trail.

A sad place, where TWA Flight 260 had taken off in a cloud-shrouded sky on February 19, 1955, and had crashed into the mountainside. All sixteen people onboard were killed. Temeke had often hiked to the wreckage site, haunted over the crew's last moments. But why there?

She copied the coordinates into her own phone, barely containing her rage when she thought of the shooter. The fact that he had shot Temeke three times brought an emptiness to her as if someone yanked out a big part of her heart, leaving a hole no one could fill.

"You OK?" The voice took Malin by surprise. Captain Fowler walked in carrying two Frappuccinos.

"*I'm* fine. It's him I'm worried about."

"Looks like shit. Apparently he lost his radio and his gun. How do you think our felon's been able to outwit the cops?"

"Temeke was shot, sir. Not much he could do about it. Why are you getting me all riled up? If these past few hours haven't been hell enough."

"A riled detective is an *effective* detective. Let's not make this any worse than it is." Fowler handed her one of the coffees. "They'll find Hannah and when they do she'll need a soft touch like you to talk to. Then she'll be all smiles and telling stories about how she escaped from the shooter."

"You really do live in a fantasy world."

"What are you so prickly about? Commander Ashton asked for you. Know what that means? He wants you out there to talk to the kid."

"And that's supposed to make me feel better?"

"It's better than sitting here staring at *him*. Not exactly talkative. They said—and don't tell him this—but he's got a very good chance of a complete recovery, except for that hip. He'll be limping around for a year and you… you'll have seniority. If I were you, I'd take a long hard look at that office of yours and imagine it with one desk."

THIRTY-NINE

Malin felt burning rage as she pushed past Hackett and Jarvis in the corridor and headed for the front lobby. Hurled the Frappuccino into a trash can and almost screamed after shutting herself into her car.

If this was Fowler's way of making jokes it was in poor taste. Either way, Temeke would prove him wrong because sore hips worked better when in motion and oh, how Temeke loved to hike.

Kate Harroway had left a message saying she was going out of town but that Malin was welcome to call her over the weekend if it was urgent. Malin found herself playing telephone tag with no hope of an informal chat on her way to the foothills.

It was Friday early afternoon and meeting Commander Ashton was a priority. To finish what Temeke had started—and that was finding Hannah. If Temeke's whispering hinted at what she thought it hinted at then she was headed to the entry station at Elena Gallegos Trail. There would be no news vans there.

She was wrong. There were three.

An officer signed her in at two forty-five and showed her a grid of the area, told her to check in by radio every ten minutes.

Her gaze hovered over his shoulder to a nosy pack of *Duke City Journal* reporters, sitting at one of the covered picnic areas. The rest of the parking lot was filled with volunteers and search and rescue dogs, who had been advised to remain by their cars. A straggle of police officers combed the scrubland and at a higher elevation she could make out the khaki colors of deputies.

According to an on-duty sergeant, the K-9 Unit and a team of Sandia Search Dogs had found blood trails along a creek bed before the climb into Domingo Baca Canyon. Trail 230. It was a disheartening discovery.

Malin shrugged on a vest and a backpack filled with snacks and water. Rifle scope against her chest and finger extended along the trigger guard, she would have preferred to throw the rifle up on her shoulder with a sling, but with a shooter out there she couldn't afford any extra seconds.

Her first challenge was to avoid journal staff writer Jennifer Danes and leg it to the trailhead. She hoped she wouldn't need the gun for that.

"Well, looky here." The last word rising. Faux-excited.

Malin turned swiftly and found the disturbing silhouette of Jennifer Danes, hand on hip, leg slightly bent.

"Hi, Jen." Malin felt the hint of a smile creeping to her lips. "Any updates?"

It was a feeble question but Malin wasn't going to enter into anything that went deeper than the weather. She had to watch everything she said or that tiny little tape recorder in Jennifer's top pocket would be a *big* problem.

"I'm sure you know more than I do," Jennifer said, swinging the blond stump of a ponytail. "How's Temeke? A little under the weather I heard."

"He's fine. Just came out of surgery and now he's resting."

"Well, that's good to know. How are you?"

"Busy."

"You're going up there why?"

"Why not?"

"No, you're going up there because there's no women in SWAT or in the K-9 Unit. I'm guessing you're here to speak to a little girl. Does that mean they've found Hannah?"

"Did someone call you with a false tip? I often wonder how you people manage to turn up uninvited."

Jennifer's nose wrinkled in amusement. "It always starts with a tip or when your editor assigns you a story."

"And what was it this time?"

Jennifer shrugged, eyes locked on Malin's rifle. "Maybe I witnessed something. The majority of what I do is watching. Talking to people, taking photos which, by the way, automatically appear on our homepage and twitter. You're looking particularly good."

Malin caught the tinkle of laughter as she blocked Jennifer's photo opportunity with a hand. "You taping this?"

"It's an informal conversation, Detective Santiago. *You people* might want to know that it's not just about getting a story for tomorrow's paper, it's about keeping citizens informed." Jennifer slipped the phone back in her pocket. "Before you go, I would like to say something. This thing with me and Matt, I don't want you thinking—"

"Dr. V did mentioned it. That you and Matt were engaged before he came along and that he didn't want to get in the way of your happiness. He also mentioned he didn't think he was right for you. Said something about preserving his independence. Sounded reasonable to me."

"I actually meant *your* feelings for Matt."

A second rumble of dread hit Malin and much less serious than the first. The thought of seeing Matt in the evening threw a dark cloud on her day. If she was honest, she liked Matt but then again every girl did. That was the problem.

"I never had any feelings for him." Malin saw the noticeable sag in Jennifer's jaw. "I'm in love with someone else. I'm sure he told you. Listen, today's a big day, Jen. I'd love to stay and chat but I've got a little girl to find."

Malin waved as she walked uphill. If it wasn't for the tragedy of a missing kid, she would have grinned her way to the crest.

She knew the site was hard to access, even if she followed the creek bed and stayed underneath the tram cables. She'd soon find out if a year of hard work was about to pay off or if she stood a chance at the promotion Temeke had suggested.

Glancing left and right, she powered uphill; the same ground already covered by the K-9 teams, two officers of which were only three hundred yards ahead. She concentrated on her breathing, trying to calm a racing heart. The wind whipped the scent of sand and shrub around her as if it was distinct as New Mexico itself.

If she thought of Hannah hard enough there was that familiar pressure in her chest, the overwhelming urge to take deep breaths to stop herself from panicking.

You'll get there in time, she kept telling herself. Only time was ticking. If the Amber Alert had been issued sooner would the search have been marshalled more quickly? Could Hannah have been found and saved? Or would there be a colorful jumble of teddy bears and posters on her memorial?

Malin was snapping angry fingers in her head. Time was of critical importance in abduction cases. Rachael had been killed in her sleep and Hannah, kidnapped by her killer, had traveled with her dead mother in the same car.

That day it had been ninety degrees in the foothills, although where she was heading it would drop another ten degrees. She radioed the two officers ahead and asked them to hold up.

"Yo-wassup. I knew you looked familiar," said the taller officer, when she caught up. His name tag read *D. Bryant*. "We were in third grade together. D'mond. You remember me?"

"No," Malin said, taking in the shiny dome of a bald head. Eyes like burnt caramel and holes in his earlobes where she reckoned he wore diamonds when off duty. "I'd remember you if we were."

Third grade? The two officers couldn't have been more than late twenties. It took her back almost ten years.

"This here is Whisky," he said, looking down at his dog. "He's a biter."

The other officer—name tag: *M. Salinas*—cut her some serious side-eye. Five feet-five inches with close cropped black hair. "Think you can keep up?"

"Yeah, I think I can manage that." Malin resisted an eye-role. Whisky didn't look too happy either.

They continued along a flat, wide trail. Today there were no cyclists shouting passing warnings or couples holding hands and dawdling in front of one of the most striking panoramic views in the world. In some ways she was glad.

A sign on their right marked the trailhead and an officer nodded them in. Told her to follow the creek beds about half a mile until she found the rough foundations of a rock shelter; another checkpoint where she'd be assigned to a group of officers.

Walking felt good and the strong tang of sagebrush cleared her head and chased away the stress. She focused on her breathing and for a good half hour as she followed behind two pairs of the longest legs she'd ever seen, she felt encouraged, almost free.

Navigating intertwining paths and keeping down near the stream bed, the elevation leveled off a little and she could see one of the tram towers to her left.

Can't be far now, she thought, following the sandy trail and noticing a ponderosa to her right, a five foot diameter trunk adorned with long scratch marks from a squirrel.

Bryant turned a full circle, grinned at her and pointed downwards. There, sunning itself on a rock about three feet off the path was a western diamondback rattle snake.

Malin paused and inched forward a few steps.

No sudden movements, she almost said aloud, creeping onward, where the path cambered through the trees. She could smell the snap of piñon in the air and her lips were already gritty with sand. They came across a clearing where ash, from the remnants of a recent campfire were scattered over the dirt.

Boy scouts, she thought, remembering how she loved camping out at night in the Sandias when she was in a church troop. Hauling food up a tree in a plastic bag, rain pattering against canvas and the howl of coyotes.

Bryant and Salinas chattered about a girl called Crazy Jane with straw-colored hair. It wasn't her real hair, judging by her ethnicity but she could rock it better than a Caucasian. How she stank of weed and always wore sagging pants. Thought she was all that.

"It wouldn't kill her to stay sober for a few days," Bryant said. "Picked her ass up three times this week."

"For real?"

"Uh-huh. She say she no hoe. She a lady. If blowing me a kiss is her way of asking me out, I'm good. Watch, we gon' see her again tomorrow night."

"*We?*"

"Yeah. I'm doing your ass a favor. Ain't like you got nothing else to do."

Malin chuckled and dropped back a little. Male talk never interested her. She wrongly assumed she could keep up, but her legs were infinitely shorter and her stride about half the length of theirs. She watched them across the distance; Bryant leaning back against Whisky's leash while bringing him to heel. They were already two hundred yards ahead, meandering back and forth over the creek bed.

She felt like she was racing a ticking clock, where the kidnapper had too much of a lead and they would never keep up.

Looking down at the valley, the desert hills, dotted with sage and piñon, sloped down to the town. Looking up, the crags dominated the skyline and an ancient rock spire rose between the pine trees like the flying buttress of a cathedral.

Malin paused briefly to study it, listening to the rhythms of the woods—the buzz of crickets and the occasional drumming of a woodpecker—knowing these sounds would stop at the slightest intrusion.

There was also a sense of peace. She was a cop, she had a gun. Nothing she couldn't handle.

FORTY

She stared along the metal enclosure, listening for footfalls in the silence.

She tried not to think of the terrible thing. *How was she going to tell dad anything after what she had done?*

She wanted to imagine she was in a flowering wood, but all she saw was a carpet of brown leaves, most of which had turned to mulch.

She couldn't see much through the small window, where passengers had once looked out onto gritty fog. Then boom! All was lost.

Did dying hurt?

Creepy rustling sounds made her skin crawl and she would have given anything in the world to be back home, sitting on the patio in front of the fire pit. Thick slices of meat spitting on a grill and a pot of beans. Or a takeout because dad always said happiness is a Domino's Pizza.

She didn't trust her memory of last night any more than she trusted Lee. There was something sick about him. Whether it was the way he spoke or the sweaty shirt he wore, she couldn't decide.

He was a liar.

Her mom wasn't here like he'd promised. Something deep down inside told her something terrible had happened.

Her eyes were sore from crying. Tiny drops crawled down her face as well as snot from her nose.

Her tongue felt swollen and the taste of sour eggs stuck in her mouth. She imagined sliding her thumbnail under the tab of a Coca Cola and then the pop before the burst of bubbles. She could smell a hint of vanilla and something sweet but that was only because she was hungry.

Camp 260 was a crash site. At least, that's what Lee had said. An airplane fuselage, where a slice had been braced against the rock she sat under. It was rotten now and there was the smell of wet porch after a downpour.

There had been an opportunity and she'd taken it. The cop had told her to do a runner and here she was. Out of sight. Out of mind. Because she didn't want to be tied up like a chicken in a roasting pan.

Thankfully, there was no sign of Lee.

And there weren't any ghosts. It wasn't that type of place.

Didn't stop her thinking about her mom. Perhaps she was slogging up the slopes to find her. She was tough. She'd find a way.

No, Mom was rolled up in a rug. Not pretty like Cleopatra but twisted and trashed among the rocks.

Dad had once said that whatever you put in your head is there forever. So be careful what you see. What you hear.

The terrible thing *kept looping in her mind and she knew she'd never stop seeing it. The cop in the black zipper pants. Shot and bleeding and lying in the dirt.*

Like it was happening again. Right now. The loud bang.

The cop went down like a rock. Had a 'why' look on his face, like someone who'd been beaten for no reason. She knew what it was like to be beaten because her mom had a heart of stone.

The cop's fingers had fluttered as he lay there and he'd murmured something. She couldn't remember what. Couldn't get close enough to hear, not with Lee squatting on the ground in front of her and pulling the rifle out from underneath the cop.

Then a strange thing happened.

Lee took the rifle and walked behind her to lean it up against a boulder. He stood there with his back to her admiring it for a while.

The cop murmured her name. He actually knew her name. Asked her if she was OK.

She thought she was dreaming. Thought he hadn't said anything but when he said it again she nodded.

"Run," he'd whispered.

Then Lee was back, boots scraping in the dirt, muttering something about leaving the cop for the coyotes. That men like him were as evil as the smirk on his face.

She never saw a smirk. Just teeth and moaning. It looked like he was trying to move but Lee stomped on the cop's back and kept his boot there for a time. Took out a large knife and held it under the cop's throat.

"What do you think, doll? Shall I cut him? Because the deeper I cut the less he'll move. We can call it anything we want. How about self-defense?"

"No! Don't!" She had been scared to bursting.

"Feeling a little squirrely? Nah, there's nothing to it. Just a quick slice and this piece of trash will be floating in the clouds. Otherwise what else are we gonna do? Sit and take turns watching him? That's a waste of time. Dogs like him fight dirty for a living and there's more where he came from."

"Stop it! Stop!"

She began screaming, big loud screams that went on and on until he dropped the knife. Came over and shook her quiet. She could still hear the teeth rattling in her mouth.

"He's shot bad," she sobbed. "You did something bad—"

"No, you did something bad. If they catch you, you'll go away for a very long time."

She twisted free and began shaking again. Ran both hands down her jeans to wipe the sweat off them.

What had she done?

All she remembered was Lee calling her a whole pile of names. Shouting, waving his arms about. That's how it was.

Nothing felt real anymore. Even the trees began to bend in and out and she was afraid she'd throw up.

Lee resheathed the knife and squatted with his back to her again. Picking at the buckle on the cop's belt, working quickly and looking around while he was doing it.

The cop's eyes were black and watery, no longer moving. She couldn't remember if they had been scooting upward or downward as if he wanted her to run that way. She had only seconds to make up her mind.

Lifting one foot after the other, she had backed up to escape a small shiny puddle that oozed out from beneath the cop.

Creeping silently up the slope to where the path forked. One trail wider and leveling around a bend, the other narrow with a sharp incline between two boulders.

Into the trees. Into the shadows. And here she was hiding behind a scrap of metal, panting and shivering like next door's dog.

She heard the soft clattering in the distance. As if someone had lost their footing along an escarpment, rocks tumbling below. Didn't sound like the wind had blown down a branch.

She had known it wouldn't be long before Lee found her. Because he'd come after her and things would get ugly.

She wanted to crawl out of her hiding place and watch the curve of the trail. Hide on the far side of the canyon high up on the rock bluffs. All she could hear was her heart.

And something else.

Crunching. The snap of twigs. And the echo of a man's voice. "Come out, come out, wherever you are."

Then a hammering on the metal frame she hid behind.
This time, Lee carried a coil of rope.

FORTY-ONE

Malin studied every bend in the trail, murmuring her position into the radio. Beads of sweat ran down her face and she tried to sweep the trees for any signs of movement. Then repeated the process in reverse order.

A young deputy walked about fifteen feet behind her, eyes gazing out over the view and not giving much attention to the trail. There were hikers who could stare at their feet and still walk in a straight line, Malin thought. Although not while carrying a rifle.

Sheriff's deputies were of the opinion that police officers—or PD as they called them—thought themselves more superior. That they rarely engaged with deputies. Malin had seen a few occasions where officers did little more than bob their heads in greeting, but that wasn't her style.

She stopped, turned and gave him her name.

"John Willoughby," he returned, smiling.

"Seen anything?"

"Not yet. Can't hear much over the radios."

"Where would a ten-year-old hide?" she asked.

"If she small enough, she might make use of a bobcat den. They're not much more than a hollow tree or a rock crevice. There's plenty of tracks—four toes without claws," he said, pointing. "Let's hope we find her before it gets dark. That's bad for us but not for the dogs. They work well at night. Air currents are better. So is the temperature."

Malin had heard that some dogs, depending on the breed, used their noses rather than their eyes. They worked more effectively when visual resources were hampered.

Willoughby turned sharply toward the trees and held a finger to his lips. "Do me a favor, keep up with the others and stay on the track."

"You know I can't do that—"

But he disappeared up a sharp incline into the trees and was lost behind a wall of shrubs. He was fast, which is exactly what she needed to be if she was going to catch up with Bryant and Salinas.

She couldn't count the times she heard boots striking rock, cracking an echo that mimicked distance gunshot. She almost crouched. It was another sound that came later. Softer, barely audible over the breeze.

She scanned the area behind her, breath hitching in her throat, while her mind retraced the sound, willing it to happen again. At the apex of the bend, she could see deep blue sky between the notched branches of towering pines and lower down, an unwooded expanse of sage and piñon. Far ahead, she could just make out the back of Salinas and radioed for him to wait.

She couldn't hear the woodpecker or the crickets. Call it intuition, but she couldn't figure out if there was someone further up the trail or a sniper perched on a nearby boulder. Could have been SWAT. There were quite a few agencies out there with a gunman on the loose.

Where the heck was Willoughby?

No point sagging under the stress, she thought, inching her way forward, rifle out in front. The breeze ebbed and flowed and sometimes she caught the stench of sweat.

The trail was little more than a tunnel of leaves and she hugged the tree line for better cover. Assuming the shooter was still armed and hadn't ditched his gun in some ravine, it was imperative to keep alert. She quietly urged herself on, thankful they were all fitted with lapel cams.

Then another sound. It took her a few moments to realize it was radio noise. Hers in unison with another officer's. Then the sound of a gun slide.

She paused and took a breath. Turned a full circle.

A snap of dried leaves, a flicker of movement. Malin tightened her grip on her rifle and angled her head toward her radio. But the crush of a man's hand against her lips, stopped her from calling for backup.

The continual chatter from his radio told her it was Willoughby, pulling her into the trees and away from danger. But the smell of him told her otherwise.

Whoever it was held her tightly against his chest. But the mountain was teeming with officers. She'd give the asshole—whoever he was—ten minutes. Tops.

There were always those precious few seconds when she looked for them, because no kidnapper was ever that vigilant. Had she been two feet away from him just as he grabbed her, she could have raised one arm, twisted around and sliced her way out. But not with a rifle out front and restrained in a chokehold.

Kicking outwards did nothing and throwing one foot backward and as high as she could, served little purpose. She had the sense he was tall, body stooped to accommodate hers. He'd only gone and thrown his legs apart so hers were swinging back and forth between them.

He gripped her harder now. As it was, both arms were pinned to her sides with one of his and the other served as a clamp around her mouth. There was no way she could move. Kick, definitely.

"If you don't quit screwing around, woman, I'll break your legs!"

It was a slight kick in the teeth to her professionalism and added to that she'd lost her grip on the rifle. Heard it clatter against a rock. Should have squeezed off a few warning shots in the struggle.

Where the heck was Willoughby?

In the split second the man lifted her up, she tried to drop her body weight to make herself as heavy as possible, driving her elbows into his chest. But he slammed her hard on the ground and she could almost feel the tremors through her ankles, shooting stars raining down behind her eyelids. There was no way she could strike out and create enough space between them to disengage.

At least, not yet.

"If you even think of kicking those little feet of yours, I'll kill a cop for every noise you make. Understood?"

Sounds melding into one as he wrenched her head from side to side. She hated to go limp but her ankles felt as if they'd been snapped in half. There was no feeling in them.

"Move!" he said, propelling her uphill between the trees.

It was a southern accent. She could tell by the dawdling rhythm even though the tension. She couldn't see much without turning her head and there was no chance of that unless he stopped squeezing the air out of her chest.

Snapping twigs and the crunch of dried leaves. Twice she almost lost her footing. And then she saw Willoughby up ahead. Lying on his front, one ear covered in blood. It was difficult to assess whether he was still alive without touching him and she prayed he'd passed out from a head wound.

To the untrained ear, the radio noise would have sounded more like a garble of words and static. Her mind tried to calculate who he was, what he was doing. Because if this was Temeke's radio she was hearing, then this was Temeke's man.

She couldn't shout, couldn't draw enough breath into her lungs. Her mind whirled around and around, thinking of the knife and Glock in her belt. If she could only pivot her upper body enough to reach her handgun and tuck it close, the other hand would be free to punch out.

Stay calm. Let him talk. Wait for that moment.

She was both mad and ashamed. On a scale of one to ten, she was more mad than ashamed.

"Before you ask me what I'm doing up here," he said, "I'm well within my rights and you know it. Just needed a little air. A little time to consider my options."

He released the pressure from her mouth just enough for her to respond.

"I don't give a rat's ass about your rights," she said. "You've no right—"

"I have rights! Here I am enjoying a few days in the mountains and here you are about to bust me for vagrancy. I feel about as welcome as a case of smallpox."

If she could have reached one of his fingers she would have bitten it. "I don't think you really understand what we're talking about here. Killing a cop and holding another against her will—"

"I didn't kill him. He's just stunned," he said, moving her further into the trees. "So what are you going to do? Arrest me? For all practical purposes, ma'am looks like I'm arresting you."

"One more step and I mean it—"

He flattened his hand hard against her mouth, pressing so hard she knew her lips were white.

"Now, let's discuss how many cops are out there," he said. "Maybe you can help me with that. Because I don't even want Smokey Bear sneaking up on me, do you hear?"

Flicking her eyes from left to right, she could see her rifle on the ground about three feet to her left. He was smart enough not to reach down and grab it because he'd need both arms to stop her from twisting free.

Was he wearing a vest? Carrying Temeke's gun? He was way strong and she could feel his breath swirling around her head.

"You scared?" he asked. "I'd say you were and if you said no, you'd be bullshitting. It's only natural to be scared, especially of a man with a hunting knife. Talking of weapons, got any more guns beside the one in your belt? I don't mind searching you but you might prefer telling me yourself."

The pressure weakened against her face just enough for her to shake her head. If it wasn't for her bulletproof vest, his arm would have felt the rapid hammering in her chest.

"I guess you want to know what I doing up here?" he said, pushing her through the trees. "Hiking. Same as you. I've always liked the name Lee and in any case my *real* name will cost you. Let's say we take a walk up this nice hill. See if we can see the view a little better from up there."

He thrust her forward, ramming his knees into the backs of her thighs. His breath came in spurts and if she wasn't mistaken, she could feel the rough brush of a beard against the top of her head.

"You want some answers?" Lee asked. "Me too. For one thing, I had the weirdest feeling those old mongrel dogs were on the hunt for some escaped lunatic. I just didn't think that *lunatic* was me."

Malin opened her lips a little.

"You want to tell me something?" he said. "I'm listening."

"You don't want them shooting at you… the cops… that's what they'll do."

"That's all right and you're the one with the vest. And besides, I've been dying a little every day. Dying, I should say, to find a way out of this mess."

Malin looked around for a sapling to kick against, a boulder. There had to be something. A small cairn on the side of the trail that had collapsed… too far for her to reach.

"Now isn't that better," he said, turning her toward the western horizon, visible in the gap between two trees. "A little hazy over Albuquerque wouldn't you say? I often sit up here and contemplate life. Get away from the humdrum of the office. And we should wait awhile until your boys have gone on a little further."

She could feel the bile bubbling in her throat and the stench from his hand was sickening. If she could only reach back a little, raise her hand to her holster…

"I've been listening to your radio for the last few hours," he whispered, lips pressed against her ear. "Think you can tell me what it all means? I'll give you a chance to talk soon. I promise. But in the meantime, I want you to feel good about the fresh air. Me. You. The view… it's striking at this time of year."

She felt him lift the pressure from her mouth, expecting a response. "Why are you doing this?"

"Because it dawned on me that sticking arrows in rabbits is different than blowing holes in people. A bow… too cumbersome. I've always been able to handle a gun. Now some big-shot judge is gonna think me a loose cannon and give me fifteen years to life. It'd be the decent thing to do."

"What did you do?"

"Whew! A little drugs. A little women. Always slows you down. You know, we can keep talking like this but it's going to get awful boring."

"That give you the right to kidnap someone?" she managed to ask before her lips were flattened again.

"I wouldn't call it kidnapping, ma'am. You're too old to be a kid. What are you? Thirty something?"

The pseudo politeness was beginning to grate on her nerves and she wasn't about to fall for it. She had no way of knowing if the man was on drugs, mentally ill, or the victim of an accident. His ramblings indicated he wasn't up for a two-way conversation.

"I'm not hurting you, am I?" he asked. "Got a feeling a tough lady like you could survive a nuclear strike. And you may have to when they open fire and empty all those big magazines into that vest of yours. In any case, me running off with a lady cop is hardly gonna come back and bite me in the ass. I'll be long gone."

He was an idiot. There were snipers at every angle, including his back. All waiting to take that fatal shot.

Again, he released his hand, palm pressed against her cheek, fingers splayed out too far away for her to bite. She studied them. Looked like someone else had got there first. Red welts and teeth marks and strips of dried blood. No wonder he was so careful.

She could feel his breath on her neck, feel him right behind her. Already picturing a blade slicing her neck from ear to ear.

Think, Malin, think! She passed on the idea of kicking him on the shins since she hadn't been successful the first time. Her legs were battered by the hammering of his knees but the feeling was slowly coming back to her feet. At the rate he was going, he'd have to take a break soon.

Sweating profusely and moisture running down her forehead, she had to keep her eyes closed from all the stinging.

Her limbs were sore, as if she'd done a marathon workout in the space of ten long minutes. But she had no desire to kick against him because the threat of feeling sharp steel against her spine was a sound threat.

They stopped on the hillside, her wheezing, him panting. The fine hairs on the back of her neck prickling.

Bryant and Salinas should have doubled back by now. All she could see were huge clusters of trees and boulders and occasionally the sky. What was worse, that's all the snipers could see too.

"I don't know what I hate more," he said. "You being quiet or me talking all the time. I'm losing my mind here."

FORTY-TWO

He didn't seem too bothered by talking to himself, Malin thought, rambling on about somebody out there, stalking him. Someone who wanted to hurt him in the worst possible way. He was high and incoherent.

"I don't want to dig up the past," he whispered. "I've talked the damn thing to death. You make me feel like I want to confess all my dirty little secrets. Maybe I should. Maybe I should get it out in the open. Let you be the judge. I'm just not sure I want to put myself through all that. We're different you and I. Our brains are different. Men enjoy a challenge. Women... too damn emotional."

Don't be so hasty, she thought. Women's brains didn't always gravitate toward emotion and intuition. They scanned the environment for challenges and threats, just like she was doing now.

"You know what would brighten my mood? Getting the hell out of this town. Think you could give me a head start?" He removed his hand just a little to let her speak.

"Where would you go?"

He chuckled. "You could say it was a journey of self-discovery. A search for the truth. There's this little trick I learned. Shoot your brains out and the demons go away. But I'm not sure I'm ready for that right now. So while I'm still here, I can tell you *she* was gonna do it for me. Had the gun in her hand. That's a shit-load of premeditation, don't you think?"

It wouldn't be long before he deflected his guilt onto Malin. She could already hear the outrage in his voice.

"If you could quit squeezing," she said, "I could start talking."

"Think I'm gonna fall for that so you can give me some snake fist. Put the hurt on me."

Snake fist? Was that some kind of joke?

"I'm not gonna let a cop—a female one at that—move in and take me down," he said, making a noise to back up how much he hated it.

Her mind almost zoned out as she tried to take in the scenery. But her brain was overloaded and not firing the way it should.

Humming sounds came from her throat as she tried to yell through his hand. He took no notice. Just kept on talking and inching up the hill, half-lifting, half-dragging, pausing only to listen for sounds.

"I can tell you're not happy right now," he said. "Probably feeling beaten and fed up. Ever think about ditching that uniform and getting the hell out?"

"Sometimes."

"This journey… the one I'm taking. Maybe I've just found a new companion. The *right* companion. Because you know a thing or two about guns."

"Where are we going?"

"*We*? I like that. I really do." He squeezed a little tighter. "But you don't fool me, cop lady. I'd sooner they kill you."

Malin tried to take gulps of air but the compression around her chest made it impossible to fill her lungs enough to shout. He knew exactly what he was doing.

Twice he turned a half-circle and began pulling her, which caused her ankles to drag and him to stagger. She felt as if her back had been sewn against his chest.

The minute he turned to face uphill again, something clicked inside of her. If she leaned back a little, let him carry her full weight, it would break his rhythm and very soon he'd have to think of another way of carting her around.

"If that's how you want to play it," he said, feeling the sudden shift," so help me, I'm gonna knee you in the butt and you'll be sorry."

She knew what it was like to be kneed in the butt. Painful, especially if bone connected with bone. He was taller. It wouldn't be her butt he would be kneeing.

"Faster, faster, dammit!"

She let her legs do the work. No use delaying. Even though a scream began to rise in her throat, she knew it would be no louder than a groan. He felt like a huge slob of a man, but his accent belied the image.

"You can't run, woman. Shit, you can't even breathe."

They picked up speed as the ground leveled off, and she heard the sound of running water as they approached a creek which had been replenished by the recent rains. A wet finger of rock, maybe four feet wide and six feet long jutted out into the middle, and Lee almost lost his footing as he dragged her across.

She sensed a drop in temperature. The tops of the trees were whipped by a new surge of wind and out of the corner of her eye she saw a yellowish column, sand boiling beneath it. The dust devil billowed out in a fine yellow haze, a rush of leaves and wind in her ears. She could hear him coughing, knew he was tiring. Even when he turned sideways and crab-walked, she made no attempt to help him.

Getting to you, she wanted to say, feeling a rush of excitement in her stomach, because the way they were going they would soon meet up with the rest of her unit.

The cloud was upon them, thick and dense and she felt him stumble several times before correcting his stride. He stopped occasionally and listened to the sounds around him: a lizard scrabbling into the brush and the shriek of an eagle. He was short of breath.

Something stirred in the shadows; he'd seen it too. Her heart was thumping so hard he must have felt it all the way to his chest.

"You say one word," he said, "and I'll drive this knife right through your spine."

Malin couldn't make any sudden movements. Sadly twisting wasn't available to her and kicking her legs might trigger a violent slash-fest. Like it or not, Lee had an arsenal of weapons at his disposal and a mind to use them.

Another wave of dizziness came over her as he lifted her up, spun her around again before her boots pounded against rock. She would be nothing but a human shield against the onslaught of police fire.

"There's someone out there," he said, keeping his voice level. "Maybe he should have picked a more convenient time because it's gonna be a bitch of an afternoon. For you."

She wondered when he'd start fumbling at the self-locking system on her holster in order to take her gun. He'd have to take his hand away from her mouth, long enough for her to shout.

"You think a cop will shoot me with you in front?" he asked, lifting his hand from her mouth just long enough for her to respond.

"You bet your ass he will and he won't think twice."

"You're lying. There's no cop out there. The feeling I'm getting here is you're disrespecting me and you don't want to do that."

Malin went quiet. He was on to her and any more stupid remarks about cops shooting and she'd wind up dead. Since Malin hadn't called in for nearly ten minutes, someone had to be looking for her.

FORTY-THREE

She lay beneath the wedge of metal. Rocking back and forth and counting rivets. Lee had told her to stay put until he came back. Otherwise the dogs would get her.

Something about dogs *made her stomach queasy. They were highly trained, he'd said, and she'd need surgery for the bites. She shuddered just thinking about it.*

What Lee didn't know was that she'd learned a few things from her friends. Like self-defense, something a weirdo with a lungful of smoke wouldn't get.

While Lee was tying her wrists out in front, she'd crossed them, rotating the lower wrist just a little so the rope appeared tight.

She'd cried out in pain and begged him to stop. Made all the right noises to make him uncomfortable. Any complaints about wetting herself and throwing up made him back up as far as he could. She reckoned that's why he hadn't knotted them too tightly.

Then he left her to all her bellyaching and carrying on.

After he'd been gone for some time, she straighten out her arms. Wriggled and twisted, cried out in pain because it wasn't as easy as her friends had told her. But she didn't give up and eventually there was enough slack to pull one hand out. After that, picking the knots around her ankles was child's play.

Crawling out of her hidey-hole, she limped for the trees. Her left leg was stiff and kept trailing behind her like a tail. But she had to keep running before the dogs came. She ran a little faster and it felt like she was soaring into the valley. Only it wasn't like she was flying or anything. But sometimes she wished she was.

Until running made her dizzy and she slowed down a little. Thought she heard a dog bark and flinched at the sound.

She couldn't hear Lee and hoped she'd gained at least ten minutes on him. If he was out there, then he was waiting for her to make the first move.

I'm not a moron, she thought.

Then an idea flickered in her mind. Was dad looking for her? Did he know where she was? She'd left her phone in the car for him to find so he was probably calling the cops, the school and all her friends. He was probably worried out of his wits.

Her mind seemed to be recalling things at a much faster rate than yesterday. Memories snapping in and out and guiding her back to the screams. Then a loud bang coming from Mom's room. And Lee... dragging her downstairs and giving her something to drink. She thought he'd started cleaning the house but everything went black after that.

If the part about mom had all been a dream, then she was in deep trouble.

"Where have you damn-well been, little girl!" her mom would say. "I've been worried sick!"

Mom always turned fights into doing chores. Brownie points, she called it. Or better still getting a real job.

"Why don't you earn some money instead of wasting time? What about a paper round?"

And she'd say, "They don't do newspaper rounds anymore, Mom. That went out with the ice age."

"They teach computer at school? If that's not a qualification I don't know what is."

"I'm ten years old, Mom!"

"You could learn to cook. Make a few dishes and take them to the neighbors. Because Lord knows I need help with the bills. You might want to think salary, *little girl."*

"You might want to think illegal *Mom."*

"I'll shake you so hard your freaking teeth'll rattle."

"Do it then."

Mom never responded to haggling. Said you got what you got and you didn't give a fit. But the 'do it then' got her all riled up last time it happened and added at least six more swats to the punishment account.

You'd think Mom would like hanging out with her because kids keep things simple. They liked to have fun. But Mom wasn't fun anymore. Called her a rag-tag-dirty-little-hag. It wasn't nice.

Anything that had once been nice in Mom had been washed down the drain because of the girls she kept looking at on the computer. One in particular got her attention. Mom couldn't stop staring at her. Started doing her hair the same way. Even bought the same dress at the mall.

There was something weird about it. People can't copy other people. They get mad. You're supposed to be like yourself and if yourself is dog-ugly then too freaking bad.

And freaking's *a bad word. It means something else.*

Mom said she seen her prowling around outside the house and staring in through the window. Little girls shouldn't be peeking. People had rights. Didn't she understand what a locked door meant or the word private?

In any case, she'd promised Mom she didn't see anything. It was a lie. She saw this one lady with big puffy lips and arched brows and sad, smoky eyes. Her mom called her Ella.

Sometimes ugly ducklings turned into beautiful swans. When her mom was downstairs, she'd sit in front of the mirror wondering if she'd ever be pretty.

Some of the girls at school were pretty. Had pretty clothes and wore makeup at parties.

Not her, because Mom said she was too young.

Didn't stop her from trying it though. A thick smear of lipstick and then you stuck out your lips like you were expecting a kiss.

If she was on her own long enough, she'd try on one of Mom's bras. The lacy one with the pink bows. The one Mom scrunched up and slipped into her handbag last week.

One day, when she was all grown up, she wanted to look like Ella because she was the one her mom liked best.

She held her breath and tried to stay focused. The wind kept blowing through the trees and she couldn't hear much over the clatter of leaves. The crags were behind her now and she was on a narrow path that wound between several large boulders.

She didn't know what was at the end of it. Him? Or a straight run to the parking lot. She was sore-eyed and tired. But there was a sick feeling of dread as more thoughts flickered in her mind.

Monsters. Big as dogs... barking.

Her dad's voice chimed inside her brain. "Why do victims always run down the middle of the road? Why don't they zigzag through the trees? Hide in a ditch or even up a tree! They're gonna get caught. They always *get caught."*

Footsteps shook the ground and she could hear harsh breaths. Words kept screaming in her head to stay low, even though panic told her to run.

Where to? Up or down?

The sun cast a hazy yellow light through the leaves, warning her of the night ahead. Although she was shielded in the shadows, he'd find her if he had a mind to. And Lee was sharp. No doubt about that.

She couldn't see him. Couldn't hear where he was coming from. She found a hiding spot behind a tree, feet steady and thighs rigid, and stared at the valley below as it turned blue with twilight.

A snap of a twig to her right. Craning her neck, she saw a man through a fringe of shrubs. As he doubled over to catch his breath, she could see he was gripping a rifle. After several minutes he squatted, fingers trailing the dirt like a tracker.

He was in Lee's gang. Had the same look about him. Hard, staring eyes and a thin mouth. Then he stood and turned his back, head tilted as if studying the crags.

She didn't hesitate. She just ran. Veering to her left and darting like a rabbit along the path, she burst through a row of saplings and into a spiny column of pine trees. In front was a ramp of boulders. Unable to stop herself in time, she staggered and fell sideways over the edge. Sliding first on her left side and then on her butt. Down, down, down, until she hit a grassy ledge.

Tremors shot through her ankles and her hands were shredded and bleeding. The pain in her shoulder and left foot caused her to wince and there was no way she could stand. Hand fumbling over the bobbing tassels of grass, she found the only way forward was a sheer drop.

She lay there until she could breathe again and over her pounding heart she heard the dogs.

FORTY-FOUR

"You like ignoring me," Lee said, turning her every which way toward the sound of snapping branches. "Like pressing my buttons."

Despite sucking in each breath and holding it for the count of three, Malin knew it was loud and ragged when she released it. If she had been facing him, she would have worn a look that expressed the appropriate degree of attention. But since he couldn't see her face, it wasn't worth shit.

Between a sapling and the edge of the boulder they were facing, she caught sight of a rifle. Couldn't be sure, but there was a red, blue and white insignia on the sling.

She wriggled a little, trying to ease her head up so she could take a good look at him. Truth was, he knew he was being followed and he was huffing and pulling and trying to get a bead on the sudden rush of sounds.

Then he stopped again and went rigid.

"Now, you let me do the talking," he whispered in Malin's ear. "There'll be no need for heroics."

She felt the pressure tighten around her waist and mouth as Bryant and Salinas emerged through the trees, mouths a grille of teeth.

"Gentlemen," Lee said. "Let's put the guns down and let's be real friendly."

Bryant and Salinas lowered the muzzles of their rifles slightly and moved forward. The dog barked up a storm, intimidating the threat rather than engaging.

Malin couldn't help thinking several things at once. A sniper could fire within an inch at about one hundred yards but if the scope wasn't zeroed right, his accuracy would be questionable. Add that to changing wind and distance it might amount to two inches at one hundred yards. What if he was holding a rifle and a K-9 at the same time?

"You might want to stop right there," Lee said. "Either way, she'll get hit first."

Malin felt faint and breathless. He was solid, built like a firefighter. Probably a good six feet.

She felt the slight release of pressure from around her waist. If Lee's legs weren't wide apart, she'd have a good chance at mashing his calf with her heel or something else if she could reach high enough. Just one small jab.

She caught Salinas's eyes as they widened a fraction, conveying he wanted to talk the perp down. She was glad he was holding a gun and Bryant was holding the dog.

It had to have been the longest minute of her life. Salinas jockeying for the upper hand and Lee sobbing. He was surrounded. Dogs barking, mouths yacking. Sometimes raised high enough to know there was some heat in those words.

Lee questioned how the dogs would know which person to bite? Him or her? That's when Bryant held up a stained t-shirt he'd found in the scrub.

"This yours? Dog thinks it is."

Malin's brain was ticking over and taking it all in and she could feel the adrenaline buzz at least four times more than before. Lee was already on the downward slide; running out of ideas and steam. A human shield wasn't enough to protect him from the dogs and he couldn't aim a gun if he was holding her.

She glanced to her right and saw a dead tree. Sprouting from the bark was a dried out twig, snapped and dangling... and on the end of that twig a dangerously sharp point.

The dry whisper of leaves seemed to goad her into action and she sensed something in Lee's stance. Rigid and trembling, arms slackening as if his mind was already made up.

She didn't need to make up hers.

Easing her hand out from under his arm, she grabbed one end of the twig and pulled. Lee couldn't hear much over the sound his flapping mouth. Kept backing up, chest no longer mashed against her back and one hand grappling with her sleeve. Seemed he was paying more attention to Salinas than to her, giving her a few precious moments.

She turned her head slightly and gauged about a foot of space between them now. Muscles tightening, she gripped that twig for all she'd got. Forced it over her left shoulder and jabbed it into his face. By the sound of his scream and a hand covering his eye, it had done its job.

Filling her lungs and energized by the sudden separation, she zig-zagged down the slope toward Salinas. Flicked back the locking system on her holster, she twisted back around. Elbows locked and gun centered in her field of view.

It could have been a foolhardy move. Lee had recovered enough to be gripping a handgun in one hand while shielding his eye with the other. But he couldn't have seen much through a haze of blood.

"Put the gun down!" she shouted several times over the officers behind her.

Six foot, dark hair and stubble, she guessed he was about one hundred and ninety pounds. Matched the description of the man who tried to break into the doctor's car. Only this one was half-naked. Hyperthermia was unlikely. A drug reaction, possibly.

He was either a material witness, an accomplice or the perpetrator. Then again, he could have been a hiker, a camper. Homeless. There were plenty of them up here.

No. Not with an AR-15 leaning up against a nearby boulder, British flag clearly visible on the sling. To be in this stretch of woodland he had to have known exactly where it was.

"Get down!" Malin shouted, gun raised, voice firm.

"Don't shoot me!"

"I *said* get down! Put your hands where I can see them!"

Malin wasn't going to let him use her as a range target nor was she going to engage him with gunfire. But the truth was, it was up to him how he was going to play this out.

He made no attempt to get on the ground, lifted the handgun to the side of his head and promised to do it himself. If this was the man who had kidnapped Hannah, she was shit-out-of-luck if he was the only one who knew where she was.

Please God, don't let him shoot.

It went stiflingly quiet, Bryant clasping Whisky's snout and watching the advance of more officers through the trees. Malin knew her training in crisis intervention had taught her how to deal with the fraught combination of high-stakes negotiations and guns.

But nothing like this.

Nothing like confronting a live gunman willing to kill himself. She didn't have FBI training on how to talk a man down and even if she elected not to go for center mass and shoot him in the shoulder, there was nothing to keep him from jerking the trigger.

In order to take the man into custody she needed to execute five things. She could only remember two.

Approach. Communicate.

She didn't like the sound of the first, but the second was good. She took a few steps forward, could see his face now. Cheeks smeared with mud and where the whites of his eyes stood out against the shadows.

"You're not going to kill yourself," she said.

"I should."

"There's no reason for anyone to get hurt. Do you understand? I need to tell you something... something important."

He tilted his head. She took it to mean he needed an explanation.

"I know a man who tried to do what you're doing now," she said. "Threatened to pull the trigger in front of someone. I'm glad he didn't because it wouldn't have been a clean shot. Not all of them are. Knowing his luck, he would have ended up a vegetable in a hospital bed, someone mopping up his waste. He would have hated that." She hoped he was frowning it through, maybe coming to his senses. "Tell me what happened. Why you're here."

"The car broke down... I didn't know what to do."

It didn't really explain it.

"Didn't know where to go. Just wanted to make it right. So I... I carried her. Set her down nice and easy. She was quiet. Didn't move."

"That must have been scary," she said.

"Yeah. Yeah it was."

Malin kept her eyes on him. Wanted him to feel like she was listening because she knew his mind was a series of scenes that had shattered into a thousand pieces. Each one telling a story or a truth he didn't want to share.

"Did you call anyone?" she asked.

"No... no."

With Hannah as an unwilling passenger, Malin guessed things didn't go quite as smoothly as he had hoped.

Had he ditched her on the way? She couldn't have been tied up and bleeding because the dogs would have found her by now...

"I don't know how she did it," he said. "I don't know how she knew. Listen, I took a hit... I don't remember when."

"What did you take?"

He shook his head, mouth open as if there were no more words. "I do a few things. Nothing heavy."

"What did you take?"

Again no reply. What voice he did have was choked with emotion and not the bluster he'd shown earlier.

"Tell me about her?" Malin asked.

His face lit up and then darkened as if he was locked in an endless nightmare. He rambled. Couldn't get his words together and Malin had no idea if he was talking about Rachael one minute and Ella the next. If only she was near enough to squeeze his hand, pull him out of the memory to focus more on her.

"She was smart, *real* smart. Could have made so much of her life. I wanted her to. But then everything changed... All the things I did to her. Don't judge me. Whatever you do don't judge me."

Malin wasn't there to judge him or tell him how to live his life. In her opinion, he'd already ruined it. Right now, her chief concern was Hannah's safety.

"What did you do to her?"

"She's dead now so we'll never know will we?"

"How? How did she die?" *Shot herself? Shot someone else? What?*

"We used to… see each other early." His eyes flicked upwards as if rewinding his thoughts.

"Early?"

"Yeah. In the mornings."

"Can you tell me who she is?"

"I had to have been blind not to see what she was trying to do." He pointed to the ground with his free hand, stabbing the air as if to make a point. "She did it because she knew what it would do. Ruin me. That's what. I had to show her. I had to make her see."

Malin took a step forward and then hesitated. He raised the gun nozzle, aligning it with his temple and moving it up and down as it to relieve an itch.

"I want to tell you… but I think I need a lawyer… to tell me what that's gonna to mean. We had something, her and me… Then it was over."

"Except it wasn't over, was it?" she prompted.

"No."

"You said it was early when you saw each other?"

"I waited for her husband to leave. I wanted to get it over with and I wasn't feeling much of anything."

"Was she asleep?"

"No. She kept talking about Ella. I didn't want to talk about Ella. Then she started shouting. Kept pointing that gun." He looked away, started panting as if the horror of the situation had finally sunk in. "I know in my heart, right now, that what I did was wrong. But I needed Ella. She should have understood that. She should have understood what Ella meant to me."

"Rachael, you mean?"

His finger twitched on the trigger guard, gun aligned with his temple.

"Doesn't matter, does it? She's gone. I wanted her to shut up. I don't know why I let her into my head the way I did. I was flattered. Stupid… I don't know."

"You said you were flattered. Do you think she was getting a divorce for you? So she could marry you?"

"Yes, yes, I think so."

Malin knew he was fading; too many winces, too many breaths.

"I tried to stop her… Then I shot… shot her."

"How many times did you shoot her?"

"I don't remember. I never would have killed her. She had a child. She was a mother. It's not in my nature."

"When you say it's not in your nature to kill, how do you feel now?"

"Terrible."

He shook his head and said he wanted to be alone. Told them to take the dogs away because they were slathering up a mouthful of foam and getting awful excited. It was the vehemence of his voice that snapped Malin back to his last word. *Terrible.*

She studied the gun in his hand. A Glock 19, semi-automatic, standard capacity magazine. Could have been Rachael's.

"Why don't you put the gun down, Lee? Scoot it toward me," Malin said quietly.

It was the sound of more dogs barking that made Lee flinch. She was still skeptical that he'd drop the gun and if it wasn't for Hannah she would have already taken a shot, and that didn't include the officers behind her.

He took two steps backwards into the shadows where a yawning darkness spread over his face. She couldn't see the direction of the muzzle or his finger on the trigger guard.

"Why are you here?" he asked.

She knew he was watching her, standing upright and completely focused in the darkness with a large boulder at his back.

"We're looking for a little girl," Malin said. "Name's Hannah. You wouldn't have seen her would you?"

"Flying..." Lee whispered. "She's flying."

The sick feeling continued to roil in Malin's stomach. It was no longer about whether he knew Hannah but the unmistakable feeling that he did. "Flying where?"

"Up there."

Malin resisted the urge to look up. She'd be dead meat if she did. All she could hear was the wind whispering dryly through pine trees. He must have heard it too.

Then a loud crack.

She flinched, recalling only a split second of disbelief as Lee slumped to the ground.

It was enough to send Whisky into the darkness; a flash of black against the gray boulders. The dog must have latched onto something. Wrist, arm, leg. He was trained to take a gun.

It took Malin a few seconds to understand what had just happened and she lurched forward on heavy feet.

Why kill himself? Why?

Salinas brushed past and crouched in front of Lee, pressing two fingers against his neck. He looked up and shook his head. Malin could feel the grief pressing against her chest, the notion that they had missed their chance. That Hannah would never be found.

Her knees hit the dirt and she scrambled for Lee's pockets. No wallet. No phone. No ID.

Salinas grabbed Lee's gun. Dropped the magazine and racked the slide. "Clear!"

FORTY-FIVE

If Malin was honest, her legs would have given way if she hadn't found a rock to sit on. Her ankles were sore, but she wasn't going to let that bother her.

It was already six o'clock by the time Malin made her way back up the trail toward the commander. Hardy presented her with her rifle and it was good to feel the weight of it on her shoulder again. She would have given Mauser a pat but he gave a warning growl and a few shrill whines.

The medical team had taken Deputy Willoughby downhill to the waiting ambulance over an hour ago. He had been slammed in the back of the head and his face was a map of bruises. Other than that, he would be back to work in a few days.

"How are you doing?" Commander Ashton said, taking Malin to one side. "Need a few more minutes?"

"No, sir. I'm fine."

"Make sure you keep drinking. It'll keep away the shakes."

Was she shaking? Were her teeth chattering? She knew her patience and skill was about to be tested and she didn't want to add physical strength to the mix.

"It's not your fault the suspect killed himself," Commander Ashton whispered. "No one could have seen that coming. I normally require an officer to head right back for counseling."

"I'm fine. Really."

"When we find Hannah she'll feel more comfortable talking with a female. But I understand if you need time—"

"No, no, sir. I'm OK."

"Good. I was hoping you'd stick around."

It was a well-known fact that female officers rarely tried out for SWAT. There had been one in the K-9 unit for two years but she had recently transferred. The best they had up here was a traumatized female detective with no SWAT training whatsoever.

A bruised sky overhead and the distinct smell of rain threatened to make progress more treacherous. What if Hannah was coiled in a ball and half buried under a pile of leaves, eyes open and no longer seeing. Malin tried to swallow the bile that had settled in her throat. Tried to think beyond the negative.

"I spoke with Temeke," Commander Ashton said, straightening to his full height. "Told him we'd found his gun and radio. He couldn't remember losing either. Total blackout."

"You called him when?"

"About fifteen minutes ago. He was asking after you. I told him you were trying to talk a man down. Might want to give him a call. Let him know you're OK."

Malin checked her phone. One missed call from Mac Webber, hopefully with a comprehensive internet report, and one from Temeke. She dialed Temeke's number as they waited on the trail.

"Listen, love, I want you back for debriefing," Temeke said. "It's important you speak to someone. Doesn't have to be me. Hell, talk to Fowler if you have to."

"The suspect's dead, sir. Shot himself. And we still haven't found Hannah." There were a few seconds of silence and she angled the phone away from the commander. "We need to get going. It's getting dark."

"Blimey, Marl, one more person doesn't make a difference."

"You wouldn't say that in a general election."

"Marl, get your sorry ass back here right now!"

Malin felt her face twist. "Sir, this isn't the first time I've helped traumatized people. I've even tried to calm down an out-of-control colleague."

"When?"

"I'm doing it now!" She hit END and caught the grin on Commander Ashton's face.

"Ready?" he asked.

"Ready, sir."

"You know he thinks very highly of you," Commander Ashton said, picking his way under a low hanging branch. "Says you're disciplined and you don't despise the details. Sounds like you hate failure."

"I do."

"You need to make room for it. We all fail from time to time and when we do we just pick ourselves up and keep at it."

She felt a flush to her cheeks as he gave her a helping hand over a boulder, where a tree branch provided a useful ladder.

"So, what was your assessment of Lee?" he asked. "Might help to talk it through."

"Said he'd took a hit a while ago. Couldn't remember when. Crack would be my guess."

The commander took a stick of gum out of his top pocket, bit off the wrapper and offered her one. "At least you didn't rush in."

Malin nodded. She was still shaking but tried not to show it. "He was a ticking time bomb. I had no idea what I was walking into."

Passing through what appeared to be a tunnel of trees, she slogged after the commander whose stride had already out-paced hers by several yards. The officers behind occasionally paused to survey the area in circular motions dogs wearing smiles and lolling tongues and from what she understood, air-scenting for raft particles.

Mauser's snout hovered inches above the forest floor accompanied by the occasional whine. Then a loud bark. Looking up, Malin could see they were directly below the tramlines and to her left were two rubber tires marking the start of the debris field. They had to be close.

"Did Temeke mention why he thought we'd find Hannah up here?" she asked, assuming Temeke must have passed on his thoughts.

"No, but my guess it's hard for anyone to find."

"We've just re-opened a case," she said, jogging his memory. "Andrea Irwin and Maria Velasquez. Two girls brought to the foothills, sexually assaulted and then killed."

The names rang a bell judging by the look on his face. "One disappeared in a mall parking lot and the other…" He had to think for a moment. "Outside Walmart. Both ended up someone where on Tramway?"

"Correct."

"Did Lee say anything significant?" he asked.

"He kept mentioning *she* and *her*. Could have talking about his mother for all I know."

"Yeah, well every perp has his little vacation from reality."

"If we find Hannah, sir, she'll be required to give a positive ID. There's no one else living who can do it."

The woods fell silent for a while and wind whispered through the trees. Malin hoped Hannah was not injured and that she would survive the ordeal psychologically.

For as long as Malin had been walking behind the commander, she had been talking to herself. Low murmurs of prayer and self-assurance that Hannah would be found.

She looked over her shoulder and saw the officers were catching up, Mauser sniffing and giving alerts. It wrestled her from each savage thought and dispelled the cold fear in her stomach.

The commander paused on the track to give them time to catch up. "Dogs scented Hannah to three piles of clothes. Men's t-shirts, water bottles, food wrappers and an empty backpack. He must have thought it would distract the dogs, while, *he*—whoever he is—was running downhill thinking he was invisible."

"Unfortunately, he stumbled across me," Malin said, knowing the commander thought otherwise. In a sick way, it was a lucky strike.

"Did he use threats?"

"Nothing degrading," Malin said. "Didn't try to depersonalize me. But then I'm a cop not a call girl."

"I'm sorry?"

"My guess is he finds his women online. Mainly to feed a drug habit. The only difference in this case is that Ella Gibson and Rachael Trandahl weren't raped. The other two were."

"So he's dialed it back?" he asked.

"No... well, I've never seen it. Unless he was cooling off between attacks because someone was on to him."

"Or he's working with someone else."

Malin knew it was a disturbing possibility and two suspects was a complication they didn't need.

Commander Ashton pointed at a boulder, where a framed plaque recorded the events of the impact site.

"I wanted to point out this is where the Martin 4-0-4 prop plane hit. If they'd been another forty feet higher they might have made it. Anyway, there's wreckage everywhere so please treat it with respect."

"Yes, sir."

Making way for Officer Hardy, who was being pulled along by a howling dog, she noticed part of the fuselage leaning up against a boulder; two fragments separated by a tree. Red painted registration numbers had faded with age and an *In Memorium* plaque secured to the metal. She wished she had time to read it.

Up ahead, she could see part of the wing and a chunk of engine, some of which resembled pleated furnace filters dented and twisted out of shape.

"Hannah?" she called.

Then behind a portion of the fuselage she saw a trail of rope—twisted hemp, by the look of it—where each strand was no more than a quarter of an inch thick. There were brown smears along the inner edge and it was clear this is what the dogs were after.

But there was no sign of Hannah.

FORTY-SIX

"That sick sonofabitch!" Malin said, both hands gripping her rifle. "He's moved her."

She felt Commander Ashton's hand on her arm, heard the words she knew he'd say. "She might have escaped."

Malin held back a sob. "He knew we were headed this way. He had Temeke's radio for crying out loud."

"We're all exhausted, brains on overload. I suggest you take a breather."

She knew the dogs had already worked five hours with short breaks in between. They could work six at a stretch but they would need at least two hours break. With only one hour remaining, time was running out.

Barely listening to comments from the medical teams on how rough the terrain was and how to watch for gullies and canyons, she poked among the leaves, anything to keep her mind active. But something caught in her throat and made her chest tight, feelings of hopelessness she'd been suppressing all day.

The moon was high above the trees surrounded by a gossamer of clouds. Other than that, the only light came from the occasional flash of a camera while technicians bagged evidence accompanied by the soft murmur of voices.

Malin's phone pinged and she looked down to see a *how's-it-going* text from Temeke. Telling him about Hannah was the last thing she wanted to do. Telling him about the bloody eye she gave Lee was a use-of-force complaint she didn't need.

She caved in and dialed his number. "How are you feeling?"

"Hip's giving me jip. They made me walk around the nurse's station three times. Know how far that is? So I got to thinking anything's better than this. If I can walk, I can work. Bad news is, I can't put my feet on my desk."

"You should be at home in bed."

"Now look who's talking."

Malin heard the sound of a gurgling coffeemaker and the clank of mugs. He was a raving insomniac.

"Do you remember anything, sir? About the shooter."

"No. Can't remember anything between calling you yesterday and waking up in here. But I can remember everything else."

Malin shuddered at telling him about Hannah but there was no easy way to do it. "Hannah wasn't at the crash site."

"Yeah, I heard. I was listening in on the radio."

"Look…" she said, rubbing her forehead in the hopes of fending off a headache, "I need to ask you something."

"Go on."

"He tied her up. There were ropes and there was blood…"

"How much blood?"

"Smears. I'm guessing she was tied by the ankles and wrists."

"Should tell you a few things," he said. "The blood indicates she struggled to untie herself. It also tells you he was gone long enough for her to do it."

"So if Lee had been found a quarter of a mile from here, either he was on his way back up to the crash site where Hannah was, or he was on his way downhill because she had made a run for it."

"And then you came along which put a sodding damper on his parade," Temeke pointed out.

Malin chuckled. Defeat and disgrace were instantly replaced with confidence.

"He was hallucinating when I found him. If he's our guy, it doesn't look good, sir."

"Don't kid yourself," he said sharply. "You know he's your guy."

"Was." Malin stiffened.

She'd tapped into her intuition and could only come up with a single killer. Not opportunistic. Someone who knew Rachael Trandahl intimately. She had originally likened the killer to Childers, where rejection had led to a death and latterly, a botched kidnapping.

But she had been wrong.

When she thought she was out of options, Lee was a suspect she hadn't anticipated.

"Where would you go if you were running from a killer?" she asked. "Hypothetically."

"Downhill. That's where the parking lot is."

Simple. Screamingly obvious.

"Do you think she's still…?" She trailed off, waiting for him to take the lead.

"There's a good chance she's still alive. So get your ass out there and keep looking."

She hung up and scanned the trail. A sliver of light poured down between the branches casting a bluish tinge on the landscape.

Then a barking dog, lips leaking trails of drool, wedged itself behind a tree. Not to lift his leg, as it turned out, but to squeeze through a narrow fissure with his handler, shoulders angled to allow himself through.

Two more K-9s lurched in the same direction, officers following in single file. They were off again. Heading along a narrow path that snaked between the boulders. If it wasn't for flashlights, visibility would have been demanding.

Apart from the gentle thud of feet easing from one bend to another, the only other sound was the distant trickle of water. As they came out into a clearing, two of the dogs gave bark alerts.

Malin hoped it wasn't another pile of clothes to discourage them or bad news they'd have to cart down the mountain in a body bag. While each negative thought collided with the next, she made a pact.

No more thinking.

The dogs were almost running now, veering to the left and ducking under low hanging branches. To her right was a slope of evergreens and towering cliffs. Malin could make out the thin blue line of the horizon and the shimmering lights of Albuquerque in the valley. There was something different about it, something unique to New Mexico. They say the city lights are luminescent; something to do with the landscape and geology.

It was almost half an hour before one dog lay down at the foot of another large boulder. Commander Ashton held up a hand and ran his flashlight across the path. Part of a white outsole lay curled in the grass and blood smears trailed to the edge of a near vertical face.

Malin walked forward and peered over the edge. Her blood chilled as she stared down in paralyzed disbelief. About fifteen feet below and lying on a narrow ledge was a little girl.

"What have we got?" Commander Ashton shouted as he pushed his way between a huddle of officers.

"Ten-year-old female," Malin said, eyes fixed on the blue t-shirt inscribed with the words *Her Royal Ten-ness*. "Bleeding but conscious."

There was no knowing the nature and extent of Hannah's injuries. As two medics rappelled down to the ledge, Malin could only stare through a mist of tears as they hauled her up on a litter.

Hannah whimpered as they set her down. It was a good sign, but the vomit on her shirt warned of a possible head injury.

Malin handed her rifle to Hardy and crouched beside her. She studied glazed eyes that stared off in the distance as if an unwelcome image had lodged itself there. Then tears and shudders.

"Hannah… Hannah, can you hear me?"

Malin had read that where victims suffered a complete shutdown, the brain could no longer process the things around them. In this dissociative state, anxiety had moved in on its own terms, refusing to give the victim space.

"Hannah, I'm a police officer," she whispered. "We've come to take you home."

FORTY-SEVEN

Malin overheard Commander Ashton radioing the mobile command center. Dai Trandahl was on his way.

"You'll see your dad soon," Malin said, tucking the blanket higher over Hannah shoulders.

There was no reaction to the comment. For a heart-stopping moment, Malin realized she had been so focused on getting Hannah to speak that she hadn't looked closely at why she couldn't.

Lee was the monster every kid feared. He had dragged her from her home and tied her up inside the shell of an old plane, where a broken window in the fuselage was the last glimpse of a world she once knew. Her own mother was the very example of that threat and Hannah would have believed every word of it.

Malin felt the commander's hand close around her forearm and steer her away from the litter.

"I need to take GSR samples from her," Commander Ashton whispered. "Not expecting them to come back positive but just in case."

Malin hoped any gunshot residue would come back negative. The procedure must have seemed odd to Hannah, and possibly somewhat insensitive but as officers' voices simmered around her, she seemed more settled.

"See if you can keep her talking," Commander Ashton said. "Find out what this guy looked like. We've got no concrete evidence Lee was responsible. Even expedited DNA tests can take days."

"She's making a little progress. But I can't push her, sir."

"It won't hurt to ask," he pressed.

She couldn't see too well with all the flashlights directed at the emergency medical teams but she had a weird feeling his eyes burned right through her.

Malin returned to the litter and crouched down beside Hannah again. "Feel like talking?"

Hannah was disoriented, brain hardly firing through the shock. Malin knew the lights inside were about to blink off altogether. But before they did…

"I know you've been through a lot, but if there's anything you can tell me, anything at all, it'll help us to understand what happened."

There were no tears, no voice choked with fear as she described Lee. But the bland whisper that followed gave Malin a chill. "He… he killed my mom. He wanted to kill me."

"You're safe now," Malin murmured. "We won't let anything happen to you."

"My mom… is she still down there because… it's getting cold."

Malin was the one choking back the tears now and nodding over a dry throat. "Everything's going to be OK."

"The dogs… will they hurt us?"

Malin felt her eyebrows shoot up. "No, the dogs won't hurt you. They're the ones that found you."

Hannah seemed to study Mauser as he fell in step beside the litter. Hardy told her that Mauser had super-human gifts. Especially the one where he could sniff out aliens as far as Roswell and whale poop in the Puget Sound. That he had three hundred million olfactory receptors up his nose compared to about six million of hers. There were a few more amazing dog facts Hardy felt the need to explain before they arrived at the parking lot.

Malin was taken aback by Hannah's stamina. It couldn't have been easy for her but somehow the danger and the blackness of the situation had been briefly forgotten.

It was almost eight thirty by the time six deputies brought Trandahl in by car. He folded Hannah in his arms and whispered words Malin couldn't hear. Mayor Oliver was waiting with his son Adam in the parking lot and, of course, Jennifer Danes with a camera crew. Some people never give up.

When Adam saw Malin he came right over, gave her a big crushing hug and showed her his newest model dinosaur. It was a Deinonychus, he said, known for having more than sixty razor-sharp teeth.

He was chirpy and appeared not to carry any scars from his kidnapping earlier that year. But she couldn't tell just by looking at him. There must have been times when he thought about it, cried about it even. Malin was just happy she and Temeke had been the two detectives assigned to his case.

Mayor Oliver took her hand in his and greeted her with his usual gushing cheerfulness. "I want to thank you for everything. I'm sorry to hear about Detective Temeke. Will you give him my regards?"

"I will, sir. We'll need to talk to Mr. Trandahl. When he's ready."

"Of course, although I should mention that he's particularly partial to the key lime pie you offered him. Said it was almost as good as mine."

"You bake?"

"Of course." The mayor grinned a little wider. "I'm a single dad now. Well, Adam sees his mother in the summer but for the most part it's just us guys."

"How is Adam?"

"Doing good. He's a great kid and I know he'll help Hannah through her nightmares. You?"

"I'm keeping on." She was almost dead on her feet.

"It's good to see you again, Malin."

Malin sank into the driver's seat of her unit and watched the mayor's car pull away. It was eerily quiet and her skin prickled with sweat.

For the first time in her hopeless, dog-eared career, she felt like a winner.

FORTY-EIGHT

Clouds hung in a thick, frothy layer as the horizon blazed with the first touch of dawn.

Saturday morning. Malin flipped through the online news while munching on a piece of toast.

Child Found Alive in Foothills Confirmed to be Hannah Trandahl.
By Jennifer Danes
Journal Staff Writer

A little girl found alive in the Albuquerque foothills has been confirmed to be missing Hannah Trandahl, authorities said today.

"We are grateful to learn that the little girl found by police late last night is confirmed to be Hannah Trandahl." Duke City Police Commander Fred Hackett said in a statement. "Hundreds of people searched tirelessly for a mother and a child and although we are saddened at the death of Rachael Trandahl, we are happy that Hannah is finally back home with her family. Our work still continues as we try to find answers."

Autopsy results for Rachael Trandahl are still pending, police said, and it's not yet clear how both mother and child went from their home to the foothills.
Hannah Trandahl, who is a student at Lincoln Middle School, was at home with her mother early on Thursday morning when she disappeared...

Malin was wrenched from the news by an incoming email alert from Mac Webber. He had sent a report of Rachael Trandahl's recent messages and a three-page diary she had written in Word.

"Rachael Trandahl didn't have a profile on WebDoc," Mac said over the speaker phone. "Nor was she speaking to a Nobel Prize-winning psychiatrist on the faculty of Harvard Medical School. She was talking to someone with the screen name NightCrawler. I might point out that his profile had been created from an IP address at the Tony Hillerman library."

"So she was having an affair with this guy?"

"Correct. But if you read the last six or so messages, it looked like he was trying to back off. Ella Gibson was the problem. There were a few text messages to a number we tried to access by GPS and WiFi. But it's no longer in any mobile network. Rachael mentioned watching the other party on a family tracker app using the shared location feature. Whether it was reciprocal or not, we don't know."

Malin thanked Mac and hung up.

She skimmed through a long list of steamy messages which plateaued for about two months and then tailed off sharply after Rachael mentioned marriage. It was these final messages leading up to Rachael's disappearance that interested Malin.

NightCrawler: *You getting divorced?*

SilentAdmirer: *I don't see any other way.*

NightCrawler: *Sounds a bit drastic.*

SilentAdmirer: *Makes perfect sense if we want to get married.*

NightCrawler: *I never said anything about marriage.*

SilentAdmirer: *You said you wanted to move in together.*

NightCrawler: *You're twisting everything out of context.*

SilentAdmirer: *Does this have anything to do with the woman in the green stucco house? Because your picture is all over her Facebook page.*

NightCrawler: *I'm calling you now.*

SilentAdmirer: *Not answering.*

NightCrawler: *Pick up. Please.*

SilentAdmirer: *I'll see you tomorrow. Same place. Same time.*

There were no further messages from *SilentAdmirer* as if she knew her time on the ever-ticking love clock had run out. After all, Rachael wasn't about to pick up the phone and make it easy for him. No, her last message was the dangling carrot *NightCrawler* couldn't resist.

Was Rachael Trandahl about to tell him she was pregnant? Or was she planning to kill him with the loaded gun under her pillow?

Malin dialed the number of the evidence custodian and asked him to check the log for a possible handwritten letter addressed to Dai. It should have been among the items removed from the house.

Then she texted Dr. Vasillion for the paternity results of Rachael's baby. The response was immediate. Dai Trandahl was the father. The results for Jewel Hansen were exactly as she expected. Gunshot wound to the head. She had been killed in the early hours of Wednesday morning.

Malin exhaled loudly. She reached for her gun, holstered it and got into the car. Grabbing two cups from the BadA$$ coffee stop, she decided to call Kate Harroway. Hopefully, Kate would be happy to hear from her which, due to playing telephone tag was a big assumption.

"I appreciate you talking to me," Malin said, surprised to get Kate on the first ring. "Any chance of meeting at your office or at the command center?"

"Command center would be better. I can meet you tomorrow morning at nine."

"That would be great. Can I ask you a few questions now?"

"It's a good a time as any."

Malin heard the squeaky wheel of an office chair and gave her a few seconds to sit down. "I heard you worked with Rachael Trandahl and I wondered what you thought of her."

"I liked her," Kate said, clearing her throat. "We all did. She had a great passion for the place. Very friendly with the customers. I used to assist her with teller training and debit card balances. Branch security was fun. She organized simulated incidents, you know, when an actor's brought in to pretend he's a hitman. Richard Meinz. He does regular performances down at the KiMo Theater."

Malin knew Richard. He did de-escalation scenarios at the police academy.

"She rewarded her staff," Kate said. "Gave bonuses every Christmas." Malin heard the sigh and knew Kate was bracing herself for the tougher stuff. "Then she changed. Began avoiding me."

"Do you know why?"

"It was after I lost weight. I bought some new clothes and got my hair colored. The boss here was pretty hot. Pretty single. Then *she* started dressing up and changing her makeup. She'd be in his office with the door shut. I thought they were talking about me."

"What made you think they were talking about you?"

"I could see them through the blinds and she'd sometimes look over at me."

"Did Rachael talk to you about it?"

"No. But I heard her on the phone talking to her mom. She said her husband wasn't happy with the long hours she was working. That her career was more important than her marriage. I'm guessing her mom gave her a sharp talking to because she went all quiet and withdrawn after that. I did wonder if she was pressing our boss for the promotion."

"What promotion?"

"He told me in confidence that he had been transferred to the New York office. Didn't want anyone to know. But I figured he'd at least told her. Maybe she was after his job. I guess that's what I meant by she'd changed. Didn't have the same... warmth."

"Was your desk outside her office?" Malin asked.

"Yes."

"So if her door was open, you could hear everything?"

"Oh yeah. *Everything*."

"Were you responsible for keeping her calendar?" Malin powered down the car window and punched in the code for the rear parking lot.

"Yeah I was. It was odd... there were these mysterious family emergencies she kept having. It happened about three times a week. Usually around lunch. Woman to woman, I wondered if she was pregnant. Did she have any other children?"

"No, no. Just the one." Malin squinted through the windshield and felt a twinge of sadness. Rachael *would* have had another baby had she lived. "These appointments she was having, your boss must have known where she was."

"No, he was usually at the gym and I didn't want to let on that I was curious. Or that I thought… well, that I assumed it was gynecological."

"Is there anything else you can tell me about Rachael?" Malin turned off the ignition. "Anything jog your memory?"

"I got the sense he didn't like it when she kept closing his door."

"Did he tell you he didn't like it?"

"Not in so many words. He just told me that he was keeping his door closed from now on. That if I needed anything to come straight in."

"Did that worry you?"

"No. But I know it worried her. She'd ask me why his blinds were drawn. I had to make stuff up. Like he was in a teleconference meeting with the chairman of the board. I could see it made her nervous."

"How long did this go on for?"

"About two weeks. Then she was gone. I never heard from her again. But I saw her outside sometimes. Sitting in her car. Watching through the window."

"Did your boss see her?"

"Yeah. He called security. I thought it was sad, honestly. Wanting a promotion that much that she lost her job over it. He never said anything to me. But I could see he was relieved after she'd gone."

"Thank you. I appreciate you talking to me. Oh, one last thing. When's Mr. Dowie back from his hunting trip?" *She knew it was Thursday. Just needed confirmation.*

"Thursday morning. I left a message on his cell phone that you wanted to talk to him. Hasn't he called you?"

"Not yet. But if you hear from him it wouldn't hurt to give him a friendly nudge."

"I'll do that."

"See you tomorrow." Malin hung up.

Malin slid the cup carrier onto her lap and eased out of the car. The lobby was buzzing as usual. Sergeant Moran was dealing with a woman's plea about a stolen car and the toddler next to her was bobbing up and down and squealing for the toilet.

Malin headed upstairs to her office and opened the door with her elbow. Temeke was taking his customary ten minutes, head thrown back against his chair and a few light snores. Sat up when he smelled the coffee.

"You read my mind, love."

Malin reached for her phone and checked the headlines. "Luckily the media hasn't got wind of Lee's death yet. I don't expect it to be announced until we've got proof of his true identity. He had a southern accent. Think Matthew McConaughey in *A Time To Kill*. 'Aah reckon he haden made up his maand yet.'"

It got Temeke laughing and wincing all at once. He told her he knew exactly what a southern accent was like without her massacring it. And *southern* was too general a term. Someone's south could easily be someone else's north.

"The mayor said to send his regards," she said, spotting a walking stick leaning against the wall. "He was sorry about what happened. I saw Adam too."

That put a big smile on Temeke's face and he fired off a few questions about Adam. Seemed like his old self to Malin, except that he was all banged up and embarrassed.

"I hope you didn't see what the nurse did to me," he said. "Thermometer in my mouth and two in my ass. I knew darn well she was grinning while she did it. Said she knew I was a smoker. Asked me when I quit. I told her it was a year ago. She said that was a bold-faced lie. More like a couple of months and I wasn't to think of smoking in the toilet because she'd smell it on my gown. And no, I couldn't have another cup of coffee otherwise I'd be headed for the freezer. A stinky decomp with a toe tag is what she said. That's why I checked out."

Malin wanted to give the nurse a pat on the back. It was about time someone lectured Temeke about his coffee intake, which had increased since he'd quit smoking, and was now through the roof.

"I'm glad you're feeling better," she said. "You look better."

"I look like I've been in a knife fight."

"At least you're alive."

He nodded as if the likelihood of death hadn't occurred to him. Malin steered him back to the present with a recent update from Dr. Vasillion and a detailed report on her conversation with Kate Harroway.

"You have to wonder if Hannah saw her mother die. Whether she'll ever get that memory out of her head." There was a pause as she gathered herself for the next question. Braced for it. "Gossip on the vine says Hannah shot you."

"What?"

"Yeah, that's what I said. Little girl, big gun. Doesn't seem real, does it? You heard something up there... saw something?"

"I wasn't paying attention, love. That's all there is to it. Should have interpreted the sounds better because he doubled back around and that's when it happened." He frowned and shook his head. "I can't remember, love. I'm sorry."

"It'll come back."

"Serena said she knew I'd get shot one day. Become a vegetable for her to look after. I was just in the wrong place at the wrong time."

"I'm glad she came to see you."

"She wasn't there for long. Said now I was on the gimpy side I was going to need a cane. She asked me if I thought it was time to hang up my hat. I said no, it sodding wasn't. Then there was this uncomfortable moment where she said she was sorry and I said nothing. It's been the problem since day one and I'm over it."

Malin couldn't work out whether Serena was sorry he wasn't ready to retire or she was apologizing for abandoning him.

"Getting used to the cane?" she asked. It was a stupid question. He'd probably only used it once.

"I can't say it's a chick magnet. But one of the nurses said 'I own it', which I believe is meant as a compliment. Anyway Serena asked after you. Sent you a high five for making the arrest. She's gone to stay with some friend in Ruidoso. I told her you'd look after me."

Malin felt a slight buzz at the comment. Call it excitement but the weight of it startled her. Felt like she was floating.

"I'm sorry I didn't have time to get those emails you asked for," she said, changing the subject. "I was on my way to your house after interviewing Emma Burnett. But Midgely's call took priority."

"Emma Burnett?"

"Manager at Trandahl's gym. I ran a background check on her. Clean as a whistle. Not even a parking ticket. She said that Trandahl confided in her. Rachael had been using a dating profile to look at women. One in particular. Ella Gibson. We know Ella was an escort but that doesn't mean she didn't escort both men *and* women."

"Trandahl have any idea Rachael liked women?"

"No. But he asked Emma to contact Ella. Find out if she was seeing anyone. Evidently Ella was. But that could have been a polite rejection on her part or it could have been the truth. And there's something else. Dai told Emma that Rachael wasn't exactly good to Hannah. Forgot to pick her up from school and slapped her around a few times. She even shut her in the closet."

Temeke wrapped both hands around his coffee cup and pursed his lips for a moment. "Maybe it's time we go out on a limb."

"And do what?"

"Interview Hannah. Yes, she'll need an adult present, and yes, it will have to be her dad."

"Hackett will never allow it."

"He will if the GSR comes back positive."

Malin saw him flinch as if one of his wounds was giving him trouble. Or from the sheer weight of what those GSR results might reveal.

"Changing the subject, sir, I was concerned by what Fowler said in the hospital. He was chatting about—"

"Yes, love. Heard every word. You know, when I get out of here I could hire someone."

"What do you mean hire someone?"

"Two pieces of pipe and a bicycle chain. He won't be quite so *chatty* after that."

Malin felt the squeal of laughter bubble in her throat and then her phone emitted a light jingle. She knew who it was without looking. "I need to take this. It's Matt."

"Think you can handle it?"

She nodded. She could handle pretty well anything.

FORTY-NINE

After Malin had stepped out into the corridor, Temeke thought of his visit with Serena.

A lazy smile, a frosty bedside manner. She neither kissed him nor touched him, refused to sit in the chair Lieutenant Alvarez provided. Even when they were alone, she stood awkwardly, hands clutching her handbag and eyes roving around the room, never settling.

Temeke had been the one to open the conversation, asking her how she was and if she was OK.

She said yes, shook her head a few times and gave him the same old spiel. That he should retire and find a decent job with fewer hours. Didn't he realize how difficult it was for a spouse? Temeke remembered nodding a few times. Not to indicate his agreement, more to hear her out. To see if she wanted to give it one last try. He was sad they had no kids to entice her. More for her than for him.

The weirdest thing was how she began talking about a sick friend in Ruidoso. How Dolly was living in a tiny little cabin in Bonita Park and dying of cancer and how there was no one to look after her. What was worse, Temeke had never heard of this friend before.

Dolly? Who the bloody heck was *Dolly*?

He wondered if the whole scene disgusted her because she kept shooting the urinary bag a grimace and then jerking her head toward the door. She must have been feeling stabs of shame and yet she couldn't bring herself to admit it.

When she left, Luis tried to make a joke of it. Kept asking where the fire was. But his face was white as if it had unnerved him too.

Temeke could still hear her listless tread along the corridor and he was ashamed to feel the prickle of tears in his eyes. But the truth was, it provided a rare moment of clarity in the darkest season of his life. A decision he hated to make.

He looked out of the office window at a humming bird; a tiny missile, hovering back and forth in some kind of aerial dance. It reminded him of Serena—dazzling in the sunlight and mysteriously disappearing into the shadows. There, and then gone.

He was snapped out of the thought as Malin came back into the room. Head down as if she'd been put through the ringer.

"Let me guess," he said. "He's been putting the moves on Alice?"

"He's engaged to Jennifer Danes."

Temeke felt his jaw drop, noticing the flat tone in her voice. "Looks like he's hung himself with his own rope, Marl."

"Don't get huffy, sir."

"I'm not being huffy. I just don't get what he sees in her. Thinks he's some numbnut celebrity, all smiles and waves, when he doesn't have the balls to tell you in person. He's a career criminal. That's all there is to it."

"So what are you gonna do? Call the boyfriend police? He wanted more than I was prepared to give. Just like captain you-know-who in New Jersey."

Temeke didn't like her defeated tone. He had that feeling again. A cocktail of spite that got his pulse revving.

"Let me tell you something. That worthless sack of monkey-shit has overestimated his importance. Seems to think he's entitled. Once Jen finds Alice's number in his coat pocket—and she will—he'll find himself out on his ass. Again. How do you think he's been able to remain single for so long? Think he planned it?"

He saw her face crumple with laughter, while darkly, his thoughts turned to Matt's balls and how far he could twist them up his scrotum.

"Get a grip, Marl. You're moving on and up. He's moving down and out. Your career takes first place. Unless you meet someone worth dating and that's a shot in the dark these days. They all want to try on the plastic handcuffs, let you take the dominant role. It's hardly a compliment is it?"

Malin was pensive, the way she always got when the present slipped away and quickly became the past. "No, sir, it isn't."

"Is there any reason why you can't call me David?"

"Just doesn't feel right."

"Better start making it feel right." He could see uncertainty behind those dark eyes. "Is there anything else?"

"After I hung up on Matt I got an email. It was originally sent to you only you never answered."

Temeke looked up at the clock. Already past midnight. Couldn't have been from Hackett. He was already tucked up in bed. Probably Fowler jawing about not wanting an invalid on his squad.

"Sergeant Thompson from Homicide," she said. "They want you back."

"Blimey, Marl, the day just keeps getting better and better."

Temeke should have been happy. But somehow the feeling wasn't there. Northwest Area Command had the monopoly on the best detectives; the ones with the sharpest minds. The ones who salivated at the thought of a murder no one else wanted. But his move, at the time, had been like a punishment posting and now he didn't feel ready to go back into a specialist squad.

Homicide—the highlight of his career—had been hostile. They said he was impossible to work with and now... now that he was vulnerable and at his lowest ebb they wanted him back?

If there was one thing he knew in his gut it was guilt. He couldn't take it as a compliment but then again, he didn't have a choice.

"Not sure they deserve you," Malin said.

"Not sure I deserve *them*." Temeke hadn't been at Northwest Area Command long enough to leave a footprint. It had been less than a year.

"After Midgely's trained," she said. "That's what I understood."

"She's a good cop, Marl. You can have my desk, if you like. Save Luis knocking the damn door against the back of your chair."

Temeke couldn't quell the feeling of sadness. He'd become accustomed to their shared office, the times they spent together in the evenings talking through each case. He'd miss that. He'd miss her.

"Hackett talk to you about a promotion?" he asked, seeing the shake of her head. "As a matter of fact, I told him you could do with seniority, especially in the shark tank. You have an opinion. I want to make sure it counts."

"Thank you, sir." Malin's eyes, briefly animated, suddenly sparkled with sorrow. "It won't be the same without you."

There was a loaded silence, a questioning look which if he had interpreted it correctly was somewhere between surprise and relief. It wouldn't be unreasonable for him to ask her out.

"We'll do coffee," he said. "And lunch."

"Of course."

Her voice was composed, but he could tell how hard she tried to contain her excitement. And he knew, with a twinge of guilt, she would walk through fire for him.

"It'll be like old times. I've got a great recipe for chicken and red wine. Dodger likes it. Does all that yowling cats do."

She was watching him intently, dark eyes gauging the interaction as if it carried great weight. "I'd like that."

"Good. So it's a date." A statement not a question.

FIFTY

Temeke turned the volume up on his computer to watch a live report from Channel 4. All the networks were crackling with pictures of Trandahl.

Cynn Wrigley, chief editor of the *Duke City Journal,* stood in front of the mayor's house with a mic. The other hand was pushed deep into the pocket of a ridiculously expensive jacket.

Mr. Dai Trandahl filed a police report shortly after two o'clock today, alleging that a waiter assaulted him outside the Ranchers Club. Mayor Oliver saved the day by escorting Trandahl to his limousine. Demonstrators shouted obscenities on the street corner and a fifteen-year-old hurled a snow cone at the passenger door. It seems Mr. Trandahl is being targeted for his part in the murder of his wife.

Temeke raked a portion of skin under the bandage on his shoulder and flinched.

There were days when it was good to be a detective. When you got a confession and watched the scumbag being cuffed and lead away. Then there were days when you had to apologize to a suspect because the browbeating he got was uncalled-for. Temeke wasn't looking forward to any mention of emotional use of force where Trandahl was concerned.

Given the urgent nature of the live commentary, and the articles in every local tabloid, everyone had spent the first few days of Hannah and Rachael's disappearance combing through statements and conducting interviews.

Trandahl's interrogation had turned up nothing but horror over a wife who at the beginning of their marriage was sweet and thoughtful and wouldn't have dreamt of running off with another man. When she went missing only the worst could have happened, right?

Wrong.

Rachael had been easily lured away by her former boss. A man with two faces, who during the day wore pressed shirts and a short boxed beard and at night, rocked the homeless look; ripped jeans and worn-out shoes. He hung out at local bars getting high, met Ella Gibson online and his career went to pot.

Literally.

More importantly, Trandahl knew Rachael was talking to someone on the internet. Why didn't he tell Malin during his first interview? Because he was embarrassed and his ego couldn't handle any media attention. It seemed the only answer Temeke could come up with.

"You watch. The minute Trandahl gets out of the car you'd think Hollywood's biggest star was taking the red carpet."

"He should be hunched in the back of a patrol car," Malin said. "Can't blame the public for exacting revenge for what he did to his wife."

"If you read the reports, you'll find Trandahl responded with the full force of his middle finger."

"He's a nut. He's going out looking for trouble. Why can't he order take-out and stay at home?" Her voice carried through the open door all the way to Hackett's sumptuous suite and she let it. "Maybe our illustrious commander can dismiss Trandahl's behavior because of his connections, but the rest of us can't."

"If he did contract Lee then why's Hannah still alive?"

A slammed door at the end of the corridor made Temeke flinch, followed by the sudden jingle of Malin's phone. It was Hackett and by the sounds of it the gunshot residue had returned positive.

"Know what that means?" she said, after he'd hung up. "We're interviewing Hannah tomorrow morning."

Then, like a cloud inching across the sun, Temeke remembered why he hadn't returned fire. Lee had been crouched down with Hannah in front of him, hands wrapped over hers as she held the gun.

"He used Hannah as a human shield. Got the upper hand and took the shot I couldn't take. Terrible thing to do that to a kid."

"Thank God." She blew out a big O of breath. "It would have been hard to prove if you hadn't seen it."

"I was too focused on her…"

It took him all of two minutes to tell Malin while her eyes took on the dead-in-a-coma look and to cap it all the redundant noises she made were hardly edifying. Hmmm… yes… I see.

What did she see? It was the brick wall everyone saw when someone else was telling the biggest horror story of their lives.

She looked down at her palms, massaged her middle finger and tapped the keyboard again.

He quickly changed the subject. "Got the forensic report from Matt Black and transcripts from Ella Gibson's computer. She was a junky all right. There were emails back and forth between her and Jewel Hansen. When Ella couldn't get the money Jewel owed her, she sent Lee to get it instead. Lee clearly had a way with women but when Jewel refused to pay up he killed her."

Malin sucked in her bottom lip, finger dancing over the keyboard, writing an email or whatever it was she was doing. He couldn't see, because they sat opposite each other. Her computer monitor bucked up against his.

Her desk against his.

Temeke studied the view beyond the window. The Sandia Mountains tapered at its northern tip, stretching toward acres of tumbleweed and sagebrush. He had come to love Albuquerque and for all his rantings on how well the police did things in England, he knew he'd found his niche.

He also studied her. When he first met Malin he would have described her as fragile. Too fragile perhaps to be doing police work. She'd lost her mother, and a boyfriend who might have been attractive were it not for a tough job policing the rougher parts of New Jersey. Her own past wasn't exactly squeaky clean—bars full of cigarette smoke and a coil of strippers around every pole—but then whose was?

Now he saw her as strong, mesmerizing, someone he found hard not to stare at. She was someone you could love bone-deep and someone he knew he couldn't live without.

He scrunched a KitKat wrapper into a tight ball and launched it against the wall. Malin caught it on the downward slide and carefully placed it in the bin. Her wrinkled brow reflected exactly how Temeke felt.

Bushed.

"What if Trandahl left home exactly when he claimed," she said. "Contracted Lee to kill Rachael and then reconstructed the scene to fit the intruder scenario. Before you ask for the motive, Trandahl finds out Rachael wants to leave him. Trandahl doesn't want to go that route because of the publicity over Uncle Bill's case earlier in the year. After all, someone might make it into a movie."

Temeke felt his mouth widened. "Lee wasn't stupid and Trandahl isn't that smart, love."

"I happen to think Trandahl's way smart. Did you see any nosy neighbors rushing to provide a statement? They didn't see anything because one: they were all getting ready for work at that time in the morning and two: it all happened around the back of the house, not the front. That's smart, if you ask me."

"Let me do us both a favor and cut to the chase. We know the timer switch for the sprinklers was set to come on at nine o'clock at night for thirty minutes and then again at five o'clock in the morning. Meaning the lawn would have been saturated at the time of Hannah and Rachael's disappearance. There were no tire tracks or footprints in the backyard the following afternoon. If you recall, the weather that day was cloudy. No sun to burn off the moisture."

"So he loaded the bodies into the Highlander and drove out of the garage as if he was going to work."

"Only he didn't use the Highlander. He used his bike. You said Porsche confirmed it." Temeke gave her one of his signature dark-eyed looks. The ones that told her he needed to come clean. "Nor was Trandahl sneaking around inside his house last night, hoping to get rid of things he didn't want us to find."

"You were there?"

Temeke nodded. "According to the bodyguard at the mayor's mansion, Trandahl was passed out on his bed. Plastered, apparently."

The ever-chiming cell phone and Malin's eyes dropped for a second to skim over the incoming call. He guessed it was Matt and he knew she wouldn't answer.

For some reason that made him glad.

"Shall we go over the internet report?" she asked, turning her phone face down.

Temeke wheeled his chair around to her side of the desk and scooted alongside her. He scanned the sections Mac Webber had highlighted.

"So, here's what we've got," she said. "The laptop at the Trandahl house was used primarily for the usual social media sites—Facebook, eBay, car enthusiast forums and what we originally thought was porn surfing under the screen name *SilentAdmirer*. Not only that, Rachael kept a Word document—a diary of sorts—saved under the initials CD. There are no dates recorded, except when the document was created and subsequently updated. You might want to read this."

Temeke studied the words for a long time, mesmerized over Rachael's torment. A symbol of desperation. A woman's plea for attention. But there was no timeline. It would be hard to date Rachael's thoughts.

You keep saying you'll call and then you don't. It's so easy, isn't it? How you just turn it on and off like a switch. First it's me. Then it's her.

I found her profile and saw pictures of you in the park. All the places you promised to take me.

You were smiling then.

Now your status says Single. *Makes me feel all used up and dirty.*

Even though I'm not your number one girl I like to think I am. It's the silences I can't stand. Not knowing if it's your footsteps I hear on the stairs or just my imagination. You and me. Our special time.

Then I start to wonder, are you OK?

Why don't you call?

Malin's eyes flicked to the window briefly and then back at the screen. "Rachael seeing all those pictures of him with Ella... it had to have been the trigger. Weeks and months of holding it all in and not knowing where to turn. She was watching him through a tracker app, which she could have set up on his device without him knowing."

"These aren't just random thoughts, Marl. Every word counts. When she writes, *are you OK?* I believe she was concerned enough to stalk him."

"He was a womanizer. Why bother?"

Temeke met her gaze, unable to tell if there was an underlying meaning behind the comment.

He wanted to ask her.

But not then.

Malin turned back to the screen. "She talks about having a nervous breakdown in 2008 where she was hospitalized. Then recently she lost her medication."

"For how long?"

"A week. She would have had serious withdrawals. Then she finds her meds in the glove pocket of the car. Takes thirty milligrams because she thought she needed to make up for lost time. But nobody takes thirty mils. They start low and work their way up. I read a case recently where a woman didn't follow her doctor's instructions and the withdrawal, including the stress and depression she suffered, was fatal. She killed a man by stabbing him over thirty times and couldn't remember a thing. It says here Rachael found herself on the couch at home with no memory of how she got there."

I have a dream. You running along a dark road and me standing inside someone's house. There's blood on the floor. And then there's her.

I wanted to warn her. Wanted to tell her what you really are.

A monster. A cold-blooded monster.

But you got there first with all your hate and now she's dead.

How could you have done that?
You paid her rent! What else were you paying for?
You took something from me. The way to feel normal.

Now I'm afraid someone will find out what you've done. There's so much shame. Like I'm the one to blame and you're innocent. It's cruel after everything you promised me.

I'm all wrung out inside and you don't care.
I want to forget. You. Her. All of it.
And now finally a text from you.
I don't know if I should feel happy or sad.

Malin's eyes scooted down to her lap this time. "In that split second of pain, anger, whatever you want to call it, Rachael made a decision. To warn Ella before Lee arrived."

Temeke tried to ignore the slithering voices in the back of his head. Saw the look on Malin's face as if her emotions had changed rapidly from pity to outrage.

"Part of me wants to feel sorry for Ella," she said, "because Lee owed her money. He didn't want to pay, so he shot her twice. That's the difference between murder one and murder two."

FIFTY-ONE

Temeke sat in the interview room with Agent Stu Anderson and Captain Fowler. They were waiting for Trandahl.

Temeke's walking stick was hooked over the top of the table and the shaft swung back and forth for a few seconds.

Suddenly he was tired. For some reason, Stu's and Fowler's voices became white noise. Like a gushing tap Temeke wanted to turn off. He felt as if he was detached, that all this was happening to someone else. That the people in the room with him were strangers.

Temeke checked his watch. "By the way, while I was barely conscious in hospital Malin told me something."

"You like her don't you?" Fowler said.

"She said something that made me want to retract all the things I ever thought about you."

"Apologies are a rare treat coming from you."

"You were right about Malin. About her having seniority."

"I never said she would have seniority," Fowler said, raising an accidental eyebrow. *How incredibly stupid.*

"It's not that hard to imagine. Take Scarlet Midgely for instance. The officer who, if you recall, gave you the one finger salute. You may have put her on your *do not call* list but I happen to think she's perfect for the job. She reminds me of a determined housefly and that's exactly the type of person you want in your squad. You don't seem too impressed by this information?"

Fowler gave a whimper that wavered dangerously between laughter and a tantrum. "You mind telling me what this is about?"

"Well, it's really about me—and here's the part where you pretend you know nothing about my return to Homicide—which means Malin will need a new partner. And that my friend requires *two* desks. Not just the one."

"Hey! Stop beating each other down." Stu had a habit of barking orders at officers who didn't have his FBI status. "Can we read the letters, please?"

If they had been outside a bar Temeke would have grabbed his Glock, chambered a round, pointed it at a spot on Fowler's forehead and given him a third eye. Instead he took two deep breaths.

"Letters, gentlemen," Stu repeated.

It still puzzled Temeke how angry he got when Fowler was in the same room. He just hoped the walls were thick enough to keep the same anger wrapped when Malin interviewed Kate Harroway next door.

It also dawned on him during those few precious moments that it would be a miracle if he could even keep his private life wrapped. Malin was on her way to his house to forward Hackett's email and he sodding-well hoped she hadn't been snooping around on his hard drive. She was the nosiest person he'd ever met.

He patted the two letters from the evidence custodian. One addressed to Dai Trandahl and one addressed to Lee. Both sealed.

And very quickly unsealed by Temeke's enthusiastic thumb. He read the one addressed to Dai out loud and then passed it around the table.

Dai

There are things I want to explain. Things I've found so hard to tell you.

I know I've been impossible to live with and I know you've been patient trying to work through everything with me. Suggesting counseling, new drugs, vacations, telling me I didn't have to work anymore. But the thing is I'm heartbroken.

I know you think it's unfair that I've taken myself off into this inaccessible place. So you can't talk to me, or reason with me, as you keep begging to do. Space and time is what I need now, anything to work through my feelings. To understand where Hannah fits best in all of this. With you. With me.

I want it to be with me and I know when the time comes you'll contest it. What loving father wouldn't?

This has nothing to do with you, Dai. What you did or didn't do. I don't have the same love I once had and I don't know why.

It would be a lie to say my feelings have just run out. They haven't. I'm in love with someone else.

R.

Temeke had been through the drill of showing surviving partners evidence that might help them work through their grief. But nothing as coldhearted as this.

Rachael had explained her decision to leave but had failed to offer an apology. Reading between the lines, she valued Lee above Hannah and Dai.

For Trandahl, there would be no unwinding, no erasing of the pain and for the first time in Temeke's career, he dreaded telling a man that his wife was about to file for divorce and seek child custody.

He was reminded of everything he had lost in the last year. His standing with Homicide which, although recently restored, would require extensive boot-licking. He tried to fend off a sudden wave of homesickness because Malin, Hackett and the rest of the team were as close to family as he got.

And then there was Serena, who was likely scratching out a *Dear John* letter in what could only be described as a long, drawn-out deluge of self-pity. He didn't enjoy being cynical, but there was no point wishing for a reconciliation when his partner was no longer his.

Tapping his fingers on the letter addressed to Lee, he tore it open. Found the ultrasound image of an unborn infant. The same infant Dr. Vasillion confirmed was Trandahl's. Perhaps Rachael never knew. Perhaps with all her deep-seated insecurities, she wanted to pin the baby on Lee.

Temeke turned the envelopes face down on the table just as the door creaked open. Sergeant Moran escorted both Trandahl and the mayor into the room.

Temeke stood and shook the mayor's hand. Noticed his eyes dropped briefly to the tray of coffee and donuts on the table before giving the hint of a smile.

"Good to see you." The mayor shook hands with all of them and took a seat in the corner of the room. "I would ask you to work your questions carefully. My nephew is traumatized. He's had no sleep since… since this happened."

Captain Fowler assured the mayor that all questions would be handled sensitively. He then gave Temeke an intimidating stare.

"Good to see you," Temeke said to Trandahl.

He noticed his eyes were dull. He was hung over as hell.

"I'm doing OK." Trandahl took a seat opposite Temeke, Agent Anderson and Captain Fowler.

Temeke spoke into the tape recorder.

"We are at Northwest Area Command, Michael King and Richard Smith Memorial Substation at 10401 Cibola Loop Northwest. I am detective David Temeke of the Duke City Police department. Present also in the room is special Agent Stu Anderson of the Albuquerque FBI and Captain Rufus Fowler of the Duke City Police. Also Mayor Bill Oliver and Mr. Dai Trandahl."

Temeke then pointed his questions directly at Trandahl.

"What I want you to do is to start with Thursday morning, in your own words and at your own speed, and provide a step-by-step re-enactment of what happened."

Trandahl took a deep breath. "I woke up, got dressed, went downstairs and made coffee. Had something to eat… two eggs, two pancakes." Another breath. "I made Hannah a peanut butter and jelly sandwich. Put it in her backpack. Then I went back upstairs and cleaned my teeth and made the bed. The spare bed. That's where I slept that night."

"And all this time Rachael was still asleep?"

"I peered around the door before I left and she appeared to be asleep."

"Did you speak to her?" Captain Fowler asked?

"No, sir, I didn't want to wake her up."

"And you didn't notice anything odd? Blood or open doors."

"No, sir."

Captain Fowler gave Agent Anderson a do-you-have-anything-to-add-look.

Temeke interpreted Stu's blank stare as a no and continued with his questions. "If you'd like to tell us what happened next."

Trandahl thought about that for a second, his face pinched. "Hannah was up. I gave her a hug and told her I'd put a PB&J in her backpack. I asked her to be good for her mom and not to get distracted at school. She got a B in geometry recently. Not a bad grade in my opinion. But Rachael thought it was. Then I left."

"So both Rachael and Hannah were in the house before you left for work. Is that correct?" Temeke asked.

"Yes."

"And there were no indicators leading up to Rachael and Hannah's disappearance? By that I mean arguments, packed bags."

"Correct."

"That you went to work that day at seven-oh-five. Got to work at seven thirty and had a normal day. Except for not getting a response to your telephone calls, which you stated began around lunchtime."

"That's right."

"According to the cell phone report, you called Rachael seven times on her cell and twice on the landline. And it didn't begin around lunchtime. Ten-thirty, it says here. Why so many times?"

Trandahl thrust out his bottom jaw, teeth clenched over his top lip. The sigh was loud.

"She... she hadn't been herself over the last few weeks and I thought it was the drugs." Trandahl averted his eyes as if the topic was uncomfortable. "Last Tuesday night, I went to bed around nine, nine thirty. Something woke me up an hour later. Rachael hadn't come to bed. I went downstairs and found the car was gone. The laptop was on in the kitchen. The screen is set to time out after five minutes, so I knew she'd just left."

"Did you try calling her?" Temeke asked, eyeing Trandahl over the rim of his coffee cup.

"No, I didn't want her to know I was worried. In any case, it was easy to hack into her stuff because the password's saved in the computer. She'd been on a singles site, talking to someone called *NightCrawler*. No picture. Not much of a bio either. But it was what she said that... well, clued me in. I don't give a hoot who he is. I just want to know how long it had been going on."

Temeke knew what he was asking. It was the same question any father would ask. "The baby was yours. Our forensic pathologist confirmed it."

Trandahl began bawling, kept looking up at them all and wiping his eyes. The mayor gave Temeke a pointed glance while patting his nephew on the shoulder.

"Would you like a break?" Temeke asked, grabbing a box of tissues from a nearby shelf and plopping it on the table.

"No, I'm OK. I... I'm tired, that's all."

"I'll be brief." Temeke turned over the letters, both sealed in evidence bags. "For the record, is this Rachael Trandahl's hand writing?"

"Yes."

"I'm going to ask you to read the first one out loud and then I want you to tell me, to the best of your knowledge, what you understand it to mean."

Trandahl took his time reading the letter and then he studied the ultrasound. His voice was low. "Rachael ran off with a playboy and had her heart broken."

"Why didn't you tell us this on Thursday afternoon?"

"I didn't want Rachael to think I was snooping around her stuff. She hates that. I wanted her to tell you."

"She was having an affair. Surely that was important enough to—"

"I was trying to be loyal and I was trying to understand what had happened. Had she run off with this guy? Made it look like a murder?"

"You mean spattered blood all over her pillow so she could disappear without a trace."

"Something like that. Yes."

Temeke saw a flicker of so-what in that look as if Trandahl didn't give a toss. That he was trying to man-up to the idea of Rachael having a boyfriend and the impact it had on his marriage. He'd likely probed even deeper and found out about Ella, but he wasn't talking.

"You said you saw a stranger in the neighborhood that afternoon."

"I don't recall." Trandahl waved a hand in the air as if there was a group of no-see-ums above his head. "Possibly."

"Either you did you didn't."

"I did."

"Remember what he looked like?"

"Blond. Buzz cut. Stocky. That's all I remember."

"Taken a polygraph?"

"Already done that."

"How did you do?"

"Passed, if that's what you mean. I'm not taking it again, OK? I haven't done anything wrong. Why do you even think I have? Why does anyone think I have? I've never hurt anyone. Rachael? Now that's different. Hannah wets the bed, gets a B and there's a dent in the wall!"

"What makes you think Rachael did anything?"

"Because she's always hollering and telling Hannah to keep out of her business. Hannah told me… she told me she heard her mother talking to some guy on the phone. Four times it happened. She didn't like the way her mom was acting around him, didn't like the touching. That's when I sat my little girl down and had it out with her."

"When was this?"

"Tuesday. Wednesday. Evening. Sometime."

"So sometime last week?"

"Yeah, yeah." Trandahl closed his eyes and then opened them again. "After I went to bed, Hannah said her mom took her for a drive up to the heights. They watched this man and this woman in some house. Hannah begged me not to tell her mom. She was scared. You know what her mom said? She said, if you ever tell your dad our little secret, you'll never see him again. You bet Rachael did something."

"How were you feeling at this point?"

"I dunno. Scared. Rachael would go on and on about how horrible Hannah was as a daughter. How useless I was as a provider. She didn't have any failures, except the killer side the world's not supposed to see."

"You don't mean that literally."

"Depends how you classify a *killer*. She never did a damn thing for Hannah. Had the nerve to tell my little girl she was on her own no matter how sick or frightened she was. All in the name of not bonding at birth… or whatever crap it's called. I'm sure you know about infants who aren't breast-fed. Hannah wasn't."

"And I'm sure you know about mothers who suffer significantly because they can't breast-feed?"

"It wasn't because she couldn't. It was a choice. Bottle or nothing. And as you've probably worked out, I did the feeding. Especially at night."

"Well, bully for you, Mr. Trandahl." Temeke caught the mayor's steely expression and continued. "So you're saying Rachael's lack of bonding compounded Hannah's feelings of rejection? And perhaps your resentment?"

"Over discovering some kind of internet activity between my wife and another man, hell, yeah. Come on guys, this isn't rocket science. Wife runs off with a man on the internet. All because it suited whatever selfish purpose Rachael had at the time. Him... obviously. A weakness she couldn't resist. And Hannah... my little girl, sees it all through the bedroom door. The one person she was supposed to trust. The one person she wanted to be like. Oh, I can talk about what Rachael did. She crushed Hannah and she destroyed our marriage. If that's not someone with a killer instinct then I don't know what is."

Temeke realized Trandahl had been chalking it up to emotional and psychological abuse, but not once had he given Rachael a break for her illness. Whatever it was she had suffered, whether it be sweating, racing heart, dizziness, thoughts of suicide, Trandahl had no mercy.

"Nobody can say she was sexually frustrated," Trandahl said. "I offered myself to her regularly."

Temeke didn't want the conversation to slide into marital intimacy and quickly responded with, "Did Hannah describe the house she visited with her mom?"

"Green. That's all I know. I just wish I'd confronted Rachael. I wish we could have talked about it." He took a few grounding breaths. "Hannah said she'd seen a man in our house early in the morning. He used to leave out the back door apparently. I didn't believe Hannah at first. I didn't want to. Then I saw all that stuff Rachael had written on the computer. Stalking someone called Lee. Then Ella Gibson. I know because I pulled up the search history. Rachael's a doll, don't get me wrong. But Ella, she's a heart attack."

"Doesn't make it right?"

"Doesn't exactly make it wrong though, does it? I'd have given Rachael a divorce if that's what she wanted. But I'll tell you right now. There wasn't a hope in hell she was taking Hannah. Over my dead body!"

FIFTY-TWO

Malin drove along Guadalupe Trail to a white house surrounded by cottonwoods. Temeke's pad was set back from the road with a suspiciously artificial lawn that had seen better days.

As she pulled into the driveway, the air was clouded with odiferous smoke. Neighbor Fats Riley was diligently burning weeds under a wide-brimmed hat. She could see the whites of his eyes as he attempted to hide his curiosity without completely turning his head.

There was a large tree in the middle of the lawn. Didn't look like an apple tree. More like a maple. But on the west side of the house were two fruit trees, one with a small birdhouse swinging on a lower branch.

She opened the lid. A front door key partially hidden under a scatter of shelled bird seed.

She unlocked the deadbolt and opened the door. The alarm began to beep and she entered the code to silence it. Pale blue walls—eggshell, she thought it was called—and bright white trim.

It was a cottage as Malin saw it. Functional and serene with hardwood floors, built-in shelves on either side of the fireplace and small front windows that gave an almost panoramic view of three sides of the house.

The bitter odor of burnt coffee alerted her to a near empty carafe and she walked into the kitchen, reached over the counter and switched off the hotplate. No auto shut-off. The machine was too old for that.

She opened the window. A lulling murmur of wind and next door, an empty swing dangling back and forth under the maple tree. The smell of freshly mowed grass and the acrid stench of alpaca dung.

Then a distant memory threatened to break through her focus.

The steady rhythm of another swing, another yard and the spurt of children's voices. A little girl swinging higher and higher, skinny legs pumping forward and back, fingers gripping the chains. Why did childhood always feel like another life?

She chased it away with thoughts of cleaning. The house was a mess. A piece of toast idled beside the sink and there was a sticky trail of butter on the countertop. Everything she saw confirmed a lived-in feel: a dent in a cushion, a bottle opener on the couch and a copy of the *Duke City Journal* slouching on the carpet.

It was the first time she had seen the intimate side of Temeke. Inside his house now and not parked in the driveway as she had done before.

Images of a crime scene spooled inside her head, questions as to how difficult it would be to hide any forensic evidence if she were the killer. For a seasoned detective with a well-thought out plan, it would have been easy. For a layperson, fingerprints might have been lost with the use of gloves, but not trace evidence; hair, fibers, soil particles under a shoe.

How calm would a killer need to be to rid himself of those?

A soft meow drew her head upward. Dodger was on the staircase, tail swishing back and forth on the carpet and a trail of gray molt between the banisters. He lifted his head at the snap of her fingers, followed her into the kitchen and sat in front of a blue plastic bowl.

The pantry was stocked with last year's cans of spam, baked beans and tuna fish and two boxes of cat food—Seafood Medley. She filled the bowl and the feeder; a white tower with a wide-angle camera. Probably had night vision function and real time sharing.

Malin looked down at the open laptop on the coffee table. Her fingers grazed the mouse and she tapped out the password he had given her. The home screen had at least twenty icons, but there was one that captured her interest. *Photos*.

Twisting her head from left to right, she berated herself for being paranoid, yet she toyed with the idea of Temeke walking in suddenly and witnessing this blatant intrusion into his private life. The gentle *tick-tock* of an English carriage clock on the mantel reminded her she didn't have much time.

So she swiped and clicked through pictures of Serena in a white beaded gown and veil, standing in front of San Felipe de Neri Church in Old Town. Serena, hand over brow at the Ruidoso Downs Racetrack, Carlsbad Caverns, Bandelier National Monument.

Her stamp was everywhere.

Malin forwarded the email from Hackett to Temeke's computer at work. The attachments consisted of a contract, job description and a generous pay grade for Scarlet Midgely. Nothing to explain why Hackett had sent it to Temeke's personal email in the first place. Unless he knew she had Temeke's password and didn't want her to see it.

Another email hung there waiting to be opened, dated yesterday.

From Serena.

David. I'm so sorry about dinner. I should have called. I don't know what made me feel so uncomfortable about meeting you. Shame perhaps.

The past few months have been hard. I've thought about it a lot. You offering to help with the car and being there when I needed a friend. I know you're not asking for much. Just a little companionship.

I was out of line thinking someone else could make me happy. Someone I thought the world of and who thought so little of me. There's no justification for what I did. Seems I've lost everything. God has a way of breaking down pride. He's certainly broken mine.

Maybe one day, David, when I've healed. When I've come to terms with being on my own. Maybe then. Serena.

Malin felt the frown deepen as she shook her head. What would Temeke do when he read it? A red pen edit? Or would he wait for her as he always had.

Malin knew what Temeke believed in. He believed that if there was any chance of doing something worthwhile it was protecting those who couldn't protect themselves. It was waking up every morning with a mission; to preserve the peace and protect the community. He took his job first.

She right-clicked on the email and was about to mark it as 'unread' when she noticed an icon on the home screen.

WMan.

It couldn't have been more than a suspicious coincidence but she couldn't let it go.

Her heart was beating so fast it filled her ears and so did the twanging of crickets that drifted in through the kitchen window. She scrolled through pages of emails, copies that had been sent to her nearly a year ago and, more recently, cut and pasted phone texts.

Wingman: You can learn so much from a marriage. A seemingly perfect family. A vulgar secret. A frantic search. There's only ever one way out.

It had always been wild speculation on her part that *Wingman* was Ole Eriksen, *The 9th Hour Killer*. She still had nightmares about it. Tied to a chair in a burning cabin and falling under the piers beneath the deck. Crawling through smoke... She had no idea how she got out but she could still smell soot and blood and it still made her gag.

Or that Wingman might have been a judge, a prosecutor, a repeat felon. But *Wingman* was none of these. He had disguised himself as a humble veteran, someone who no longer saw himself in the lead. He had been flying off her right wing for the last year. Warning her of threats, watching her back, boosting her career, even at the cost of his own.

There were letters Temeke had sent to Commander Hackett and the Chief of Police. Letters of commendation, endorsing her bravery and recommending her for the True Blue Award because she had gone above and beyond her duty in every case.

She no longer needed a mentor.

Malin forced herself to read the many questions she had asked *Wingman*. The many answers he had given her, going deeper and deeper until the shock melted away.

It had been an education.

FIFTY-THREE

Interview room 3 was mainly silent except for the sound of sobbing. Kate Harroway took off a pair of retro cat-eye glasses and raked another tissue from the box. She asked to be excused. Said she wouldn't be long.

Well, she *was* being long and Malin had exhausted her limited supply of patience. Her eyes kept veering out of the window where a jet dew a chalky line across the sky. Even Maggie beside her was huffing and that wasn't like her.

They both decided to play *monkeys always look* and when that failed to entertain, they decided to sing a version of *What'sa matter you? Hey. Gotta no respect? Ah, shaddap you face.*

Until Hackett squeezed his belly around the door and wagged a finger, told Maggie to go into the bathroom and check on their witness.

Malin rolled her eyes. It wasn't like Kate was lost. The bathroom was less than fifteen feet from the interview room and she was probably just slapping on another layer of makeup over that perky little nose.

The fan clattered overhead, air twitching a piece of hair on her forehead and she was tempted to scratch, scratch, scratch.

What the hell is wrong with you?

Her own voice amidst her tangled thoughts. She was still mad at Temeke. Then she blew out her cheeks and did it all over again.

"Right," said Maggie, pulling a reluctant Kate behind her. "She doesn't feel well. Gippy tummy."

"I'm sorry," Kate said. "This whole thing makes me want to vomit."

It made Malin want to hurl too, only she was a dab hand at keeping her emotions in check. Wasn't she?

"Take a seat," Maggie said, pushing Kate's shoulders down on the nearest chair.

Malin got that niggle of irritation every time Kate blew her nose and squinted through her glasses. If she couldn't see through them then why was she wearing them?

"After I spoke to you yesterday," Kate said, "I felt bad. There were a few things I wanted to tell you but I needed to talk to Cal first. So I texted him. But there was no answer. He always answers."

Malin heard the soft lisp in her voice. It was attractive, just as Kate was.

"Last Wednesday evening I followed him after work. OK, so I was stalking. But I was worried about him."

"So let me get this straight," Malin said, staring at blunt bangs and hair so black it could have been colored. "You followed Mr. Dowie why?"

Kate wiped her nose and bounced a look from Malin to Maggie who was anchoring the box of tissues to the desk with both hands.

"He'd been distracted these last few days. Forgot his office key three times and that's not like him. Walking around in a daze like all of us have suddenly become white noise. But then I found a prescription bottle of Roxicodone in his desk drawer."

"How many tablets?"

"One hundred. It was filled about a week ago."

So Kate had checked that too. "Do you know what that is?"

Kate shook her head.

"It's an opioid analgesic," Malin said. "Very habit forming. Another name for oxycodone hydrochloride. Didn't happen to count how many he'd taken?"

"No, ma'am. But he liked his booze."

Nasty combination. "Did you confront him?"

"He said he was addicted to a lot of things. Never been high before he met this friend. With her it was all day, every day. Sometimes it was two days straight and then he'd fall asleep and wake up again with another hit. She had a hold on him. It scared me." Kate dropped a wadded up tissue in the trash can. "Anyway, after he got back from having lunch with the chairman he was all rattled. Closed his door. Started emptying his drawers, pulling things out of the filing cabinet and shredding it all. Had a strange look on his face while he was doing it. Then he left. For about an hour."

"And that's when you followed him?"

"No. That's when I went into his office. The drawers were open and the whole place was a mess. I didn't know if I was supposed to tidy it. So I texted him. He said he'd do it when he got back and not to worry. But I was worried because the shredder was jammed and he'd taken a file out of the office."

"Was that unusual?"

"Yeah. He's a neat freak. And it's against office policy to take files out of the office."

"What type of files was he shredding?"

"Rachael Trandahl's personnel file. There were all kinds of stuff in there. Weird stuff."

"Like what?"

"Poems."

My, my, little Katie you're an even bigger snoop than I thought. "Poems, you say?"

"Love poems."

"Whose handwriting?"

"His. He liked Shakespeare. Had a book on his shelf. Told me to read it, only I couldn't make head or tail of it. So I gave it back."

"Anything else in the file?"

"A letter he'd written to the chairman before Rachael was let go. It said she'd committed company personnel and resources to a customer Cal didn't trust. As her manager, she'd gone over his head."

"So it was a violation of company police and code of conduct?

"True. But it wasn't Rachael's fault. Cal oversaw every letter that went out. He would have signed it off."

"So he blamed her for something she didn't do?"

"Yeah."

"And why would he do that?"

Kate shrugged. "He wanted to get rid of her, I don't know. I thought maybe he had a thing for her and she rejected him. I know how stupid that sounds, but you have to wonder if it was personal."

Malin was getting a very clear picture of Mr. Dowie. Freakily neat and freakily freaked out. By what, she couldn't imagine, but with a jammed shredder what else was he supposed to do with file he wanted to destroy.

Hurl it in the dumpster?

She made a brief note to call Waste Management for their collection days. If Rachael Trandahl's file was anywhere it would be in the landfill by now.

"Anyway I found two photographs on the floor by the shredder." Kate scooted two photographs across the table.

"It's her, isn't it? The woman in the news. The one that got shot."

Malin stared at the pictures, felt her neck prickle with ancient warning. They were so far removed from the polished images the media had published. Selfies. Head slanted upward and a hint of mystery coiled behind her eyes. Natural. No makeup.

The girl—she could hardly be called a woman—had the palest face Malin had ever seen. Especially in New Mexico where you couldn't dodge the sun unless you lived under a rock. Ella Gibson could be called beautiful if you liked your sculptures smooth and cold.

She passed the photographs to Maggie while keeping her eyes on Kate.

"I heard him coming back so I shoved the photographs in my pocket and nipped to the coffee station. I tried to look normal but I know I didn't *feel* normal. Him in his office and me unwrapping a coffee filter, grounds everywhere. Then he told me he was leaving. Wouldn't be back tomorrow morning, or the morning after that because he'd been fired. I started crying and he gave me a hug. Said he saw it coming. Then he left."

"And you followed him."

"Yeah. I hate being kept in the dark, don't you?"

"You didn't think it was a good idea to put those photos back where you found them?"

"They *were* on the floor where I found them, only when he came back they weren't. So if I put them back when he came in the second time he'd know something was up." Kate stared down at her hands and bit her lip. "I knew it had to have something to do with *her*. I don't know why. Just a feeling."

"Was anything else missing?"

"I don't believe so." Kate twisted the corner of a tissue and dabbed it behind her glasses. "I've always done whatever Cal told me. Covered for every tiny mistake. But this was different. It *felt* different. I couldn't bear to think of what he might have done. There were things I wanted to ask him. So I rushed out into the parking lot."

Malin allowed herself a general overview of the lot, which she Googled using a hybrid map.

"I kept two cars behind," Kate said. "Kept my head down and eased in behind him on the freeway. He drove along Paseo all the way to Louisiana. Hung a left and then parked on Elena Drive. I couldn't exactly sit there on the curb idling behind him so I drove up the hill. I saw this woman through my rearview mirror. I know it was her." Kate tapped a fingernail on the photograph. "I made a U-turn at the next intersection and drove back down the hill. His car was still in the driveway but there was no sign of him. Oh, God, you don't think he had anything to do with it?"

"Not unless Cal isn't his real name. Does he have an accent?"

"South Carolina, I guess."

"Can you describe him?"

"Tall. Six something. Fit. Hair about this length." Kate patted her shoulder. "Beard. Nice looking."

"Does he go by any other names?"

"Well that's the thing. I found a driver's license in his office a month ago. Spitting image of Cal. Only it wasn't Cal. It was a Lee Petit."

Malin opened her mouth, then closed it again. There were things she couldn't say, not even to Kate. "Tell me something. What type of car does he drive?"

"Most of the time he drives a gray SUV. But when that's in the shop I've seen him drive a sedan. White, I think. Why?"

FIFTY-FOUR

It was early afternoon when Temeke received a call from Hackett. He had requested Hannah's interview be moved forward to two o'clock today. Too many sleeps after the incident and a victim was likely to omit valuable details in their statement.

Hackett wanted them to meet in his office, where there was a couch and a plate of cookies on the coffee table. Mainly for Hannah but also to lessen the blow that Trandahl had, up until now, been under the microscope.

Temeke sat in an easy chair staring at a wall of paintings; large black and white photographs which had been splattered with red paint. He remembered doing something similar in tenth grade.

The school had a picture of Einstein hanging in the lunch room, which he and his brother artistically disfigured with a few flicks of ketchup. The punishment his father dished out was, if Temeke recalled, a damn good thrashing in the woods behind the soccer field. But a punishment shared was a punishment halved in his eyes, even though that particular thrashing left both of them with knees like jelly and bums on fire.

Temeke felt a stabbing pain in his shoulder and he failed to suppress the wince. He'd already thrown up his breakfast into the shiny white toilet downstairs. Now he felt a twinge in his stomach too.

"You overdoing it?" Lieutenant Alvarez asked, standing in the doorway.

"Just need some ice."

"Or a good night's rest. Malin's worried about you. Said you were working nearly thirty-six straight. You're on restricted duty and any more ibuprofen and you'll burn the lining in your stomach. I'm not an expert in post-traumatic stress, David. But crimes like these are like a heart attack. You either pull through or you don't."

"Blimey, Luis, that was tactful."

"Are you sleeping?"

"Like the dead." It was a lie. He hadn't slept at all and Luis had read him right through to the bone.

"I've got some Melatonin if you need it."

Temeke shook his head. He didn't want Luis digging around next door and pulling out a host of health-nut tinctures for insomnia. It would only knock him out, what… six minutes sooner. And there was no proof they would work on someone who had been marinating in caffeine since he was ten.

"It's Hannah I'm worried about," Temeke said. "Especially with the press camped out in their front yard."

"Her dad's been contacted by the victim advocates. They'll offer mentorship and support for as long as they need it."

Temeke knew there were financial resources and grants available to victims of violent crimes. He hoped the community would rally and that Trandahl's boss would give him time off.

"Yeah, you're right. She's got plenty of resilience. It's what got her through the ordeal in the first place."

That wasn't why Luis was propped up against the door, head poking around the frame. Temeke knew he was checking on him. Committing his image to memory as he sat in this particular chair and in Hackett's hangar of an office.

Because Temeke would be gone soon. Back to Homicide.

Voices in the corridor forced him to stand, hand gripping his walking stick and he wondered when the fire in his hip would go away.

Reaching out a hand to Trandahl and the mayor, he looked down at Hannah. He told her she looked lovely in a red dress and a new crossbody leather handbag.

Malin brought an icepack, dumped it on his knee. Told him to stop staring at her and to jam it against his shoulder.

Temeke opened the collar of his shirt and placed the icepack against his skin. He listened to Malin as she took the lead, black hair piled on top of her head in an intricate bun and, if he wasn't mistaken, some kind of frosty lipstick.

There was something else different about her, at least something he'd sensed in the last twenty-four hours. When he had asked her a question her answers were snappy, eyes floating over his shoulder like he wasn't there. It was the embodiment of his worst fear.

She knew.

"When did your mom start getting angry?"

Malin's voice snapped him back to Hackett's office and the little girl who sat opposite with a scrunched up tissue in her hand. He wondered why his mind kept clicking in and out of the present. Why he couldn't focus.

"I don't know. It's been a while," Hannah said.

"You said your mom found your diary. Last weekend, was it?"

Hannah stared at the floor. "She threw it across the room because I wrote 'I hate the way mom treats dad.' I didn't mean to upset her."

Temeke couldn't stop assessing Hannah. Dark blonde hair to her shoulders, legs long and spindly beneath her dress. The same legs that kept her away from her attacker. The same mind that kept her alive.

"She said I wasn't allowed to have a diary if I didn't write nice things. I don't have one now."

Aren't diaries supposed to be private? Temeke thought. When did kids not have rights? When they kept unhealthy secrets and parents had to turn into detectives.

"She said I shouldn't listen in to all her phone calls either. I wasn't listening in. I just wanted her to sign my permission slip."

"Was it a field trip?" Malin asked.

"Yeah. The rock climbing wall."

"The Stone Age Climbing Gym on Cutler," Trandahl butted in.

Malin told Hannah the closest she'd got was the Ninja Fitness Gym but that she was no Ninja nor was she fit. That was the thing about, Marl. Always trying to find ways to bond with the kids. She should have had a kid. Should have been married. But she was married to her job, Temeke thought. Same as him.

"What happened next," Malin prompted.

Hannah took a breath and looked at her dad. He told her it was OK. That she should tell the truth as best she could.

"She liked going out at night. She said it was our little secret. We'd waited until Dad went to bed. She made me promise not to tell."

"Did you like sharing secrets with her?"

"Yes. I liked it when she was happy."

"So where did you go?"

"To see the big houses in the heights. The ones with walls and gates."

"Did you go to one in particular?"

"Yeah, the green house next to the buffalo field. Sometimes there's one near the fence."

"A buffalo?"

"Well, actually they're American bison. At least that's what my teacher says."

Temeke pictured the beasts with their long, shaggy beards and humps. He hadn't seen one near Ella's house, but he could sure smell them.

"Mom parked outside. We watched them through the windows. They were kissing and talking. Mom kept wiping her eyes and pretended she wasn't crying. But she was. I said I was sorry for getting a B in geometry but she said that's not why she was upset. I thought she'd be happy I was with her."

"Would you have preferred to stay at home?"

"Honestly? I wanted to watch reruns of *Friends* but I didn't want to hurt Mom's feelings. She said I could watch the moon behind the Sandias instead and drink caramel milkshakes. She said we had to go and see someone."

"Who?"

"Ella."

"Who's Ella?"

"The lady on the computer. I sometimes watch her with Mom… through the window without her knowing."

"So you'd go outside the house and look in through the window? At your Mom on the computer?"

"She kept locking the door and I wanted to know what she was doing."

Malin smiled. "Could you hear anything?"

"No."

"Why do think your mom was looking at Ella?"

"Maybe she knew her from school. Maybe she wanted to find her in real life."

"Have you been to Ella's house before?"

"Yes. About ten times."

Hannah gave her father quick look and he smiled. Kept saying it was OK. That she was doing really well. Temeke was thankful he was there.

"When was the last time you went to her house to watch?"

Hannah looked down at the half-eaten cookie balanced on her knee. "It was the night before we were stolen."

"On this particular night," Malin said, "what did you see?"

"Ella was talking to Lee. They were holding hands and kissing." Hannah looked sideways at Malin and squinted. "Then he was angry."

"How did you know Lee was angry?"

"He pushed her and it looked like he was shouting. Only we couldn't hear. Than he slapped her. Mom started crying again. She said we had to do something."

Malin leaned forward a little more. "What did you do?"

"She said we had to go inside."

Temeke felt a drag of sickness in the pit of his stomach and his mouth was dry. He could almost hear the dialogue in his head before the shots rang out.

"Do you remember if the front door was open or closed?"

"Closed."

"How did you get in?"

"Mom... she opened the door. It was dark inside. She told me not to touch anything." Hannah inched back into her chair as trying to put distance between herself and the memory. "And then... I heard a bang."

"How many bangs?"

Hannah's eyes scooted to the ceiling and down again. Then she held up two fingers and mouthed the word *two*.

"What did your mom do then?"

"She went to the kitchen and... the lady ... Ella was on the floor. Bleeding."

"Where were you?"

"By the door."

"And your mom?"

"By the patio door. She was shouting at Lee outside. But he wasn't answering."

"What happened next?"

"We left and drove home. Mom kept saying, 'I knew it, I knew he'd kill her.' And I'd have to hand her tissues to stop her nose from running."

"Lee... had you ever seen him before?"

"Yes. He comes to see Mom after Dad goes to work. They laugh and stuff."

"At your house?"

"Yeah."

Trandahl's expression darkened briefly at the word *stuff* but he had the grace not to let it linger. Just sat there with his hands on his knees, smiling at his little girl.

"Did you see him on Thursday morning after your dad had left?"

"Yeah." Hannah said, staring at her knees in awed silence for a moment. "But he never saw me."

Temeke barely heard Malin's questions about the time, how Hannah often woke early and how the man used to get in and out through the patio door at the back of the house. A man Hannah knew as Lee.

Temeke felt prickles of anger crawling up his spine. Rachael had driven to an undisclosed location in the heights to watch the man she had come to love coiled around a woman she had come to hate. And her daughter had seen it all.

"Can you tell me what happened next?" Malin asked.

"They were shouting. It made me throw up."

"Did you stay in your room?"

Hannah nodded. "But I wanted to see if she was OK. So I went to her room. She was sitting up. He kept telling her to be quiet. Then she was lying down and he was holding her, pushing her. He… he had a gun… and a pillow… I couldn't see her face. It was so loud I screamed."

Temeke could visualize what Hannah had seen and heard. The indecipherable chatter of two people in the next door room, rising to a crescendo of shouts before a gunshot.

"I-I tried not to look." Then came the grimace and the tears. "He took me downstairs. Gave me some pills because I was sick."

Hannah's memories were sporadic then, moving in and out as the drugs wore off. She said she woke up in the car and there was no one there so she went to look for her mom. Saw her lying on the ground in the woods.

Or was it the woods?

She wasn't sure. But her mom was wrapped in the hall carpet and every strand of her hair had turned red.

"I kept asking if my mom was OK because she wasn't moving. Lee said she was fine. She'd be up soon to join us at the camp. He wouldn't let me see her."

Images of Lee backing up the hill and Hannah trying to duck and roll out of his arms. How he must have dragged her up the mountain and told her the worst things he could have told a ten-year-old. That cops and K-9s were the enemy.

It was the water that had made her dizzy. She had been plied with pills so she wouldn't remember anything. Wouldn't have been alert enough to call out for help. As Lee took her deeper and deeper in the mountains, he would have told her to feel pity for him because the world was against him.

Hannah wasn't equipped to understand a hard-luck story was a con and now it was a therapist's job to unpick all those lies thread by thread.

"He made me hold the gun. I didn't want to. I didn't."

The rest of her statement came out in a gush of sobs and Temeke could see tears sliding down her cheeks. She didn't bother to brush them away.

More replays. Temeke didn't want to remember. He'd seen it so many times. But as far as he recalled, Lee stood behind Hannah, hands wrapped over hers around the grip. Temeke couldn't recall if Hannah's finger was extended against the frame of the gun but he knew they weren't squeezed inside the trigger guard.

It was Lee's finger curled around the trigger. There was no way the front sight was clear and on target because Hannah flinched and the gun moved out of alignment. That's what had saved Temeke's life.

"He was lying on the ground," Hannah said, looking at Temeke. "He told me to run. So I ran."

Everyone turned to look at Temeke, many sets of eyes glistening. He was suddenly very cold. Melted ice ran down the inside of his shirt. He'd been gripping onto the icepack the entire time.

"You didn't shoot me, love," Temeke said. "He did. I remember now."

Hannah told them how Lee tied her up and how she ran downhill. She didn't remember falling but she did remember Malin's face.

Temeke knew she would piece together the fragments of that night when she was older and able to process it all.

And Malin would be here to unravel it for her when the time came.

FIFTY-FIVE

Three days later, Temeke sat in the board room surrounded by the officers of Northwest Area Command.

Hackett was dressed in the same suit he had on last night. He'd slept in his office again and it looked like it. Sandra Buckingham, his assistant, brought him a plate of dried toast and a pair of sunglasses. It was a beer migraine.

Captain Fowler was his usual snippy self, flashing like a Christmas tree in the corner and giving Scarlet Midgely a glance here and there.

Midge was more spit and dirt than the rest of them and she was a bad-ass cop. So far everyone liked her, including Malin. And that was important to Temeke because Malin had taken over his desk and Midge had Marl's. They would be overseeing Detective Cornwell's double homicide at Hunter's Run Park, which was still unsolved.

Everyone was happy.

Temeke wiped off a glaze maple icing from his mouth. Thanks to *Stand True 4 Blue*, the command center was once again rolling in Krispy Kremes.

"So," Hackett barked, squinting at Temeke as if the light was hurting his eyes. "Any connection with the Andrea Irwin and Maria Velasquez case?"

"We understood Calvin Dowie was on some hunting trip so I called the New Mexico Department of Game and Fish. According to a staff member, all sportsmen are required to fill in an online form requesting vehicle description and license number. Calvin Dowie's name was not in their database of regular hunters. He could have been hunting turkeys in Artesia for all they knew. But there was a Lee Petit. The same Lee who drives a white sedan, sir. The same sedan that has a scrape along the passenger side fender which matches the scrape on Trandahl's back wall. Of course there are worse things than poachers. Liars, for instance, and those guilty of driver's license fraud. Managers who tell their gullible assistants they're out hunting when they're cruising for chicks and getting high in the foothills. The same Lee Petit who, according to Hunters Residential, pays Ella Gibson's rent, which is odd since the real Lee Petit is dead."

"So Lee Petit is Calvin Dowie?"

"Correct. Ms. Harroway, his assistant, confirmed it."

"Any links to Irwin and Velasquez?"

"Andrea, Maria, Ella and Rachael. What a squirrel. Picks up women in parking lots and leaves them dead in the foothills. Only this time, Cal got careless. He left a few prints behind when he emptied Jewel Hansen's purse of cash and bank cards. Dr. Vasillion was latterly able to confirm the blood spatter found on Rachael Trandahl's thigh belonged to Calvin Dowie."

"Probably thought he had it all stitched up."

"He didn't know shit. Had a hell of a career in the bank before he started snuggling up to Rachael Trandahl and sleeping with his junkie."

"So he dumped Rachael for Ella." Fowler smiled and wiped his mouth with a napkin.

"I wouldn't say dumped. More like he was keeping her on a back burner, which was thoughtless given the accessibility of social media and Rachael's state of mind."

"A man with two faces. Quite a part to play."

Temeke gestured to Malin to complete the report. She was, after all, the new senior detective. He was damn proud of her as she stood at the head of the table.

"Since then the CSI teams have completed their examination of Mr. Dowie's residence," she said. "Not only did they find the bloody pillow from Rachael Trandahl's bed but there were boxes in Dowie's garage dating back to 2004. Newspaper cuttings, items of ladies underwear and photographs of Irwin and Velasquez alive in his car and photographs of both ladies dead in his car. Tied with twine. The same twine he used all those years ago to anchor his roses to a trellis in the back yard." Malin took a slug of coffee. She was also suppressing a grin. "Looked like he entertained these ladies and took pictures while he was doing it. On his couch, in his bedroom and in his garage. I can't say I've been to his house. But the field investigators had the pleasure of filtering through all the evidence. This is their report.

"There were citizen complaints pertaining to narcotic activity at Mr. Dowie's address on Topeka Street in the southeast part of town. We also know both Irwin and Velasquez lived one street over on Hinkle and, according to their files, were picked up several times in South San Jose Park for a liquor violation. Mr. Dowie was also present but not arrested.

"When I interviewed Beverly Herrera, it became obvious to me that Rachael never told Beverly about Cal. And so naturally Beverly assumed the *he* she kept talking about was Dai. Rachael Trandahl didn't want her best friend to know she was having an affair with Calvin

Dowie but the connection wasn't through narcotics. He was her boss. A clean-cut bank manager turned drug addict. And latterly a cold-blooded murderer.

"Rachael didn't know what she was dealing with. Nor did she know Dowie was seeing other women. When she retreated more and more into her online world, Trandahl assumed it was because of her depression. Even though they slept apart—him in the spare room, her in the bedroom—he had no idea she was seeing someone else until the week of the incident. And worse, he had no idea it was her former boss.

"We know Jewel owed Ella several hundred dollars. Ella sent Dowie to meet Jewel at the back of Smiths to pay a debt which, as we know, went bad. His blood was found under her fingernails.

"Ella seemed to fit Dowie's romantic ideal but she was also a junkie. When Dowie spent hours on Facebook talking to other woman, this sparked Rachael's worst fear. For a woman who craved love in every aspect of her life, Dowie changing his Facebook status to single, was significant.

"Although Dowie was exercising his right to privacy and wanting out, Rachael couldn't bear it. She had no idea these women were merely supporting Dowie's drug habit. She googled Ella Gibson. Found her address and went out late one night after Trandahl had gone to bed. Why she took Hannah on several occasions we don't know. Trandahl was a capable babysitter and Hannah would have benefited more by being left to sleep.

"The night before Rachael and Hannah disappeared, they saw something different through the windows of Ella's house. Not the intimacy they'd witnessed previously. But anger and violence. Dowie hadn't just gone over there to socialize. He needed a fix and he was also in debt to Ella to the tune two thousand dollars. We know this because our media compliance officer found a sequence of angry email exchanges between Ella and Dowie.

"In the case of Ella Gibson, these emails also confirmed she knew about the crimes he had committed in 2004. Dowie had made the mistake of telling her about them while under the influence. He had also made the mistake of telling Ella about Rachael. Ella left Rachael a warning note on the windshield of her car, telling Rachael she was in danger. That Ella had proof Dowie was a killer. Consequently, Rachael confronted Dowie about it. He insisted it was all a lie, that Ella was a jealous ex. According to Rachael's diary, she was very afraid of him. She was also afraid for Ella. Rachael bought a gun to protect herself two weeks before the incident. The same gun Dowie used to kill her.

"Hannah confirmed that her mother went into Ella's house to help her. But they were too late. Hannah stated that her mother was shouting at someone through the back door and we can only assume Dowie made a dash for it. It would be true to say that whatever Rachael planned, she went beyond rationality and instead of calling the police she took matters into her own hands."

So now we have the homicide triad, Temeke thought. A mechanism by which risk markers and danger signs were present before a homicide. The psychology of the offender, high risk markers and triggers that push a homicide to happen. Damage to anyone's reputation was a big trigger. If he could bet on it, Ella had been to Dowie's house and found the evidence the crime scene investigators had latterly found. But she was killed before she could do anything about it.

"When Dowie arrived that night," Malin said, "Telephone reports revealed that Ella was expecting him. She let him in since there was no sign of lock-stripping or scratches on the front door, and instead of paying her he threatened her. Evidence suggests that she ran down the hall toward the kitchen, kicked off her sandals but didn't get as far as the back door before she was gunned down. We think Dowie knew Rachael was in the house at the time before making his escape. That she had witnessed him shooting Ella.

"The following morning he drove to Rachael's house. As far as he was concerned, she had threatened both his career and his reputation."

"In your opinion," Hackett asked, "Was Dowie of sound mind?"

"I doubt an attorney acting for Calvin Dowie could have claimed diminished responsibility because there was intent to murder. He had a plan. The suicide note as we know wasn't a suicide note," Malin said. "Probably more like a calling card because Cal had screwed up. He knew he was running out of time."

"What made you think Trandahl had something to do with it?"

"We know Rachael used Trandahl's computer to stalk Dowie online. Initially, it appeared as if *SilentAdmirer* belonged to Trandahl since the screen name was linked to women. Then I got to thinking that Trandahl wasn't aggressive enough. I was expecting him to make more noise about it. He used the computer regularly enough to find out about Rachael's online love affair. His only mistake was not telling us sooner."

"Perhaps he didn't want to cause the mayor any undue publicity."

"Perhaps he just didn't want his pansy-ass in a sling," Temeke said, watching the frown that always spread across Hackett's face every time he spoke.

"Another job well done," Hackett said, patting his belly and staring at another donut.

Temeke thought he would feel better leaving Northwest Area Command behind. But he actually felt a hollowness in his chest, as if someone had removed all his organs. He spent his whole life comparing it to Homicide, and now he had what he wished for. There was only Malin left to bat for, and Midge if he was counting her, and he would. She was a damn solid cop.

"I can't thank you all enough," Hackett said, although his voice was beginning to crack.

He dabbed his eyes with the tissue Sandra handed him, stood at the head of the table and raised his cup.

"As we say goodbye to one of our best employees—myself since I'm retiring..." Everyone laughed. "And Temeke since he's going back to Homicide." Everyone booed. "We say hello to our newest recruit. Scarlet Midgely. I say raise your glasses to another fabulous year at the Duke City Police Department."

FIFTY-SIX

Malin dropped the Trandahl file in the filing cabinet drawer and closed it with her hip. It was her last evening with Temeke in their old office. The last case she would share with him.

It was his idea to drink a toast to her promotion with the whisky he had secreted behind a file marked *Arrest Warrants*. A small bottle of Johnnie Walker Double Black and two plastic cups. It had been there for the past year. Maturing, he said.

She took a seat at her desk, wrapped her hands around the cup. Took a few sips and made a face. It was the most disgusting stuff she had ever tasted. But she'd done it for him.

Temeke was listening to noises of revulsion, even if he wasn't watching. Clicking his keyboard and signing out of that old dragon of a computer.

She reminded herself again and again that it was nothing personal. That he must have had his reasons.

It would have been tempting to lay into him as he sat there. But the truth was, he had shared valuable information under an assumed name. She couldn't say she wasn't grateful. Every case they worked was as much about protecting critical details as it was about uncovering new ones. But what did Temeke know that the rest of them didn't?

Albuquerque's favorite detective—the protector of lost children—had been given a promotion rather than early retirement; an ignominious end to a fantastic career. This time he hadn't overstepped his responsibilities and got fired for use of force.

Well, he wanted to beat the crap out of Fowler. Who didn't?

The suspense had gone on several beats too long and she wondered how he'd take it now she knew.

Wingman would come to an end and she felt strangely abandoned. Like a young child who had been left at the school gates.

Remember, Malin, her mother used to say. *You're like a sheep running through a pack of wolves. Don't draw attention to yourself.*

Temeke's eyes were shining as he looked up from the file he was consulting, as if he sensed she wanted to talk.

She tapped the rim of the cup against her bottom lip, brain spinning like it often did after she'd been for a run to burn off the stress.

She preferred the honest, straightforward approach. "You saw the letter I forwarded from Hackett?"

Temeke nodded.

"And you opened the attachment concerning Scarlet Midgely?" Malin felt the hairs rise on the back of her neck and saw him nod again. "I helped myself to a few other files on your computer. I thought you should know."

"So much for trust."

"I don't think you can say anything about trust."

"I'll say what I want, and I hope you didn't go as far as opening the email from Serena."

The way he said it implied enough. Malin perched on the edge of the chair trying to remember if she had marked Serena's message *unread* before closing the computer. But she knew she hadn't and there was no covering a failure like that. She should have felt betrayed but she didn't. Just flat out mad because she was confident she'd gotten away with it.

"I've got cameras and microphones," he said. "They captured everything you did."

"Bullshit."

But then again it could be true.

Maybe Temeke was a sicko closet voyeur. He'd chased enough sickos every day. Maybe they left some kind of residue behind that had stuck to him. Made him into one of them.

Temeke? Nah. Not kick-ass Temeke.

"So what else do you watch?" she asked.

He took another swallow of whisky, eyes wide awake now. Something in his face told her he knew. "You."

The room began to blur into a barely visible haze but she had to say it. "Wingman. Why the mystery?"

He didn't appeared baffled that she had asked him. Just sat there and cleared his throat.

"If you recall, I asked you a few questions when we first met. Wanted to get an idea how your mind worked. I could see you had an excellent short-term memory, repeated things word-for-word *and* you recalled the smallest details the rest of us would find hard to remember. I admit I doubted you. You probably sensed it."

She nodded.

"I didn't think you'd take instruction from me. The guy everyone hated," he said. "So I invented someone you could identify with. The criminal mind. What is it you once said? 'Evil is slick. It knows you inside and out. Your secrets, your despairs, your regrets. It makes it all the more dangerous.' When I asked why you gave evil so much credit, you said, 'Because before evil became evil, it was once good.'"

Malin sat back in her chair and gawked at him. Surprised he remembered the details.

Especially *those* details.

So why feel guilty about going through his stuff?

He'd done exactly the same. Gone through her dossier and possibly her apartment. Probably hunkered down behind the shrubbery when she pulled in, or climbed a tree to peek through half-closed blinds.

Seriously, who does that? Temeke, that's who. Although never in plain sight.

"I don't pretend to have the ability to mind-meld with psychopaths," he said. "My training with the Behavioral Science Unit has made me question the skill behind criminal profiling because no two crimes ever fall neatly into one camp. I wanted to teach you everything I knew."

"It would have been good if you'd told me."

"I'm telling you now. If you hadn't looked in my computer, I'd still be telling you."

Malin loudly slurped up a few swallows of whisky, tension easing as she swirled what was left of her drink. Her throat was on fire and her belly was warmer than the inside of a wood-burning stove. If she opened her mouth, she wondered if she'd see a spurt of Smaug-hissing fire.

Wingman. Temeke. Her. It was like the royal three. Joined at the hip.

"Wingman was a counselor. A nurturer. I guess he was the closest thing I've ever had to a father," she slurred.

There had always been something about police work that fascinated her: the adrenaline buzz and the responsibility. It certainly wasn't the money.

"I bet you don't remember your father," he said. "Probably don't know what it's like to have a dependable man in your life. You told me how you paid off your student loan and how you'd closed the chapter on a broken relationship in New Jersey. Someone you no doubt idolized and trusted. Then you became Malin Santiago. Breadwinner. Loner. So why trust any man?"

He was right. Her father was no more than a shadow and she had pushed working for an escort agency to the back of her mind, regardless of what it took to pay off her loan. At least Temeke had the good nature not to mention Matt Black who, if she had her way, would be taking a poly for all the lies he'd told.

"Remember last year when we drove out on Highway 14 to the penitentiary?" he said.

She nodded. Recalling dark clouds and the smell of rain. It had been December.

"I said something about correctional officers being better leaders to inmates than those they looked up to on the outside."

Malin remembered. "You said, '*We* are leaders to someone. The question is, who is that someone? Because that *someone's* counting on you.'"

"I took my role in that very seriously."

"Who do you think I counted on?" Before Temeke could answer, Malin added. "I get it. It was one hell of a responsibility. But you and Wingman were the only constant things in my life."

"It doesn't bother you that I kept it from you?"

Malin shrugged. "I wanted to learn and you're a natural teacher. No surprises there."

He had that look about him: the kind that told her he could surprise even the best of them through sheer presence alone.

"When I first met you, I saw a mirror image of myself," he said. "A cocky little smart-ass. Although I do have to add your version was more modest. We made the same mistakes you and me, and we've learned." Temeke quit gripping the bottle on his desk and refilled his cup. "You didn't feel like you were being played?"

Malin held back a smile. "You have no idea."

"How about I make it up to you? I can do coq au vin?" he said.

Malin caught the smile in his eyes. "Sounds a little ambitious."

"I have a little coq. That'd be *cock* to you. Though it would sound a little less vulgar if we refer to the bird as a rooster."

"Fresh?" Malin swallowed, trying her hardest to keep a straight face.

"Absolutely. I have one that has rested beyond rigor mortis and about to be loaded in a Dutch oven. A long, slow braise with Burgundy, new potatoes and pearl onions. I can see your mouth's watering."

Malin was more familiar with the tough-as-rubber kind which had put her off rustic farmhouse dishes. But if Temeke could cook something she had a shot of chewing, then why not?

"There are two things that will change your mind," he said. "A great chef and a good thriller. Actually, make that three things: my impressive wine collection. It's the best Burgundy you've ever tasted. How about we leave right now?"

She didn't have to think too hard. In fact, she couldn't really think at all. But the one thing she could think about was spending the evening with her favorite man.

And, if she played her cards right, the rest of her life.

ABOUT THE AUTHOR

Claire Stibbe grew up in Norfolk, England and now lives in the USA. Having lived in Albuquerque, New Mexico for twenty-seven years, she is the author of the Detective Temeke Crime series - *The 9th Hour, Night Eyes, Past Rites, Dead Cold, Easy Prey* and *Silent Admirer*. Winner of the New Mexico/Arizona Book Awards for crime mystery, her books have also been Amazon bestsellers, reaching the #1 spot in the top 100.

She is also a reporter for Stand True 4 Blue, which features a Nationwide Newsletter dedicated to law enforcement, supporter of the Victim Impact Program and a member and graduate of the Citizen Police & BSCO Sheriff's Academy. A former journalist and magazine editor, she now writes full time.

Find out more about Claire at www.clairestibbe.com Twitter and Instagram @CMTStibbe.

For those who would like to hear more about new book releases and deals, please sign up here at http://eepurl.com/bqCQhv. You can unsubscribe at any time, and your email address will never be shared.

If you loved *Silent Admirer,* please could you write a review and tell your friends and family. Reviews and word-of-mouth recommendations are so valuable and help new readers discover my books.

I'd also love to hear from you! Feel free to drop me a line on my Facebook page, through Twitter, Goodreads or my website, which you'll find at www.clairestibbe.com. There are many more books to come. I hope you'll stay in touch!

https://www.instagram.com/clairestibbe/

A Letter from Claire

Thank you so much for reading this book and for entering into the world of Detectives David Temeke and Malin Santiago. I sincerely hope you have enjoyed reading the series.

Thank you to the amazing team at Book Lab and to all the editors I have worked with: Jeff Gardiner, Sandra Mangan, proofreaders Babs, Jean, Kris, Karen, Mark and Cherith.

Thank you to the Albuquerque Police Department for feedback and advice on police procedure. To Officer Michael King for the inspiration and the laughs, and to those of you I interviewed. Any liberties taken with fact are mine.

A massive thank you for my husband, Jeff for all your love and support, and for putting up with closed doors and the rapid fire of typing. For your hugs and those precious early morning chats. All awards are yours.

Thank you to my son, Jamie. My bright and shining star. You do me proud. For your unconditional love and for making our days so bright and full of fun. Coffee always tastes better with family.

And lastly, to all my wonderful readers, book bloggers, writing groups and reviewers worldwide.

Thank you!

ALSO BY CLAIRE STIBBE

THE 9TH HOUR
DETECTIVE TEMEKE BOOK 1

New Mexico/Arizona 2016 Book Award Finalist

Everyone has secrets. Some more deadly than others.

When the ninth young girl falls into the clutches of a serial killer Detective David Temeke faces a race against time to save her life. The Duke City Police Department in Albuquerque, New Mexico is no stranger to gruesome murders, but this new killer on their block keeps the body parts of his eight victims as trophies and has a worrying obsession with the number 9. The suspect is incarcerated in the state's high security penitentiary but Unit Commander Hackett is faced with a dilemma when another teenage girl goes missing.

Detective Temeke and his new partner, Malin Santiago, are sent to solve a baffling crime in the dense forests of New Mexico's Cimarron State Park. But time is running out. Can they unravel the mysteries of Norse legends and thwart the 9th Hour killer before he snatches his next victim?

More in the Detective Temeke Series

NIGHT EYES
PAST RITES
DEAD COLD
EASY PREY

ature and Climatology is essential.

SILENT ADMIRER

www.ingramcontent.com/pod-product-compliance
Lightning Source LLC
Chambersburg PA
CBHW020245030426
42336CB00010B/618